Section 6
HOW TO STYLE YOUR KEYBOARD SOUNDS

Section 7
JAZZ IMPROVISATION

Section 8
TECHNIQUE SESSIONS (PART 1)
Classical Skills and Studies for the Keyboard

Section 9
TECHNIQUE SESSIONS (PART 2)
Pop/Jazz Skills & Studies for the Keyboard

Section 10
THE ORGAN STUDIO

Section 11
SPECIAL FEATURES

Contributing Editors

Judy Carmichael
Raphael Crystal
Debbie Culbertson
Gary De Sesa
Michael Esterowitz
Ronald Herder
Bill Horn
Bill Irwin
Stuart Isacoff
Mark Laub
Becca Pulliam
Samuel Sanders
Ed Shanaphy
Lou Stein
Paulette Weiss

Section 1
BASIC MUSIC THEORY AT THE KEYBOARD

Guide To Music Notation

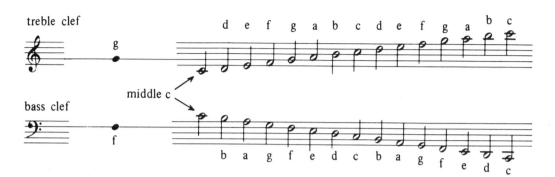

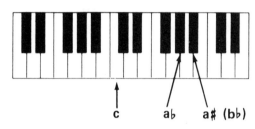

c a♭ a♯ (b♭)

♭♩ = *a* flat ♯♩ = *a* sharp

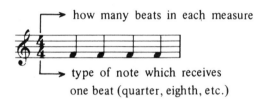

→ how many beats in each measure

→ type of note which receives
one beat (quarter, eighth, etc.)

Name	Rest Symbol	Note Value
Whole		𝅝 = 𝅗𝅥 𝅗𝅥 = 𝅗𝅥 𝅗𝅥 𝅗𝅥 (3) = ♩ ♩ ♩ ♩
Half		𝅗𝅥 = ♩ ♩ = ♩ ♩ ♩ (3) = ♫ ♫
Quarter		♩ = ♫ = ♫ ♪ (3) = ♬ ♬
Eighth		♪ = ♬ = ♬ ♩ (3) = ♬ ♬
Sixteenth		𝅘𝅥𝅯
Thirty-second		𝅘𝅥𝅰
Sixty-fourth		𝅘𝅥𝅱

11

A note with a dot next to it has its normal duration increased by half again its value.

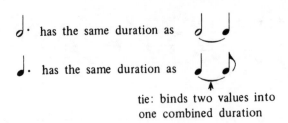

♩. has the same duration as

♪. has the same duration as

tie: binds two values into
one combined duration

Repeat the material enclosed by these signs:

After playing the first ending, go to the beginning;
the second time around use ending number two.

phrase mark divides music into phrases

Stress Marks

Dynamics

pp	very softly
p	softly
mp	moderately soft
mf	moderately loud
f	loud
ff	very loud

crescendo

decrescendo

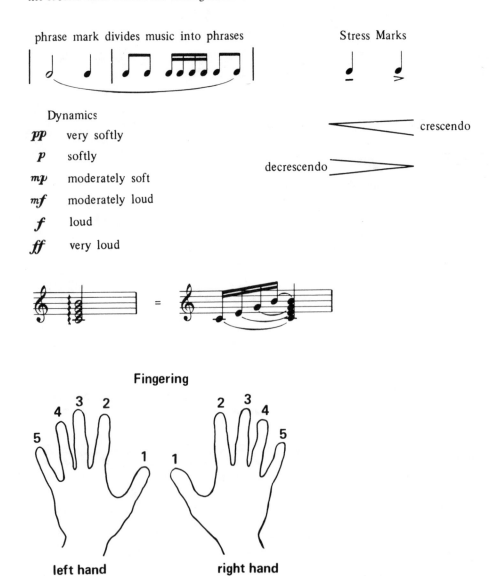

Fingering

left hand   right hand

"A/S/K"

A New, Easier Way to Understand Musical Steps

by Ronald Herder

Semitones and Half Steps

INTERVAL means "space between." A MUSICAL INTERVAL is *the space between any two pitches.*

We measure this *musical* space by using a convenient, standardized unit of measure, just as we do when we measure *physical* space by figuring inches, feet, centimeters, and so on.

In music, our most convenient unit of measure is called the SEMITONE or HALF STEP.

In the traditional chromatic scale, the semitone or half step on the keyboard is the distance between any pitch and its closest neighbor, either higher or lower:

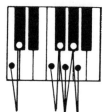

What is "A/S/K"?

"A/S/K" is a new, easier system of measuring intervals.

"**A**" stands for ALPHABET.
"**S**" stands for STAFF.
"**K**" stands for KEYBOARD.

Why a new system?: *To try to eliminate the confusion that often surrounds the identification of intervals.*

An example of the usual confusion happens when we try to distinguish between two intervals that sound the same but are written differently (which we call "enharmonic intervals") — for example, the **chromatic half-step** C-C# and the **minor 2nd** C-Db;

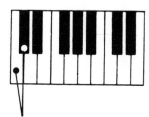

Let's apply the "A/S/K" system to these two very similar intervals.

"A/S/K" describes the Chromatic Half Step

"**A**" (Alphabet) / We describe C-C# in terms of *the musical alphabet:*
"*C and C# have the* same *letter names.*"

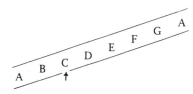

"**S**" (Staff) / We describe C-C# in terms of the position of these pitches on *the music staff:*
"*C and C# are on the* same *line or space of the staff.*"

"**K**" (Keyboard) / We describe C-C# in terms of the position of these pitches on *the keyboard:*
"*C and C# are one half-step apart* on the keyboard."

"A/S/K" describes the Minor 2nd

"**A**" (Alphabet) / We describe C-Db in terms of *the musical alphabet:* "*C and Db have* different *letter names.*"

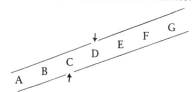

"**S**" (Staff) / We describe C-Db in terms of the position of these pitches on *the music staff:*
"*C and Db are on a* neighboring *(adjacent) line and space of the staff.*"

"**K**" (Keyboard) / We describe C-Db in terms of the position of these pitches on *the keyboard:*
"*C and Db are one half-step apart* on the keyboard."

Things to Think About

This simple comparison on three levels — the music alphabet, the staff, and the keyboard — lets us examine these intervals in a clear, simple, uncluttered way.

What have we learned?

That the chromatic half-step C-C# and the minor 2nd C-Db are truly alike *in only one way: Both intervals are one half-step apart on the keyboard.*

Otherwise, they are completely different: The two intervals have different letter names. The two intervals occupy different positions on the music staff.

"But that's so simple!" I hear you saying. "It's so obvious!" That's what I hoped you'd say! ◠

A complete description of Ronald Herder's original "A/S/K" system appears in the author's forthcoming publication, "THE PLAIN-LANGUAGE ENCYCLOPEDIC HANDBOOK OF MUSIC THEORY."

ASK For An Interval

By Ronald Herder

We've used the A/S/K system to define half steps and whole steps on the keyboard. Now, let's see how it can be used to find any interval. Below, we'll describe a Major Third by seeing how it appears in three ways: by *Alphabet* name, place on the *Staff*, and position on the *Keyboard*.

"A" (Alphabet) / Describe the interval C-E in terms of the musical alphabet:
"C and E *skip one letter of the musical alphabet.*"

"S" (Staff) / Describe the interval C-E by looking at the position of these pitches on the music staff:
"C and E *are on two neighboring lines* or *two neighboring spaces* of the staff."

"K" (Keyboard) / Describe the interval C-E by looking at the position of these pitches on the keyboard:

"C and E *are four half-steps apart* on the keyboard."

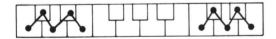

CONCLUSION: An interval is *always* a MAJOR 3rd if these three conditions exist:
  (A) its letter names skip one letter of the musical alphabet;
  (S) its pitches are on two neighboring lines or two neighboring spaces of the staff;
  (K) its pitches are four half steps apart on the keyboard.

Note that the minor 3rd and major 3rd are IDENTICAL in their letter names (disregarding sharps and flats) and in their staff positions. But they are DIFFERENT on the keyboard. ⌢

Major And Minor Triads

By Joan Stiles

One of the best ways to improve your musicianship is by taking the time to SING and ACTIVELY LISTEN to musical materials you use everyday. Let's consider our most basic chords: major and minor triads. These chords are made up of different combinations of major and minor thirds. A major third (M3) spans the distance of two whole steps (G-B); a minor third (m3) covers one-and-a-half steps (G-Bb).

You can construct these triads by using the formulas: Major triad = M3 + m3; minor triad = m3 + M3 (spelled from the bottom up). If you know your major and minor scales, you can refer to these relationships between the degrees of the scale. Try the following exercises at the piano to review thirds and triads.

Using the numbers 1 2 3 4 5, sing the first five notes of a major scale starting on G. Check yourself on the piano. Next, break the triad down into its two stacked thirds. Sing 1 2 3 and then leave out 2, singing 1-3 (G-B, a major 3rd). Next, sing 3 4 5, then just 3-5 (B-D, a minor third). Finally, sing 1 2 3 4 5, then 1-3-5. Congratulations! You have just sung a major triad (G-B-D).

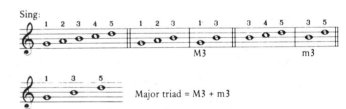

For a minor triad, use the minor scale as your reference. Remember, a minor scale has a half step between scale degrees 2-3, so Bb is scale degree 3 in G minor. Follow the same steps as above: 1 2 3 4 5. Then 1 2 3, 1-3. 3 4 5, 3-5. Finally, 1 2 3 4 5: 1-3-5. Congratulations! You have just sung a minor triad (G-Bb-D). Do this same excercise starting on other notes within your voice range and you will improve your ability to quickly construct and recognize thirds and triads BY EAR.

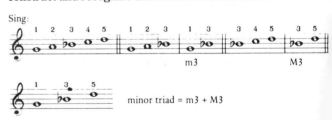

1,000 KEYBOARD IDEAS

From The Editors Of
Sheet Music Magazine
Keyboard Classics Magazine
& The Piano Stylist

Edited by Ronald Herder

223 Katonah Avenue, Katonah, NY 10536

How To Use
1000 KEYBOARD IDEAS

Welcome to the greatest single source of keyboard ideas you"ll ever find! In the following pages there are sections on Basic Theory, Harmonic Tricks, Rhythm, Arranging Skills, Melodic Tricks, Keyboard Style, Jazz Improvisation, Technique, Organ and much, much more!

If you are a voracious keyboard lover, just browse at your heart's content. It is not necessary to follow a particular order (though the articles within each section are arranged to lead logically from one idea to the next).

If you need information on a particular subject, just check the table of contents and turn to the article that supplies you with just the right tip or explanation.

Being a keyboardist has never been more exciting. Happy reading ... and — more importantly — happy playing!

Table of Contents

Section 1

BASIC MUSIC THEORY AT THE KEYBOARD

Section 2

HARMONIC TRICKS OF THE TRADE

Section 3
THE RHYTHM WORKSHOP

Section 4
ARRANGING SKILLS

Section 5
RUNNING WILD!: MELODIC TRICKS OF THE TRADE

Harmony at the Keyboard

Constructing Simple Chords

A chord is a group of notes played or sung simultaneously. In popular music the chords are usually represented by symbols that appear over the vocal line. If the pianist wants to vary the written keyboard part, or make up a completely new one, he or she will use those symbols as a basis. Here are the melody and chord symbols for the first four bars of "The Twelve Days of Christmas."

The letters refer to the chord "roots," the notes on which the chords will be constructed. Ordinarily those notes appear at the bottoms of the chords, so the bass part will look something like this:

Above those roots the chords are built up in "thirds." A third is an interval that spans three letter names. For example, the interval C-E is a third because it includes the letter names C, D, and E.

There are two kinds of thirds: major and minor. They can be defined in terms of the "half-step" —the distance between two adjacent notes on the piano. The major third consists of four half-steps and the minor third consists of three. C-E is a major third, since it includes the half-steps C-C#, C#-D, D-D#, and D#-E. The minor third D-F consists of the half-steps D-D#, D#-E, and E-F.

Let us look back at the chord symbols for "The Twelve Days of Christmas." The first chord is represented by the letter "C". When a chord symbol consists only of a letter name, a "major" chord is indicated. The major chord is made up of a major third and, above that, a minor third; thus, the C major chord includes the intervals C-E (major third, four half-steps) and E-G (minor third, three half-steps).

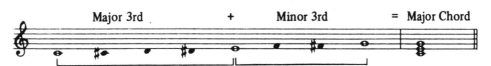

Continued next page

The abbreviation "min" after a chord root, or simply a lower-case "m", stands for a "minor" chord. Here the lower interval is a minor third, and the upper is a major third; thus, the A minor chord includes the intervals A-C (minor third) and C-E (major third).

The numeral "7" after a chord root stands for a "dominant seventh" chord. This is a four-note structure, consisting of a major third, a minor third, and then another minor third. The G7 chord is made up of the intervals G-B (major third), B-D (minor third), and D-F (minor third).

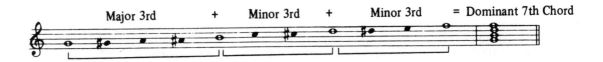

With these chord-types in mind we can now translate the chord symbols of "The Twelve Days of Christmas" into notes. Let us put the chords in the left hand, underneath the melody.

This represents the simplest kind of chordal accompaniment; however, the same chord structures can be arranged in much more interesting, musically sophisticated forms.

If you would like to gain facility in constructing chords, try building major and minor thirds on all twelve tones of the chromatic scale. Then go on to construct major, minor, and dominant seventh chords on each tone. Do this on paper and also at the keyboard. At first you will have to laboriously count out the half-steps—four to a major third, three to a minor third—but soon you will become familiar with these intervals and you will be able to pick them out immediately. Eventually the chords themselves will become second nature to you.

RC

16

Harmony at the Keyboard

The Three Primary Chords

How do you go about harmonizing a melody? It helps to know that in any key there are three chords that are especially important. Those are the chords built on the first, fourth, and fifth notes of the scale. Our first example shows the scale of C major. The roots of the three primary chords — which we have labeled I, IV, and V — and C, F, and G.

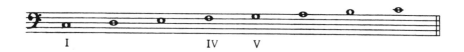

In major keys the chords built on I and IV are major chords. The chord on V can be either major or a dominant seventh. The next example shows the three primary chords in C major: C major, F major, and G7.

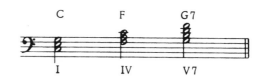

Those three chords will suffice for the harmonization of many simple tunes. In many others they serve as the backbone of the harmony. Let us look at the first four bars of the traditional student song *Gaudeamus Igitur*, in C major. Play through this melody and try to imagine how you might harmonize it using the C, F, and G7 chords.

It isn't possible to lay down hard and fast rules for harmonizing a melody. In the last analysis your ear must be your guide. But ordinarily the main notes of the tune will be present in the chords that accompany them. For example, in the first bar we find the notes C and G. These notes are both present in the C major chord. In the second bar we find the note A; of our three primary chords that note is present only in the F major chord. In the third bar the important notes are B and D (the C functions as a "passing tone" between them). Those two notes are present in the G7 chord. Finally, in the fourth bar we encounter the notes C and E, which form part of the C major chord. This completes our harmonization of these four bars. We will put the chords into the left-hand part.

Another way of arranging this passage would be to play only chord roots with the left hand, and put the chord tones into the right, underneath the melody. (Notice that in the first bar the C and G are already present in the melody, so only the E must be added to complete the chord. In the third bar the B and D are present, so only the F and G must be added.)

17

Continued next page

Because the I, IV, and V7 chords are so important, it is very worthwhile to become familiar with their positions on the keyboard. Our final example shows three basic forms of the I-IV-V7-I progression, with chord tones in the right hand and roots in the left. If you practice this exercise in all major keys you will be taking an important first step in developing the ability to harmonize melodies at the keyboard.

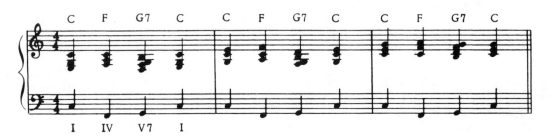

RC

18

The Dominant Seventh Chord

By Andy LaVerne

The evolution of music has resulted in an abundant variety of sounds. One of the most important and versatile products of this evolutionary process is the dominant seventh chord. Chords were first formed as the horizontal consequence of vertically moving melodic voices (lines). This combination of harmonic intervals first brought us the simplest chord, the triad — a chord of three tones obtained by the superimposition of two thirds (major and minor).

The root, third, and fifth of the triad can be joined by a fourth tone superimposed a minor third above the chord. The seventh (so named because of its intervallic distance from the root) first appeared in music as a melodic, non-harmonic tone. The seventh is often seen in a purely melodic capacity when used on the dominant (V) chord. The inclusion into the harmonic vocabulary of this vertical cross-section became known as V7.

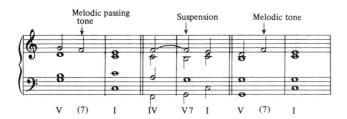

Present in the dominant seventh chord are two dissonant intervals: 1) the diminished fifth between the third and seventh; 2) the minor seventh between the root and seventh. Tones set up by the dissonant intervals move in the direction where they are no longer dissonant, thus no longer having a tendency to move.

The tendency of the diminished fifth is to contract to a third, major or minor. The inward movement by step gives us contrary motion. If the lower voice (leading tone) were to move alone, the following interval would still be dissonant, the perfect fourth.

The tendency of the seventh is for the upper voice to move downward by step. If the lower voice were to remain, an imperfect consonance (sixth) would result. When the lower note (the dominant) moves up to the tonic, a third is reached. This gives us a better resolution.

The tendencies of the tones in the inverted forms of these intervals remain the same.

Regular resolution: All dissonant chords usually progress in a harmonic manner called regular resolution. This is usually expressed in terms of root movement. As you probably guessed, the regular resolution of V7 to I is undoubtably the most fundamental harmonic progression. The addition of the fourth degree (seventh in the dom. seventh) supplies the missing important factor from the V-I progression, giving us the perfect progression for defining tonality. ∎

More Seconds!

By Stuart Isacoff

This is the first in a series covering the most popular chord in popular music, the celebrity you'll find on every lead sheet and under the fingers of every cocktail lounge keyboardist from New York to Nome: the seventh chord. Actually, there are six types of seventh chords you'll find used with some frequency.

Let's look at the major scale to learn something about the formation of seventh chords. Adding sevenths to the triads (3-note chords) that occur naturally on the various pitches of a major scale will result in several different chord types:

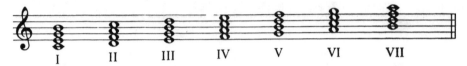

Adding a seventh to the major triad on tone 1 of the scale produces what is known as a Major Seventh Chord — in this case, a C Major Seventh, indicated by the symbol C maj.7 or C(+7) or sometimes $C^\triangle$. This type of chord is formed naturally on the I and IV in a major key (in this case, the result is C maj.7 and F maj.7).

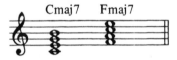

To gain familiarity with this chord type, form and play Major Seventh chords on the following roots. Just use the pitches of the major scale that begins on that root. The first two are written out for you.

To construct a Major Seventh chord on any pitch, use the formula for a major triad — 2 whole steps + 1½ steps — and add two whole steps for the seventh:

You can use this formula to build Major Seventh chords on the following pitches:

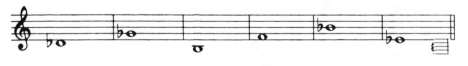

Stuart Isacoff is the author of The 20 Minute Chords & Harmony Workout, *published by Ekay Music.*

The Half Diminished Seventh

By Stuart Isacoff

Here is an unusual seventh chord that occurs on the seventh note of the major scale:

This may be seen as a diminished triad with a dominant seventh. It is in fact called a Half Diminished Seventh (often indicated by a circle with a diagonal line going through it, as in $C^{\varnothing}7$).

The Half Diminished Seventh chord may be built by constructing a diminished chord (1 1/2 steps + 1 1/2 steps) and adding a dominant seventh. This time, to create a dominant seventh interval from the root it will be necessary to add 2 steps on top of the fifth of the chord, since the fifth of this chord is diminished:

This chord is often seen as a substitution for the V chord. In the key of C, for instance, the $B^{\varnothing}7$ can often function in place of the G7 chord:

For practice, build Half Diminished Seventh chords beginning on the following roots:

The Minor Seventh

By Stuart Isacoff

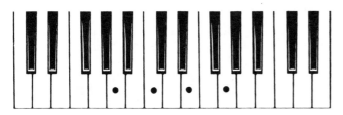

Continuing our survey of the different types of seventh chords encountered in pop music, we'll concentrate this time on the Minor Seventh chord. It occurs naturally on tones 2, 3 and 6 of the major scale:

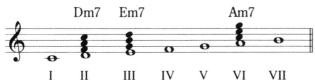

This chord type is simply a minor triad with a dominant seventh added (designated in pop music with the symbol m7 or min.7 or -7). It can be built by constructing a minor triad (1 1/2 stpes + 2 steps) and adding a minor third (1 1/2 steps) on top:

For practice in learning this chord type, construct the following minor seventh chords by first finding the correct root for each key:

The II chord in the key of C:

The III chord in the key of F:

The VI chord in the key of G.

The VI chord in the key of F:

The III chord in the key of Bb:

The II chord in the key of D:

The VI chord in the key of Eb:

If you've been following the exercises given in the earlier articles in this series, you should be able to accomplish the following drill. It's fun and really helps you to learn the differences between various seventh chords!

Change the following seventh chords from one type to another as indicated. Play each chord before moving on to the next:

Cmaj.7 to C7:

Fm7 to F7:

G7 to Gm7:

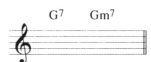

Amaj.7 to Am7:

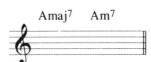

Bbm7 to Bbmaj.7:

Eb7 to Ebmaj.7:

Consulting editor Stuart Isacoff is the author of "The 20 Minute Chords And Harmony Workout," published by Ekay Music and available from Songbooks Unlimited.

21

Symbol Simon Says

Chord symbols — those funny little markings you often see above the melody and lyrics on a song sheet — can be a great help for anyone interested in working out his or her own arrangement or playing style. But they can also be terribly confusing. Even pros often disagree about the proper way to notate a chord in this special shorthand language. For example, a major seventh chord may appear in any of the following ways:

M7   Ma7   maj.7   MA7   MAJ7

This issue, we'll begin a dictionary of chord symbols; a helpful guide for the beginner *and* the seasoned player. It will cover the many symbols you'll find in the sheet music you play.

The place to begin, of course, is with the chord root. Every symbol begins with a letter naming the root of the chord it represents. **C** indicates a C major chord.

Cm indicates a C minor chord. **C dim.** indicates a C diminished chord. In each case, the root is spelled out first — then the chord *quality*.

How do we translate that into notes on the keyboard? If we take the chord *root*, and build a major scale on it, we can find the major chord of that root by selected tones #1, 3 and 5 of the scale.

To find the minor chord on that root, we simply lower that middle voice — #3 of the scale — by a half step.

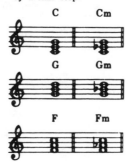

The minor chord is most often represented by a small m, as in Cm, Gm or Fm. It may also appear as a minus sign, as in C– or G–.

To find the diminished chord, we lower not only the third tone of the scale, but the fifth as well. The diminished chord is sometimes represented by the symbol dim., and sometimes by a circle °.

When professionals use these symbols, they don't just plunk down the chord in the left hand, and play the melody in the right. There is an art to "voicing" these harmonies — that is, to placing the notes of the chord in different orders on the keyboard in order to make them sound just right for each musical situation. But even in voicing these chords, players will use the same pitches outlined here; so this information is essential to any pop or jazz performer.

Next time we'll continue with more chord types, including the augmented chord, and a hodge-podge of sevenths.

More Chord Symbols

Last issue we began to decipher the most common chord symbols found in today's sheet music. Let's continue with a look at the augmented chord. It is sometimes indicated by the abbreviation **aug.**, and sometimes by the sign **+**.

The word *augment* is from the French *augère:* to increase. In an augmented chord, the size of the *interval* between the third and fifth of the chord is what has been increased. You will recall that in a major chord, the interval (or distance) between the third and fifth is 1 1/2 steps:

In an augmented chord, that distance is lengthened to 2 steps:

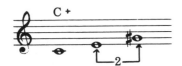

Note that in the augmented chord all pitches are exactly a major third (2 whole steps) apart from each other! Because of that symmetry, a C augmented chord contains the same notes as an E augmented chord and a G# augmented chord. So there are really only four different kinds of augmented chords!

Seventh chords come in so many different varieties there is bound to be some confusion about them. We'll begin our survey of seventh chords here, and continue next time.

Looking once again at the major scale (the basis of our chords), note the seventh chord which occurs naturally as our I (tonic) chord:

This is called a major seventh. It is indicated by **Maj. 7** or **MAJ 7** or **M7** or **Ma7** or by a triangle △.

The seventh chord which falls naturally on step 5 (the dominant) of the scale has a different kind of sound. Here, the interval between notes 1 and 7 is a half-step shorter than in the major seventh chord:

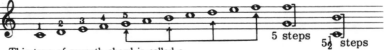

This type of seventh chord is called a dominant seventh. It is indicated very simply as **7.**

Take These Sevenths... Please!

We'll continue our overview of chord symbols by moving on to sevenths you'll find based on the minor, diminished and augmented chords. The seventh which occurs naturally with a minor chord is — like the dominant seventh for a major chord — five whole steps above the root:

The symbol for a minor seventh chord is **m⁷**, as in **Cm⁷**, **Fm⁷**, and so on.

Occasionally, you might find another kind of minor seventh chord, but it appears very infrequently. This is a minor chord with a major seventh, and it is indicated in the following way: **Cm⁽maj 7⁾**.

Two types of sevenths occur with the diminished chord. The first is a diminished seventh. In order to understand the spelling of this chord, it is important to remember that perfect intervals (octaves, fifths and fourths) are diminished by lowering them a half step, but major intervals, such as major sevenths, are diminished by lowering them a whole step. In the diminished chord, the fifth is lowered a half step:

But the seventh is lowered a whole step:

This type of chord is spelled as **Cdim⁷** or **C°⁷**.

Another type of diminished seventh chord is the half-diminished seventh. In a half-diminished seventh chord, a dominant seventh, rather than a diminished seventh, is used. The spelling for this kind of chord is **Cø⁷**.

The augmented chord — as is true of most "altered" chords — uses a dominant seventh. Here is the way it is spelled: **C +⁷** or **Caug⁷**.

Sixths and Ninths

Now that we've looked over the basic chord types and their symbols (see the past several issues), we're ready to tackle chords with added numbers, like **C⁶**, **Dᵐᵃʲ⁹**, and **F¹¹**. First, a review of sixths.

Adding the sixth member of the scale to a chord is a matter of simple arithmetic. If the chord is a **C⁶**, you will be adding an A to the C triad.

A minor sixth chord would appear in this way:

That's all there is to it!

Ninths are found in the same way (a ninth is the second scale degree transposed up an octave), except that, since 9 comes after 7, the seventh of the chord is included. That's where the complications occur, since sevenths take on different forms themselves.

C⁹ is used to describe a **C⁷** (a dominant, not major seventh) with the ninth degree of the scale added:

Cm⁹ describes a minor seventh chord (**Cm⁷**) with the ninth degree of the scale added:

Cᵐᵃʲ⁹ or **CM⁹** is used for a major seventh chord (**Cᵐᵃʲ⁷**) with the ninth added:

Then there are "altered" ninths. These are used with *dominant* sevenths. The ninth may be flatted, to form a **C⁷ᵇ⁹** or **C⁷⁻⁹**:

Or it may be augmented, to form a **C⁷ᵃᵘᵍ⁹** or **C⁷⁺⁹**:

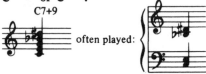

Next time we'll look at 11ths and 13ths!

Elevenths

Counting up the major scale, we find that the 11th is the same pitch as the 4th, only an octave higher. When a chord uses the fourth, though, it is usually referred to as a "suspended chord." In a suspended chord, the third is most often omitted; it is indicated by the symbol **sus** or **sus4.**

Infrequently, a suspended chord may also contain the minor third, as in **Cmˢᵘˢ⁴**.

When an 11th is used, the chord is assumed to contain a 7th and a 9th as well. Here is a typical voicing for an eleventh chord:

As we know from our earlier look at seventh and ninth chords, there are many variations that may occur. The 7th is most often a dominant 7th. The 9th may be altered. The 11th may be sharped as well (in which case the 3rd may be played, and the 5th may be omitted). Here are various kinds of eleventh chords you may find in today's sheet music.

Next time, we'll continue our survey of chord types with thirteenth chords.

Thirteenths

We can apply the same rules we used for forming ninths and elevenths when putting together our thirteenth chords. Eleventh chords, remember, use the fourth degree of scale, placed an octave higher (above the seventh). Thirteenth chords use the sixth degree of the scale, placed an octave higher. (Most thirteenth chords use a dominant seventh.)

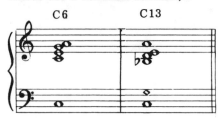

That thirteenth member of the scale can be altered, as in **C⁷ᵇ¹³**:

Most often, though, the lower members of the chord — the third or seventh or ninth — will be the tones to watch. Here is a catalogue of various thirteenth chords.

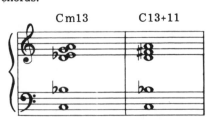

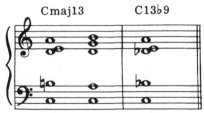

Next time: slash chords and voice-leading (moving from one chord to another).

Slash Chords

Now that we've covered the many kinds of chords found in pop sheet music, let's consider a special case. Sometimes a composer or arranger will want a specific *voicing* for a chord — not content to write simply C^{11}, for example, he or she might want this very particular sound produced:

And so, you will read the following in your sheet music: **Bb/C.** This means, "Play a Bb chord, and put a C note underneath."

Slash chords are used to convey such voicings, or, at times, inversions. (An inversion of a chord places a note other than the root on the bottom. A chord in first inversion places the third on the bottom; second inversion uses the fifth on the bottom.) For example, **F/A** means an F chord in first inversion:

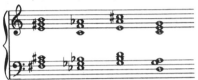

These chord symbols are helpful not only for indicating the specific sound a songwriter has in mind, but for conveying bass lines and the movement of chord voices. By following the slash chord directions below, a keyboard player will end up with a nicely flowing bass line which descends in half-steps: (See above.)

Finally, here are a few slash chords which place chords, rather than single notes, on the bottom. You won't find these often, but in sophisticated music of today's pop and jazz worlds they can make the difference between sounding ordinary, or like "the real thing."

Reader Wes Barringer wrote to ask for more information on chord suspensions. He found a definition of suspensions in a recent column, but wonders "what actually happens to a C^7 chord suspension?"

Actually, suspensions are used in two very different ways. The term "suspension" comes from a technique developed in early classical music (we associate its origins with the Baroque era). When a dissonant note is placed on a strong beat in place of an expected consonant one, and when that note then moves to a consonance, the result is a slight delay or "suspension" of the harmonic movement. We are forced to wait for a resolution of the chord progression, and feel temporarily "suspended."

Here, for example, is a simple II-V-I chord progression. First, it resolves clearly and directly to a C chord. Next, it moves into a C suspension (an F is used instead of an E in the C harmony); this suspension then resolves when the F moves down to an E.

An End To The Suspense

Sometimes this suspension-resolution formula appears in a form associated with hymn and gospel playing.

But there is another type of suspended sound, and it doesn't follow these rules. It occurs in very contemporary pop and jazz pieces. Simply put, this kind of suspension is a chord sound in which the fourth is used instead of the third. It is a sound enjoyed for its own sake, and it doesn't resolve or move in any particular way. Here it is in a V-I progression using dominant seventh harmonies.

The best way to fully understand the way suspensions are used is to try them in as many situations as possible.

The chord formed on step VII of the major scale is called "half-diminished." It is a diminished chord with a dominant seventh on top. A "diminished seventh" chord lowers the dominant seventh tone by ½ step.

The VII is called "half-diminished". Its symbol is ⌀.

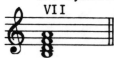

A "diminished 7th" chord lowers the dominant 7th another ½ step.

Although these very specific intervals determine the type of chord you are playing, the *order* the notes appear in on the keyboard is not rigidly determined. If we were to play all chords in the "close" position used in the preceding examples, the sound would be boring and at times ugly. Once the correct notes for a chord have been decided, there is great leeway in arranging those notes between the hands.

The art of "voicing" allows a musician to produce just the kind of sound he or she wants.

We can begin our look at this art with a very practical and standard voicing: the root and fifth of the chord in the left hand, and the third, seventh, and third again in the right. Here is a series of major seventh chords, using this voicing, in the circle of fifths.

The symbol for a major 7th chord is △ or Maj. 7.

The same voicing can be used with dominant seventh chords.

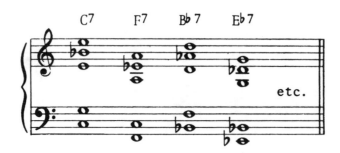

Continued next page

"VOICING" YOUR CHORDS

The chords formed by the major scale are easy enough to locate and play, but the trick of making them sound full and professionally polished requires study and practice. Here are the chords of the C major scale: C Major, D Minor, E minor, F Major, G Major, A Minor, B Diminished.

If we add sevenths onto our basic triads, we arrive at the most commonly used chord qualities: Major Seventh, Minor Seventh, Dominant Seventh, and Half-Diminished Seventh.

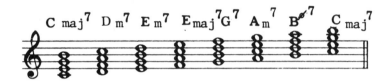

We can create any chord type by remembering the distance (the interval) between each of its tones. A major chord, for example, is built by the interval of 2 whole steps, followed by 1½ steps; the minor chord consists of 1½ steps followed by 2 whole steps; a diminished chord uses two intervals of 1½ steps each.

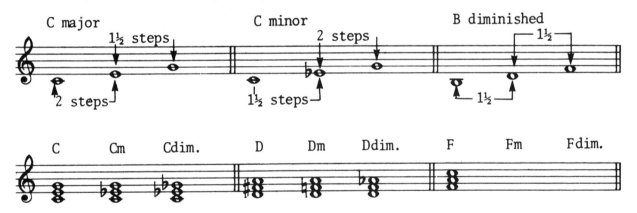

In the above example, fill in the correct notes for the Fm and F^dim. chords.

The major seventh interval is 5½ steps wide.

The dominant seventh interval is 5 steps wide.

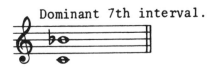

Here it is with minor seventh chords.

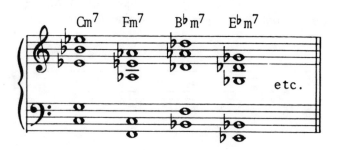

One key to good voicing is the technique of making changes from one chord to another as smoothly as possible; often, this involves holding "common tones": those notes shared by both chords. Here is an example using the circle of fifths.

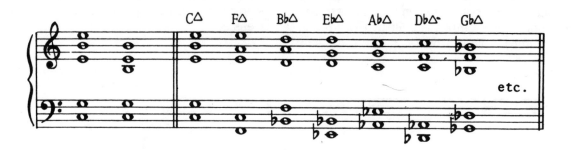

Here is another example, remaining within the key of C.

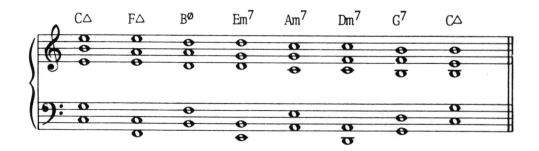

Up until now we've been using a fairly "open" voicing. The notes of a chord can be arranged in much closer proximity to one another, however.

Here's another type of voicing, which also makes use of the common tone technique.

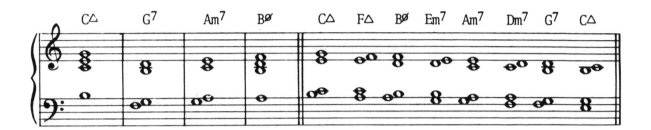

Any progression can be made to move in numerous ways on the keyboard. Turning again to an open voicing, we can play the circle of fifths so that the bass line descends. Here we are not using the same voicing for each chord, but constructing the right hand configurations so that they sound uncluttered and effective above the bass notes.

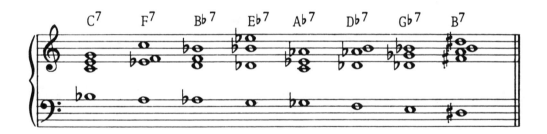

We can also keep our common tones in the bass!

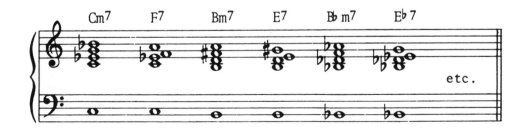

Continued next page

29

From Close To Open

There is a simple way in which band arrangers change the instrumental sound of an ensemble from very dense to spacious, and we can apply their method to keyboard arranging. Let's look at our "close" or dense voicing, in a circle of fifths pattern within the key of C.

If we take the note second from the bottom and drop it down an octave, we will change the voicing to a semi-open sound.

We can take the top note of the voicing and drop it down to the bottom as well. We now have an open voicing.

If we like, we can arrange the notes of these chords so that they expand outward — creating a more and more open sound as we play!

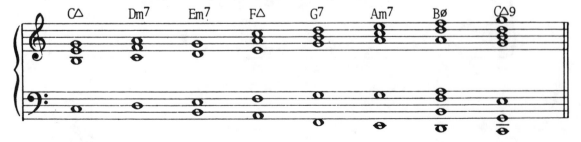

This is the complete opposite to the "locked hand" or block chord style made famous by George Shearing, in which the top and bottom notes are the same, and the spacing between tones remains very tight.

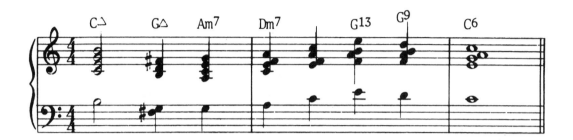

Altered Chords

Today's music uses many different kinds of chord qualities. Complex chords are sometimes referred to as "altered" chords, because the player is often asked to sharp or flat chord members, or alter the usual chord in some way.

Here is a list of most of the sophisticated chords you'll find in contemporary arrangements.

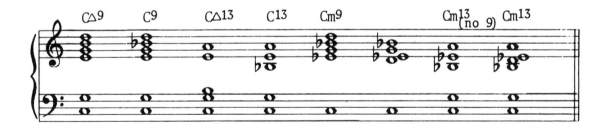

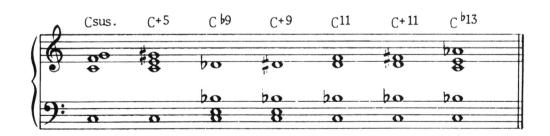

Continued next page

31

These chords can be "voiced" just as creatively as the simpler chords we've been reviewing. Here are some examples of sophisticated chords used in II-V-I and circle of fifth progressions.

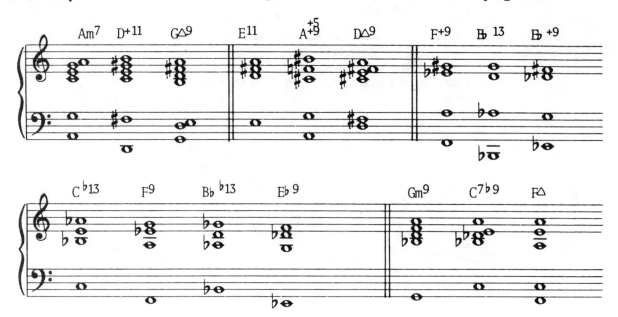

Often, these complex chords are voiced in a way that leaves out many of the chord tones. It takes a lot of experimentation and practice to achieve a complete command over these sounds, but in time they can become additional colors on your arranging palette. Use these examples as beginning guides to the world of chord voicing — the more you experiment, the better you'll sound!

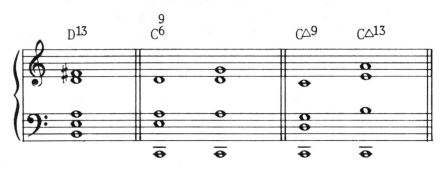

SI ♪

Striking A Common Chord

Many of who have studied the piano for years are now beginning to play organ, and vice versa. In fact, some people are choosing to become "multi-instrumentalists," which gives them the chance to experience the best of both worlds. As the saying goes, variety is the spice of life.

But keyboard instruments, though they may look alike, can sound very different. Playing full piano chords on a powerful, rich-toned console will reduce any piece of music to "Mud Gets in Your Eyes." After getting over the initial shock of that murky sound, a pianist would have to consider certain elements of chord voicing, especially the concept of "optimum range."

Take this piano voicing, for instance:

An organist would use much simpler voicings, which fall within the "optimum" register:

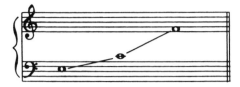
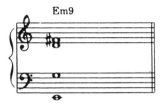

In fact, organists often play chords in inversion so that the notes of the harmony lie in a good-sounding place on the keyboard.

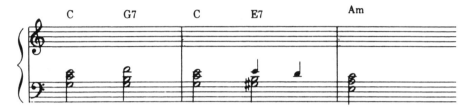

Some pop pianists do follow a similar routine; early swing players made sure that the chords they played fell so that middle C rested somewhere near the middle of the harmony. This helped to make the "swing piano" sound distinctive.

An organist, however, who plays his voicings on a piano will also run into a problem: some of the simple organ voicings will sound too bare. Pianists will tend to include half-steps and altered chord tones. It is possible, however, to develop a chord vocabulary that will fit either instrument. The following examples are useful in the song "I Love Paris" **SI** ♩

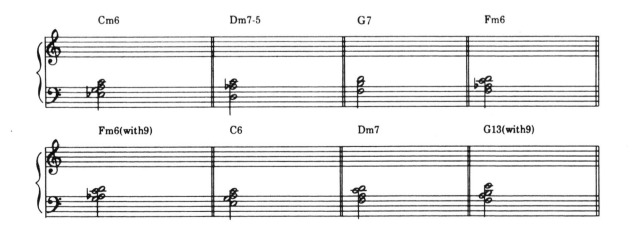

Cadences

BY ANDY LAVERNE

The term cadence can be used in various ways — to describe a cadenza, a rhythm, or the ending of a musical phrase. Our discussion here will focus on the cadence as a phrase ending. As such, the cadence provides "breathing" places in music, and helps establish the tonality of a piece.

The most common harmonic formula in Western music, V - I, is called an **authentic cadence.** Sometimes the V chord is preceded by either a II or a IV chord. These added chords often lead to a tonic six-four chord (the tonic chord in second inversion), resulting in one of the strongest final cadences: $II_6 - I_4^6 - V - I$.

Other embellishments to the authentic cadence may be: 1) precede the V by its dominant, 2) ornament the final tonic chord (i.e. using a suspension or appoggiatura), or 3) use the V chord over the tonic in the bass, then resolve to the tonic chord.

The authentic cadence is by no means restricted to final phrases. It is used elsewhere, but with less feeling of finality.

"Cadences provide breathing places in music."

When it appears with dominant and tonic chords in root position, and the tonic note in the top voice at the end, it is called a **perfect cadence.** All other forms of the authentic cadence are termed **imperfect,** implying less finality.

The matter of determining which are perfect and imperfect cadences is not strictly black and white. Gray areas result from the degree of finality, with varying contributing factors, such as the use of inversions, affecting the result.

Authentic cadence (perfect)

The **half cadence** finds the V chord at the end of a phrase. Some common formulas: $IV - I_4^6 - V$; $II - I_4^6 - V$; $VI - I_4^6 - V$; $I - I_4^6 - V$.

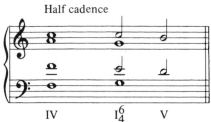

The **plagal cadence** IV - I (sometimes called the "Amen" cadence because the word Amen is sung to it in gospel music) is usually used after an authentic cadence as an added close to a movement. The minor form of the IV chord can be used in the plagal cadence at the conclusion of a movement in a major key, yielding a different harmonic color.

Plagal cadence

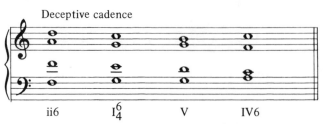

The **deceptive cadence** is similar to the authentic cadence, except that some other chord is used in place of the final tonic. A great variety of deceptive cadences can be employed, as there are many different chords to which the dominant may lead. Some, however, yield a more "deceptive" result than others. One of the most frequent alternatives to V - I is V - VI. Some other common deceptive cadences are V - IV_6, V - V_7 of IV, V - VI_7. The deceptive cadence near the end of a piece helps sustain interest at the moment when the final authentic cadence is expected, thus providing the composer with an opportunity to add an extra musical phrase or two at the conclusion.

Deceptive cadence

Modulation

BY ANDY LAVERNE

As a composer and performer I find that one of the most valuable musical resources at my disposal is modulation. Modulation is the passage from one key into another. This passage results in a change of tonal *center*.

Any chord or group of tones can be analyzed in relation to any one of the twelve tones chosen as a tonal center. For example, a C major triad can be a V chord in the Key of

The technique of modulation involves three steps.

Andy LaVerne

F, a IV chord in the Key of G and so on. The ambiguity of these possible interpretations provides the basis of the technique of modulation. This technique involves three steps.

1. The initial key — The establishment of the first key can be confirmed by the strong appearance of the dominant chord leading to a tonal center. It is not essential that the tonic chord appear.

2. The pivot chord — The second step in modulation involves the choice of a chord which will help change the tonal viewpoint already established. This should be a common chord between the initial key and the new key. This pivot chord can thus absorb a "double" analysis. A C major triad, for example, could be used as a pivot chord in a modulation from C to G. Indicated as:

(Pivot chord)

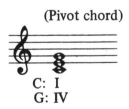

C: I
G: IV

The pivot chord should preferably not be the V of the new key, it should rather be placed in advance of the appearance of the dominant of the second key. The following demonstrates a modulation effected by means of the pivot chord just illustrated:

C: IV II V I
   G: IV II V I

3. The new key — The new key is established by way of a cadence which ends the phrase. However, strong progressions may occur in the new key before the cadence. (See the article on cadences in the January/February *Keyboard Classics*.)

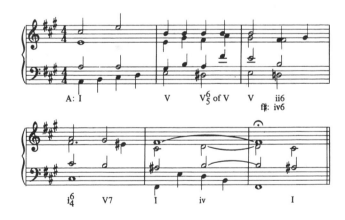

The modulation illustrated here moves down a minor third (up a major sixth). This modulation takes us from A major to F# minor (its relative minor). The initial key is established strongly by the use of tonic and dominant chords. The II chord is used here as a pivot chord and as such can be analyzed as the IV of F# minor. The cadence in F# minor confirms the establishment of the new key. The surprise use of a major third in the final tonic chord is called a Picardy Third.

The Numbers Game for Key Signatures

The first number in this key signature game is 5. If you can count to five you can always figure signatures for every key. For example, everyone knows that the key signature for the key of C is no sharps and no flats. The rule is: everytime you count up 5, add *one* (1) sharp. Count five keys up from C:

C - D - E - F - G.
(1) (2) (3) (4) (5)

The new key, G, gets one sharp, or one sharp added to the key signature of C.

Similarly, if you count up five from G,

G - A - B - C - D,
(1) (2) (3) (4) (5)

the new key of D gets two sharps, or one sharp added to the key signature of G.

Simple so far? At this point, you can figure out every key signature for the "sharp" keys. Counting up five from D gets you to. . . . Go to your keyboard and find the key which is 5 above D before reading any further. (Remember to count D as #1.) If you arrived at A, you are correct. And how many sharps in the key of A? Add one to the key signature for D to get your answer. Remember the rule: every time you count up five, add one sharp. The key of A has three sharps.

But which notes are sharped? (Not sharpened, by the way. If you sharpened notes they'd look like this: ♩ .) It's all well and good to know how many sharps there are in the key of A, but how can you figure out which ones they are?

The number you need to figure that out is "7." Some people prefer "–1" (minus one). To find out which note gets the new sharp, count up seven (7), or down one (–1). For example, going back to the key of G, count up seven notes for the new sharp thusly: G - A - B - C - D - E - F.
(1) (2) (3) (4) (5) (6) (7)

F is the 7th note, and the one which gets the new sharp. The key signature for the key of G is F#.

For the key of D, we keep the F# and add a new sharp by counting up seven from D.

D - E - F# - G - A - B - C.
(1) (2) (3) (4) (5) (6) (7)

The key signature for D is F# and C#.

Can you figure the new sharp and key signature for the key of A? Remember to keep the sharps you have already established for the previous key, and just add one new one.

Now you should be able to figure the key signatures for three additional keys, E, B and F#.

What about flats? We'll look at the flat keys next issue.

The Numbers Game for Key Signatures

The Flat Keys

In the last issue you learned how to determine key signatures for the keys containing sharps in the signature (the 'sharp' keys). This time you can apply a similar formula for signatures for the flat keys.

As we did for the sharp keys, we will start from the neutral key of C, neutral because its key signature has no sharps and no flats.

The magic number in this key signature game is 5. Count down five notes from C in the C scale to find your first flat key.

C - B - A - G - F
(1) (2) (3) (4) (5)

The first flat key is F.

The rule is: every time you count down 5, add *one* (1) flat. The first flat key, F, has, therefore, one flat (one more than the previous key).

But which note in the scale gets flatted? (Not flattened. A flattened note looks like this: ✏). Count down 5 (our magic number), to find out which note gets *flatted*.

F - E - D - C - B
(1) (2) (3) (4) (5)

The B gets the flat.

Key of F key signature:

Now that we know that the key of F is our first flat key, how do we find our second flat key? Count down 5, of course, from F in the F scale.

F - E - D - C - Bb
(1) (2) (3) (4) (5)

(Since the F scale has a Bb in it, that's the 5th note we hit rather than the B♮).

So our second flat key is the key of Bb. How many flats does it have in the key signature?

(Hint: The rule is: every time you count down 5, add one flat.) If your answer is two flats, you are correct.

Key of Bb.

And which note gets the new flat? (Count down 5 again from your new key.)

Bb - A - G - F - E
(1) (2) (3) (4) (5)

E gets the flat.

Key of Bb:

E flat.
B flat.

To get your next flat key, count down 5 again from Bb, in the scale of Bb. You should arrive at . . . .(?).
(When you find it don't forget that you are playing the Bb scale and you might have to put a flat in front of it.)
Can you continue on your own to find three more flat keys and their key signatures?

It gets a bit more difficult as you continue to add flats, but you will begin to understand scales better, and you will also memorize your key signatures sooner, too. ⌒

Chord Chart

Root	TRIADS			SEVENTHS				SIXTHS		NINTHS
	Major	Minor	Augmented	Dominant	Minor	Major	Diminished	Major	Minor	Dominant
C	C	Cm	C+	C7	Cm7	Cma7	Cdim7	C6	Cm6	C9
C#	C#	C#m	C#+	C#7	C#m7	C#ma7	C#dim7	C#6	C#m6	C#9
Db	Db	Dbm	Db+	Db7	Dbm7	Dbma7	Dbdim7	Db6	Dbm6	Db9
D	D	Dm	D+	D7	Dm7	Dma7	Ddim7	D6	Dm6	D9
Eb	Eb	Ebm	Eb+	Eb7	Ebm7	Ebma7	Ebdim7	Eb6	Ebm6	Eb9
E	E	Em	E+	E7	Em7	Ema7	Edim7	E6	Em6	E9
F	F	Fm	F+	F7	Fm7	Fma7	Fdim7	F6	Fm6	F9
F#	F#	F#m	F#+	F#7	F#m7	F#ma7	F#dim7	F#6	F#m6	F#9
G	G	Gm	G+	G7	Gm7	Gma7	Gdim7	G6	Gm6	G9
Ab	Ab	Abm	Ab+	Ab7	Abm7	Abma7	Abdim7	Ab6	Abm6	Ab9
A	A	Am	A+	A7	Am7	Ama7	Adim7	A6	Am6	A9
Bb	Bb	Bbm	Bb+	Bb7	Bbm7	Bbma7	Bbdim7	Bb6	Bbm6	Bb9
B	B	Bm	B+	B7	Bm7	Bma7	Bdim7	B6	Bm6	B9

basic training _____

A Chart of 7th Chords

The chart on these two pages contains eight types of 7th chords, in all keys.

These include *the major 7th; the major 7th with a raised 5th (+5); the dominant 7th; the dominant 7th with a flatted 5th (-5); the minor 7th; the minor/major 7th; the half-diminished 7th;* and *the diminished 7th,* sometimes renotated for easier reading.

Although a few seldom-found chords are included, the chart omits chords that are either very rare or unusually awkward in notation.

Below each chord type is a breakdown of its intervals, *always calculated above the root.* The dominant 7th, for instance, contains a root, major 3rd (M3) above the root, a perfect 5th (P5) above the root, and a minor 7th (m7) above the root.

NAME:	MAJ 7th	MAJ 7th +5	DOM 7th	DOM 7th -5	MIN 7th	MIN/MAJ 7th	HALF-DIM 7th	DIM 7th (alternate notation)
7th:	M7	M7	m7	m7	m7	M7	m7	dim 7
5th:	P5	aug 5	P5	dim 5	P5	P5	dim 5	dim 5
3rd:	M3	M3	M3	M3	m3	m3	m3	m3
Root:	root	root	root	root	root	root	root	root

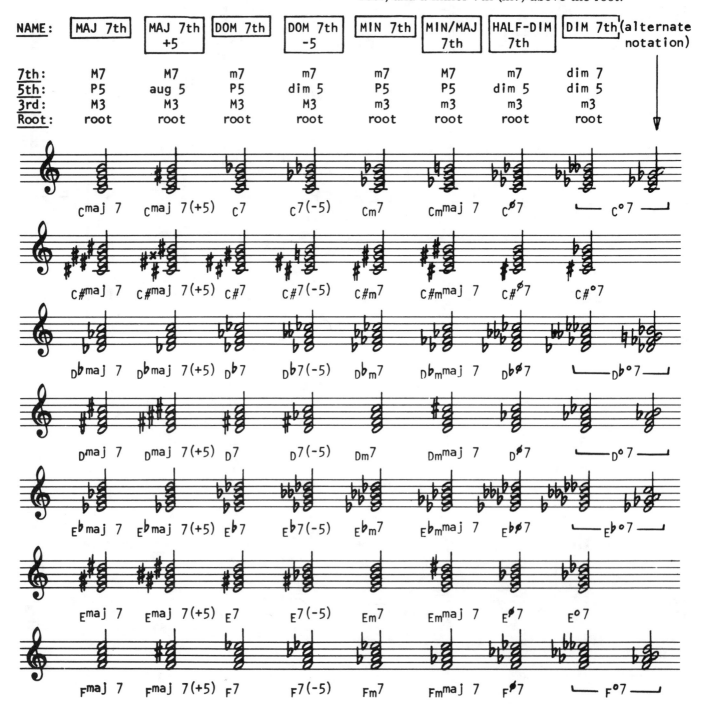

38

39

basic training
A Dictionary of 9th Chords

The eight kinds of 9th chords listed in this chart are identified and analyzed as extensions of the various 7th chords discussed in previous Basic Training articles. In each case, they consist of either a major or minor 3rd added above the basic 7th chord. In addition, the chart lists all of the intervals contained in each kind of 9th chord, calculated from the root of the chord.

1. *Dominant 7th chord + major 9th:* The most widely used 9th chord. Mildly dissonant. Used as rich substitute for any Dominant 7ths.

2. *Dominant 7th chord + minor 9th:* Useful and colorful, but infrequently found in sheet music. Interesting substitute for Dominant 7th or for Diminished 7th chord (the 9th chord minus its root).

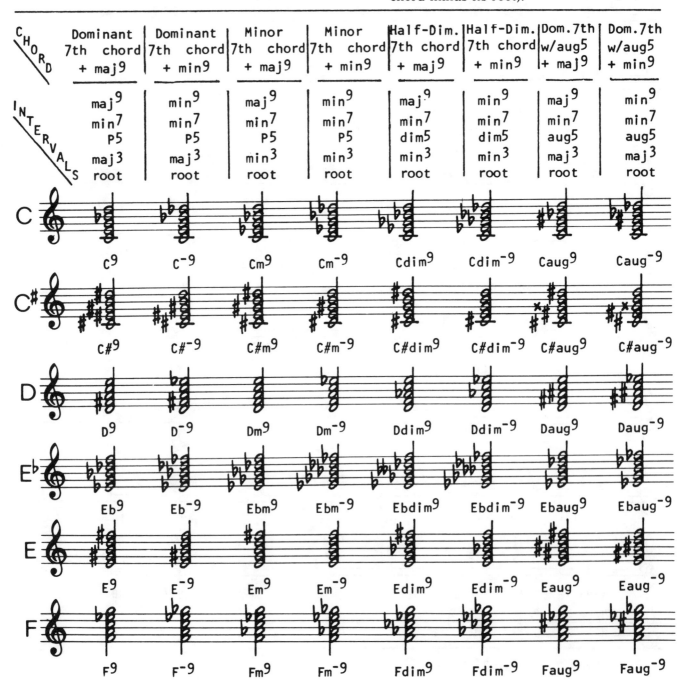

3. *Minor 7th chord + major 9th:* Lush harmony. Good substitute for Minor 7th chord, occasionally for Major 7th chord (the 9th chord minus its root).

4. *Minor 7th chord + minor 9th:* An intriguing color, especially in the Blues, as substitute for the Minor 7th chord.

5. *Half-Diminished 7th chord + major 9th:* Rare and interesting dissonance. A substitute for any Half-Diminished 7th chord where added harmonic "bite" is appropriate.

6. *Half-Diminished 7th chord + minor 9th:* Good substitute for the plain Half-Diminished 7th chord, especially where the minor 9th fits a more blues-y mood.

7. *Dominant 7th chord with augmented 5th + major 9th:* Despite its complicated label, this chord is nothing more than an augmented triad with an added minor 7th and major 9th. It is very rare, and best used with discretion because of its exotic quality.

8. *Dominant 7th chord with augment 5th + minor 9th:* Another chord built on an augmented triad, with an added minor 7th and a *minor* 9th. An intense dissonance, best used sparingly for special effect.

RH ♩

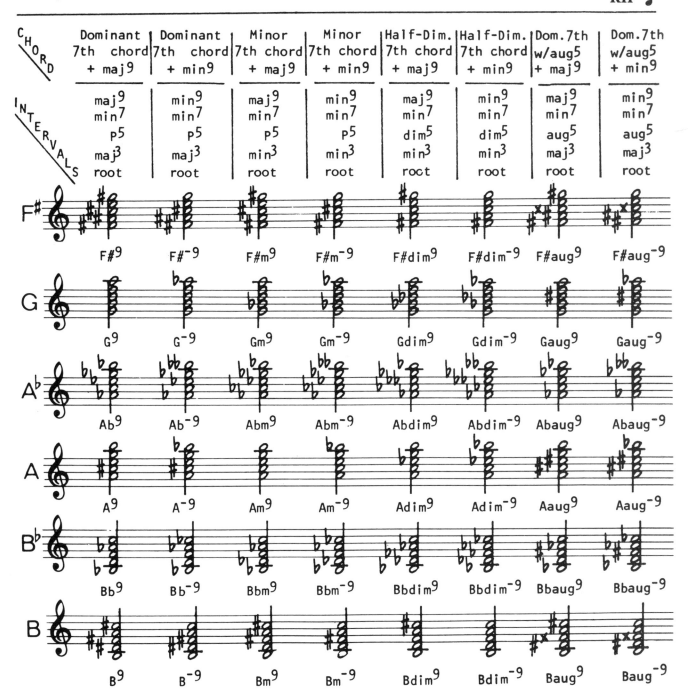

41

Section 2
HARMONIC TRICKS OF THE TRADE

Finding Thirteenth Chords On The Keyboard

By Dr. William L. Fowler

Of all the common chords, thirteenths are the biggest — and the hardest to visualize on the keyboard. Any given type of thirteenth, for example, makes twelve different visual patterns of black and white keys, one for each root along the chromatic scale. Each pattern, of course, can be individually memorized. But such learning by rote is tedious. Here's an easier way to learn thirteenth chord patterns, a way that requires only the recognition of Major and minor thirds or the recognition of Major and minor triads.

MAJOR AND MINOR THIRD RECOGNITION

White key Major thirds always enclose two black keys; white key minor thirds enclose only one:

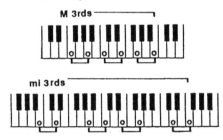

Black key Major thirds always enclose another black key; black key minor thirds do not.

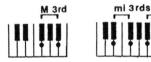

Black and white key Major thirds always enclose two white keys; black and white key minor thirds enclose only one:

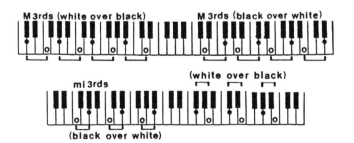

THIRTEENTH CHORD STRUCTURES

Alternate letters along the musical alphabet specify chord com-

ponents above the root. As the next example shows, thirteenth chords contain all seven:

> *"Here's an easier way to learn thirteenth chord patterns. Just spot the Major and minor triads."*

THE MODEL THIRTEENTH CHORD TYPES

Among all the types of thirteenth chords, three predominate. The first type, the Major thirteenth (#11), alternates Major and minor thirds upward:

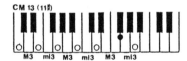

The second type, the minor thirteenth, alternates minor and Major thirds upward, just the reverse of the first:

The third type, the Dominant thirteenth (#11), groups its inner thirds in orderly pairs. It encloses two successive minors then
continued on page

45

two successive Majors between its bottom Major and its top minor: Major, minor-minor, Major-Major, minor.

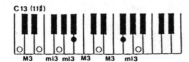

The three types also look like stacked triads: Major-Major-Major for the first; minor-minor-minor for the second; and Major-minor-Major for the third, as the next example illustrates:

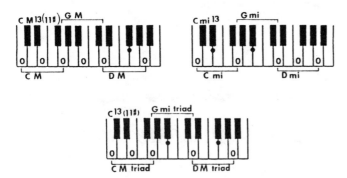

Altered notes within any of the three above models produce additional types, as in the next example:

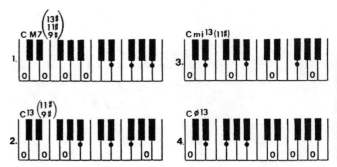

The final example provides a way to find all the possible thirteenth chord types. Either position of the third (Major or minor) combines with any position of the fifth (Perfect, augmented, or diminished) to yield six types. Then, mixing in various positions of the seventh, ninth, eleventh, and thirteenth multiplies the number of possible types to more than two hundred. For keyboard chord explorers, the final example can furnish a feast!

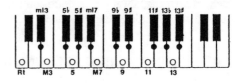

Dr. Fowler is Professor Emeritus of the University of Utah and the University of Colorado at Denver, where he was named Teacher of the Year. He has written extensively for Downbeat Magazine *and* Keyboard Magazine.

46

Harmony at the Keyboard
A Sound Experiment
Freshen Up Your Chord Playing

Example No. 1

So many of us get into the same old rut, playing pop tunes with the standard seventh chords in root position, that we often wonder what can be done to add new sounds and interest to our playing. Here's something which may be the perfect answer.

Play the chords in Example no. 1. Listen to the clear, open sound they produce. Notice that each chord has exactly the same voicing. The voicing consists of *two elements*: a triad in second inversion super-imposed on a 4th chord* consisting of three notes. (The triad and the 4th chord share the mid-tone of the entire chord.) Look at Example no. 2, then experiment with this voicing on different tones around the keyboard before going on.

Example No. 2 (Analyzing the two elements)

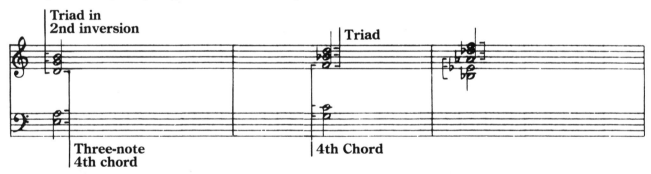

In Example no. 3, the isolated chords we started with are given chord names to create a progression in the key of F which could be used as a bridge-fill, or an extended ending, or put to any number of uses. Notice how the bass note can be a different chord tone to give each chord-name a totally new profile, e.g., the bass can be the 3rd of the chord, or the 5th, the 7th, etc.

*As triads and seventh chords are made up of super-imposed thirds (major or minor), 4th chords are made up of super-imposed perfect 4ths.

Example No. 3 (Progression)

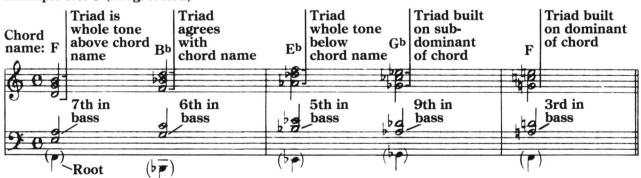

47

Continued next page

In the above example the roots are provided in parentheses in order to demonstrate more clearly how the voicing relates to each chord name.

Example no. 4 demonstrates how the same voicing can provide four distinctly different sounds to the same F chord. The voicing simply starts on a different chord tone in the bass to produce these sounds. Transposing Example no. 4 to all major chords would be an excellent way to help make this new sound become a part of your thinking.

Example No. 4 (Four ways to play the same chord with the same voicing)

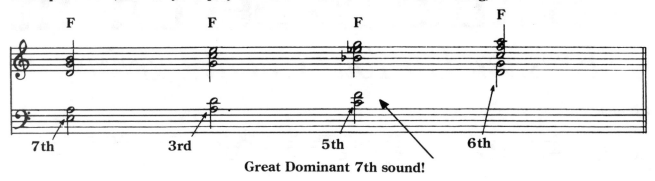

Play all four inversions on a C chord, on a G chord, on a D chord, and so on through the circle of 5ths. 𝄐

-ES

Enhancing Harmony With Passing Tones

The addition of passing tones to the harmony of a song can make the overall sound more interesting. As you can see in Example I, the passing tones form a melody of their own:

Now, take a look at Example II. Here, you have the complete sound, with the inner voices of the passing tones complementing the melody:

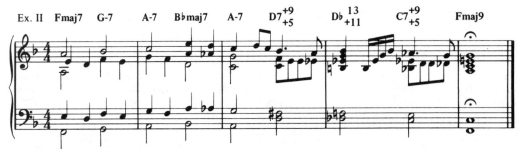

Listen to how the use of passing tones beneath the melody line creates a more pianistic sound that enhances your playing.

The passing tones utilized here are derived, primarily, by resolving the 7th of the chord downward by a whole or half step. Passing tones are also created by resolving the 9th of a chord step-wise, as in the 3rd and 4th beats of measures 3 and 4.

You can experiment by playing a series of 7th and 9th chords, and resolving them down step-wise. Try it on some songs you already know, and see if it doesn't spruce things up a bit.

LS

Want To Learn About Pop Chord Progressions? Ask Bach!

By Stuart Isacoff

The geniuses of the classical age are often described as "The Masters" because they can serve as a model for us even today. Take the subject of chord progressions. Pop and jazz musicians often talk about V-I, II-V-I and I-VI-II-V-I patterns as if they are deep dark secrets invented in the backrooms of smokey nightclubs sometime during the 1950s. But even back in the time of J. S. Bach, these progressions were considered a mainstay of musical structure.

What are these patterns? To put it clearly, look at the chart below of chords built on the notes of a major scale. In this case, they are the chords found in the key of C:

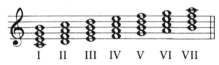

When musicians talk of a V-I progression, they are describing the V chord moving to the I chord:

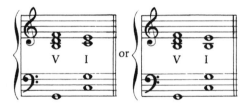

A II-V-I progression describes the movement of the II chord to the V chord to the I chord:

Here is a I-VI-II-V-I progression:

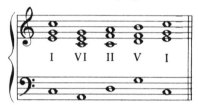

Now, in real music these chords don't always appear in *root* position — that is, with the root of each chord on the bottom. A V-I progression in the key of G might look like this:

instead of like this:

Which brings us to Bach. Here is an excerpt from the first Prelude of his monumental work, *The Well Tempered Clavier.* Try naming the chords in each measure (here Bach *arpeggiates* the chords, which means he breaks them up in a harp-like manner). To give you a hint of which chords he is using, here is an analysis: Bach first uses I-II-V-I in the home key of C. Next, he duplicates that progression in the key of G, and G — which is the V of C — leads us back to the C major harmony once again. (See below.)

This is not to suggest that there aren't more and more levels of sophistication to investigate on the topic of chord progressions. But whatever your interest, it always pays to check the work of the classical masters. You'll find without fail that they did it first!

49

POP CHORD PROGRESSIONS
The Basics

Most pop tunes are based on a few simple chord progressions; even the most complex contemporary songs are variations, or sophisticated "twists" on basic harmonic relationships. We can begin examining some of the simple progressions used in songwriting with a review of the chords which occur naturally in any major key. These chords are built from the notes of the major scale.

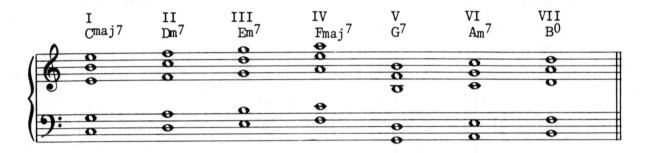

Sometimes a song is constructed by simply moving up and down the chord series I, II, III, etc.

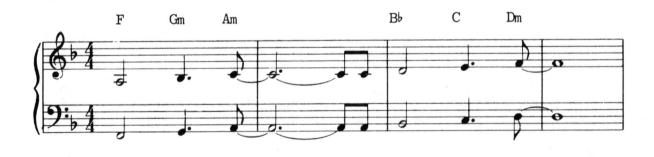

But most often the chords in a song will revolve around the use of a "cadence" — a formula for giving the impression of a momentary or permanent conclusion. The two types of cadence most encountered in pop music are IV to I (plagal or "gospel" cadence), and V to I (authentic cadence).

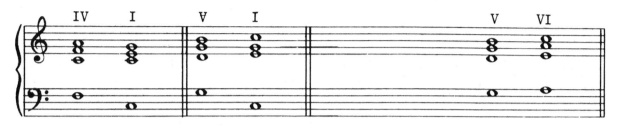

The sound of the IV-I cadence is illustrated nicely in the opening of "Swing Low."

Continued next page

Many well-known tunes make use of the V-I cadence; in "Skip To My Lou," the entire song is built on I going to V, returning to I.

"Hot Time In The Old Town Tonight" stays on the I chord (G) for most of the tune, then switches briefly to V in order to end with the V-I cadence.

Another example of a tune based solely on I-V-I is "La Bamba." Many Latin tunes follow this simple formula.

53

Continued next page

There are also songs, though, which use both types of cadence. Think of all the times you've played a tune (especially rock and folk songs) which uses only three chords. More than likely, those three chords are the I, IV, and V! "Morning Has Broken" is a good example.

Longer Progressions

The V-I cadence is so strong that whole progressions can be formed by simply placing the V of any chord before that chord, wherever it appears in a sequence. If we stay within a key, C for example, the II chord (Dm) can act as the V of the V chord (G), since it is located a fifth above that G. The VI chord (Am) can act as the V of the II chord (Dm). So, the progression VI-II-V-I is really a series of V going to I over and over. When we string out all the chords in a key so that their roots keep descending a fifth, we have the "circle of fifths" in that key.

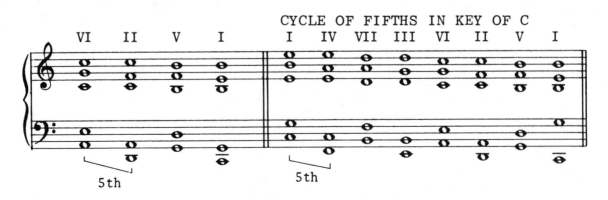

One piece of this circle, II-V-I, is so commonly used that you should be able to spot it in just about any popular song you play.

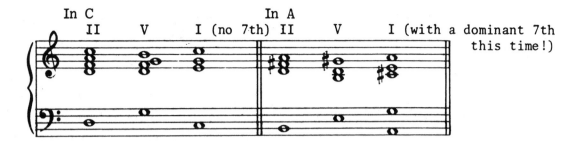

In fact, you can create your own tunes easily just by writing down a series of II-V-I progressions, and finding a melody to fit the chords!

Occasionally you'll spot a song that uses just the II-V section of the progression; a number of rock tunes (such as George Harrison's "My Sweet Lord") make use of this "partial" progression.

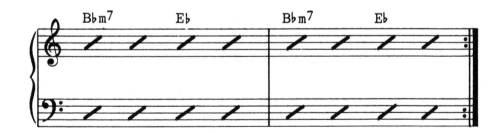

Circles of Dominants

The strongest possible cadence is a V-I progression in which the V is a major chord with a dominant seventh added (in the key of C, for example, a G^7 leading to a C major chord). We can easily create a chain of V-I sequences, therefore, in which each chord is a dominant seventh chord. (We saw earlier how II-V-I in the key of C — Dm-G-C — works as a kind of V to I sequence. D^7-G^7-C is even stronger.)

Continued next page

The resulting sound should be very familiar, as the following example, using a "Charleston" rhythm, demonstrates.

The last two lines from the next example show a sequence of dominant seventh chords which form a chain of V-I patterns leading back to the original D chord.

56

Variations

Looking back at the VI-II-V-I progression, let's add the I chord onto the beginning. The resulting I-VI-II-V-I was used for practically every song written in the 1950's! Note the movement from I to VI — it doesn't fit any of our previous categories of chord motion. We've now covered harmonic motion of IV-I, V-I, step-wise movement, and, in this last case, third relations.

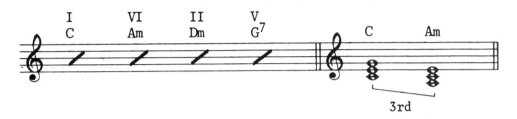

One variation on the I-VI-II-V-I progression is I-VI-IV-I (we've changed the cadence to our "plagal" alternate).

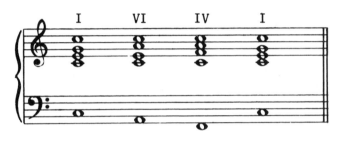

Here is a section of "Jeanie With The Light Brown Hair." Note the opening progression: I-VI-IV-I, followed by II (Major) -V-I.

Another type of variation can be formed by inserting the V^7 of any chord before that chord is played. One example of this would be to place an E^7 before the Am in the progression C-Am.

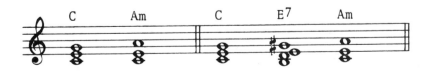

In "Wait Till The Sun Shines Nellie," this technique is used in several places.

Continued next page

57

etc.

Voice Leading

One other consideration in harmonizing pop melodies is the use of voice leading: the smooth transition from one note to another in changing harmonies. "We Wish You A Merry Christmas" utilizes a series of V-I patterns, but the harmonic movement is solidified through a bass line which moves smoothly through the chord changes through the use of inversion.

etc.

More extended variations on these basic pop progressions can be created through creative voice leading, and through chord substitution — a topic investigated on the following pages.

SI ♩

The New Chord Symbols

Today we hear a more open sound in keyboard voicings than in the past, and a new shorthand has developed to express it. You've seen the new symbols in sheet music:

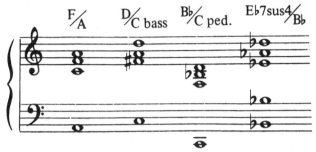

These "slash" chords summarize a number of important changes in keyboard style.

Until about 25 years ago, chord symbols* in piano lead sheets were becoming more and more complex. Extensions* (9, 11, 13) and alterations* (b9, #9, b5, #5) added colors to seventh chords. Usually the pianist clustered these extensions and altered pitches together in dense left hand chord voicings* while the right hand played active, linear solos.

Jazz doesn't necessarily sound that way today. With the contemporary two-handed voicings, the chords have a wider spread and greater openness now than in the past. Slash chords signify this two-handed approach by telling you what to play with each hand.

How To Read Them

The simplest way to interpret a slash chord is to read it as

RIGHT HAND CHORD/LEFT HAND ROOT.

If the left hand root* is a member of the right hand chord, then the slash chord calls for a simple inversion*. For example, F/A means an F triad* in the right hand over an A root in the left. This is a first inversion of an F triad.

You're likely to find inversions in a Gospel-flavored passage. For example,

Pedal point is another current sound that is well described by slash chords. The left hand sticks with one root while the right hand chords change. Here's a progression with triads floating over a stationary pedal point, written as slash chords.

Slash chords often denote fourth chords or inversions of them.

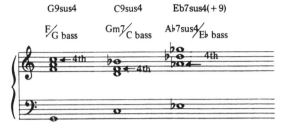

You can translate any slash chord into a complex conventional symbol and vice versa. In doing so, you'll often find that the slash chord is much easier to read.

C13 (#11, no 3, no 5, no 7) becomes **D triad/C bass. C9sus4 (no 5)** has pitches identical with **Bb triad/C ped.**

The Left Hand May Be Voiced

So far we have restricted the slash chords to single note left hands, but the left hand may play a voiced chord as well as the right. For instance,

You'll discover that this is identical with

C13(#11).

is slash shorthand for **CMa7(#9,#11).**

But don't dismiss slash chords as a lazy form of complex conventional symbols. Slash chords lead to fresh sounds and modern progressions. Now's the time to start becoming familiar with them.

Play all the slash chords we've used so far and listen for the individual notes in them. Sing the pitches one at a time as you build the chord from bottom to top. Spend some more time at the keyboard experimenting with the sounds of stationary triads over changing roots, and changing triads over stationary roots. Listen for these sounds in contemporary music. You'll hear them everywhere.

Harmony at the Keyboard
The Chord Next Door

The lovely and unusual melodic shape of *The Boy Next Door* creates some startling but eerily beautiful harmonies. They bring to mind that old adage (or did I make it up?) that any note on the keyboard can be made to belong to *any* basic chord—no matter how far out it may seem.

Take the note F, for example. What chord could that note fit? Well, an F chord, certainly. A D^b chord, or D^m, or B^b or G^7, too. Let's not stop there!

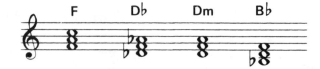

It could be the 9th of an E^{b9} chord, or the flat 9th of an E^{7b9}. It could be the suspended 4th of a C^{sus} chord. Or the major 7th of a G$^{b\ maj.7}$.

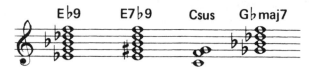

You get the idea; perhaps you're asking, "So what?" This musical truism presents a great potential for your own arranging abilities. By experimenting with the different *qualities* created by making a note fit twelve or more different chords, you will open up a whole new world of sound for your own playing.

Below is an example of how this idea can be used to move in contrary motion across the whole keyboard. Try making up other exercises using different kinds of harmonies to support simple melodic lines. Let your ear be your guide—before you know it, your playing will be filled with great sounds found in "The Chord Next Door!"

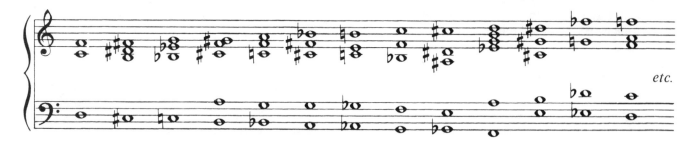

-SI

Harmony at the Keyboard

The Two-Sided Tritone And Other Puzzles

Many keyboardists feel right at home with simple triads or seventh chords, but run into difficulty when it comes to some of the more sophisticated, "jazzy" harmonies in "big band" and contemporary music. Where do these sounds come from, and how can they be used by someone without a Ph.D. in musicology? Here's a new way to think about those sounds, and a simple technique you can use to spruce up any harmony with them.

Let's begin with one of the most basic chord progressions in both pop and classical music: $V^7 - I$. In the key of F, this would represent a C^7 chord moving to an F chord. Everyone will be familiar with this progression; there is no question that it "works." But many people are not aware of why it works. The answer is "voice-leading." The notes of the C^7 chord move smoothly and logically to the notes of the F chord.

This is most apparent if we telescope in on the two notes in the C^7 chord which form the interval of a tritone: B^b and E.

The tritone is a very jazzy but unstable interval, and in the $C^7 - F$ progression, it finds stability by moving outward — the B^b down to A (the third in the F chord), and the E up to F. This resolution is pleasing, and it gives the progression a strength and inevitability.

The same two notes, called by the names $A^\#$ and E, occur in the $F^{\#7}$ chord, which is the V^7 of B. Here, though, the notes of the tritone move inward to find their resolution in the notes of the B chord.

The fact that our tritone interval can lead strongly in either direction makes possible the art of chord substitution; contemporary players will often substitute the $F^{\#7}$ for C^7, and vice versa. (These chords lie opposite each other on the "circle of fifths.")

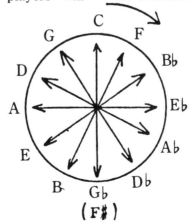

Continued next page

Harmony at the Keyboard

Musicians can make use of the two-sided tritone to add new flavors to old chord progressions. Suppose, for instance, you were faced with the progression $F^{\#7}$ to B^7. Remember, that interval of $A^\#$ and E can move outward as well as inward. In the example below, the base line moves from $F^\#$ to B, but the tritone in the right hand acts as if we were playing C^7 to F. We have purposely confused the harmonic movement, taking advantage of the vagueness of the tritone.

Try playing a whole circle of fifths using this concept. If you keep in mind the idea that each hand is capable of "voice-leading" in its own direction, the result can be refreshing and quite beautiful. To start you off, here is a sample using $C^7 — F^7 — B^{b7}$.

-SI

THEORY CLASS
Keyboard Qualities

When creating their own arrangements of the great hits, professional musicians often consider changing chord qualities or rhythmic qualities for added color and variety. Here is another important element for all keyboard players: the changing quality of sound from octave to octave as one moves from the lowest to the highest part of the keyboard itself.

Keyboardists use this natural phenomenon in many ways. Here are some examples to keep in mind.

1) Harmonies can be sparser in the lower end of the keyboard and still sound full; "close" voicings which feature clusters of notes sound best in the mid-range; the treble can sound thin, and often calls for doubling of notes.

2) Chime effects and other high pitch tinkles work best when played in two octaves at once, to avoid being too "thin" or weak sounding.

3) Different keyboard sections can be combined for various sound qualities. High and middle can imitate woodwinds and high strings.

Low and middle form the typical accompaniment sound.

Low and high can create an interesting "impressionistic" effect.

4) Single note lines can be made more powerful by playing them two octaves apart, or in thirds or sixths.

5) For a truly orchestral sound, use *all* of the keyboard at once! If you've got it, flaunt it!!

S. Isacoff

-SI

CHORD SUBSTITUTION & HARMONY WITH THE CIRCLE OF FIFTHS

PART I

An exercise to help familiarize you with the 'circle' is to play it on the keyboard as single notes, selecting any random location on the keyboard. For example: starting at the top of the circle you play a C, any C. Say Middle C. The next note in the circle is F. Play any F. It doesn't necessarily have to be the F below Middle C. Next play any B♭, to any E♭, etc. Memorize it as you play. Once you've done that you know the fifth below every note in the scale and you are on your way to changing your entire concept of pop harmony, which is really traditional harmony as epitomized by Bach.

The following exercises will help familiarize you with the circle of fifths and perfect its use in your playing.

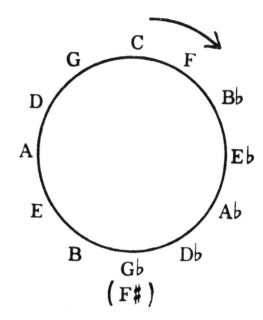

A. The circle of fifths starts with the top note of the keyboard and descends a fifth on each succeeding note, never repeating a note until it winds up on the lowest C of the keyboard. It progresses through all twelve tones of the scale before repeating a tone.

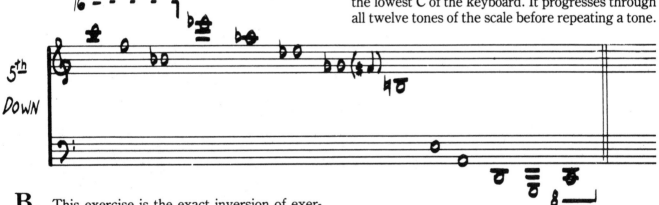

B. This exercise is the exact inversion of exercise A. The series of notes are exactly the same, except you are ascending. It is still called the circle of fifths because it is a fifth descending, but you are playing it upside down so it becomes a fourth ascending. Start memorizing the circle of fifths, beginning with the first four notes.

63

C. This exercise is a combination of descending and ascending fifths, alternating between the two. This is used in the base line of many pop songs and recordings.

D. This exercise is a mixed bag of descending and ascending fifths without any particular pattern. Memorize the first six notes of the circle and play them without looking.

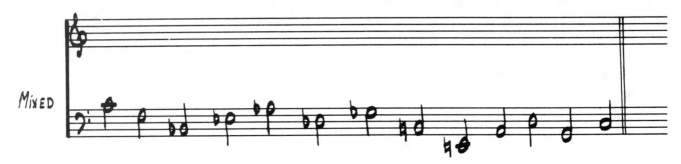

E. This exercise is a series of major chords built on a root which travels a fifth with each succeeding chord. Alternate ascending and descending fifths are found in many pop pieces.

F. This is an exercise to warm up your fingers and to develop your technique, as well as to help you memorize the circle of fifths. This exercise will also help you to use arpeggios in your playing. By now you should have memorized the first eight notes of the circle of fifths and can get this exercise up to speed.

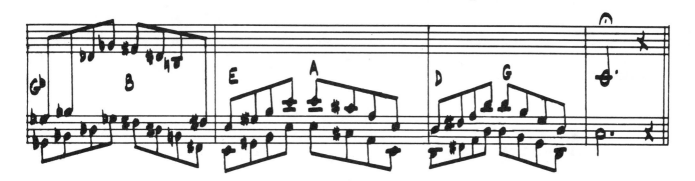

G. This exercise shows the progression of dominant seventh chords structured on each root in the circle of fifths. It can also be called a series of secondary dominants. You should have memorized the entire circle of fifths by now.

H. This exercise is the same series of dominant chords as in exercise G, but it creates finger exercises to help you learn runs and put them into your playing. Play the exercise slowly with two hands. Only the first four chords have been written, the rest are left to you. If you have not yet memorized the rest of the chords in the progression, refer to exercise G for the next chords. Practice until you get it up to speed.

I. This combination of ascending and descending fifths loosens fingers and is good for practicing the circle of fifths. Again, only the first four chords are written. Repeat this exercise and progressively make it faster until it is up to speed.

J. This exercise is an important element for chords which travel through the circle of fifths. It is a combination of a minor seventh chord and a dominant seventh chord. It is sometimes called the II-V^7 progression in harmony. Repeat the progression until fully memorized.

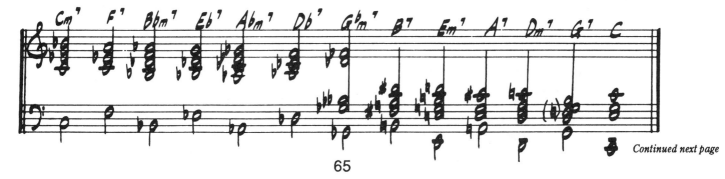

Continued next page

K. This exercise is one of many ways to practice the circle of fifths. It uses thirteenth chords, but augmented ninth, or dominant ninth chords can also be used.

PART II

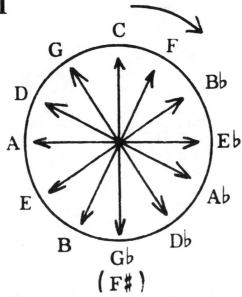

The illustration above is the one you will use to find chord substitutions and passing chords. Here are the three rules to remember:

Rule 1: You can often use the chord directly across the circle as a substitute for the chord you are playing.

(Example: If you are playing an F7 chord, follow the arrow across to find the likely substitute: B7.)

Rule 2: You can often use that same chord, the one directly across the circle, as a passing chord in addition to the original chord. (Example: If you are playing an F7 to a B♭ progression, as written in a piece of sheet music, you can slip that same B7 in between as a passing chord.)

Rule 3: You can often precede the chord you are playing with the chord which precedes it in the circle. (Example: You are playing a G7 chord for two beats and would like to "fill" a chord before you hit the G7. Delay the G7 until the second beat and play the chord which precedes it in the circle on the first beat. The chord which precedes it in the circle is a D. In the example below we use a Dm7.)

Let us now apply these rules to a portion of Jerome Kern's "All The Things You Are."

Before we substitute chords, take a quick look at how Kern composed this song around the circle of fifths, and also uses the 'jump-across-the-circle' technique we've discussed. His first chord is Fm. Next chord if Bbm (next in circle); his next chord

Eb7 (next chord in circle); next chord (can you guess?) is also the next chord in the circle, an Ab: the next chord is (how can you miss?) a Db, the next chord in the circle. (You could practically play this song 'by ear' if you knew the circle of fifths.)

Continued next page

On the next chord, Kern throws a little curve. He gives us a G7. The G7 is not the next chord in the circle after D♭7 . . . but it is the chord which is located directly across (follow the arrows) from the D♭7. He has used the 'jump-across' technique to continue his song. And now he starts using the circle all over again beginning on the G7. The next chord is C. It changes to Cm before going on to Fm,

the next circle chord. Analyze the rest of the example yourself to see Kern follow the circle and jump across.

Now let's put in some of our own chords using the rules we discussed here.

In the third measure we will use another chord instead of the E♭7. To find a possible substitute, look directly across the circle. An A7.

Now that we have that A7, let's apply Rule 3 to put a 'filler' or 'passing' chord in front of it. Find the

chord which precedes A7 in the circle, and use it just before you use the A7.

By using the circle, we have substituted two chords for the E♭7, and now you are leaving the sheet music arrangement for your own styled interpretation.

In measure 11, there is a B♭7 chord and we can apply the same technique. First find the substitute by looking across the circle. The substitute is E7.

Now use a filler chord by finding the chord which precedes the E7 in the circle. A B chord. Since

there's a D in the melody, Bm chord is the logical choice.

68

And finally, in the 14th measure, we can apply all three rules.

There is a D11 for four beats. An Am7 played before the D11 (Rule 3) and an AB7 played after the D7 (Rule 2):

Or you can simply ignore the original D7 altogether by substituting the A♭7 for it (Rule 1) but still keeping the Am7 as a filler chord.

This demonstrates how the filler chord (Am7) for the D7 can also become the filler chord for the D7's substitute. Another DISCOVERY! Ah, the circle is full of 'em!

ES

Substitute Changes
Helpful Hints

Many tunes share common progressions, and, depending on the particular melody being used, they can all be varied according to the principles outlined in the preceding articles.

Take the I-VI-II-V progression, for example. This chord sequence has been used in tunes such as "I Got Rhythm," "Cottontail," "Blue Moon," and "Tuxedo Junction." The original sequence,

Continued next page

$$B^b - Gm - Cm^7 - F^7$$

can be varied in many ways. It sometimes appears as:

$$B^b - Gm - Cm^7 - F^7 - Gm^7 - E^{dim} - Cm^7 - F^7.$$

The last four chords, however, can be substituted with the chords

$$A^{b7} - G^7 - B^{b7} - F^7$$

as a circle of fifths progression leading to F^7 (with substitutions borrowed from across the "circle"):

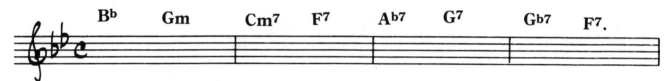

Even the Blues progression can be spruced up through chord substitution. The typical Blues in F would look like this:

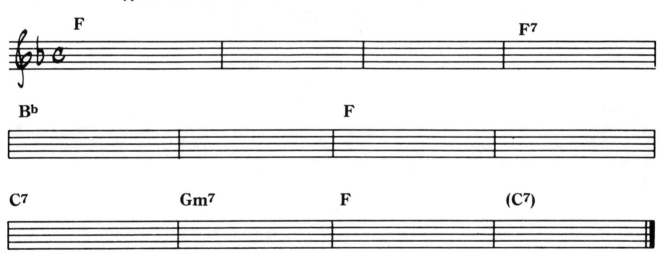

Here is a revised version using chord substitution:

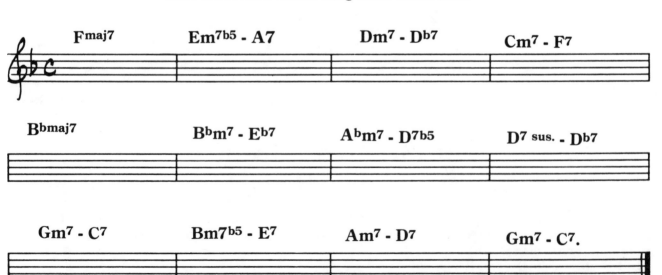

Try using substitutions on your favorite tunes. There is always a new way to play any song — the fun is in finding one you never thought of before!

SI ♪

Variations on a Triad: Suspended 4ths and Added 6ths

In early classical music, a triad was often made more colorful by delaying the arrival of one of its notes — usually the 3rd of the chord — in this way:

In this example, we do not hear the complete F major triad (F-A-C) until the "suspended" B finally resolves downward to the A.

Jazz harmony adapted this suspension to its own purposes, simply by keeping the suspended B and ignoring the resolution note A. The result is a "chord of the suspended 4th" or, in jazz short-hand, "F$^{sus\,4}$" ("4" refers to the interval between the root of the triad and the suspended note):

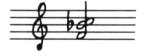

All "sus 4" chords have the same construction: a root, and both a perfect 4th and perfect 5th above the root.

Since the absent 3rd would have given the chord its major or minor feeling, the "sus 4" chord is neither major nor minor; it is simply a colorful, mildly dissonant variation of the "normal" triad.

The chart below contains all "sus 4" chords:

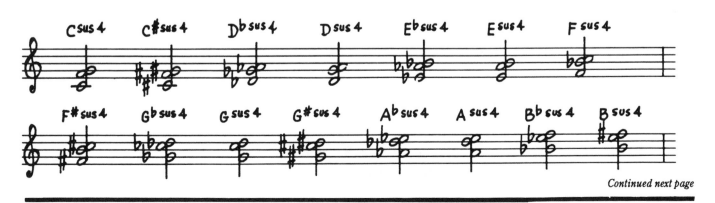

Continued next page

The "chord of the added 6th," or "6th chord," is a triad with a 6th added above the root. The 6th is always a *major* 6th unless otherwise marked. The notation " 6" or "-6" indicates the addition of a *minor* 6th above the root.

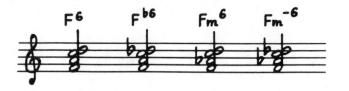

The chart below contains all 6th chords commonly found in sheet music. Chords in parentheses are "enharmonic" spellings: that is, they sound the same as the previous chord but are notated differently.

RH ♩

72

Keyboard Workshop

Old Pants and New Suspenders

—Suspensions add a different flavor to worn chord progressions

There was a time when pop music relied on very simple harmonies and straightforward rhythms; it's hard to imagine a George M. Cohan tune arranged with the kind of contemporary, sophisticated panache associated with Christopher Cross and Burt Bacharach. Today's music is something else entirely. But the new sounds we find in songs like "Best That You Can Do" (theme from the movie *Authur*) are not too difficult to understand. They just make use of a kind of harmonic tension that occurs when some of the well-worn simple progressions of Cohan's time are placed over unexpected additional tones.

Any tone can be a part of a countless range of harmonies. The note C, for example, can be part of a C chord, or of an F chord, or of a D^7, or a G^{11}, or a $B\flat^9$. By the same token, a simple F chord takes on a new identity if you place a D below it: Dm^7. If you place a G below it, it will miraculously transform into a G^{11}.

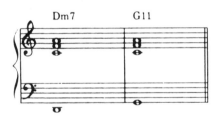

That sound of harmonies shifting over a steady bass is an important part of the contemporary sound; inevitably, the shifting treble harmonies create a "suspension"—a chord in search of resolution. There are plenty of examples of suspensions sprinkled throughout "Best That You Can Do."

In the above example, no sooner does the E chord resolve than we find a new suspension on the A chord. Still another suspension of sorts occurs when the common progression E–A (V–I) is placed over a held A in the bass. The dissonant sound produced when the E chord is struck resolves pleasantly into an A major sound; this is similar to a classical technique called *acciaccatura*. If the held A in the bass were absent, the harmonies would sound quite ordinary.

Continued next page

At other points in the song, typical step-wise progressions in the key of A, such as F#m–E–D–E (VI–V–IV–V) or F#m–E–D–C#m (VI–V–IV–III) take on new dimensions because of the bass tones below them.

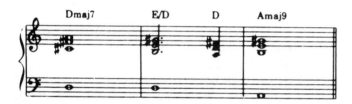

The technique of placing these simple harmonies over held bass tones results in chords with 9ths 11ths, 13ths, and so on. To continue this sound in sections where the held-bass approach is missing, simply add as many of these extra tones as possible to the chords indicated on the music.

SI

Mark Levine

Sus and Phrygian chords

by Mark Levine

Some of the musicians with whom Mark Levine has recorded are Cal Tjader and Carmen McRae, Joe Henderson, and Poncho Sanchez. His own album, Smiley and Me, *is on Concord Jazz. Mark teaches jazz piano at Sonoma State University and lives and works in the San Francisco Bay area.*

This article is an excerpt from The Jazz Piano Book *by Mark Levine, soon to be published by Sher Music.*

Although Duke Ellington was playing them in the 1930's, **sus** chords have been an everyday sound in jazz only since the 1960's. The simplest voicing — whether you're playing a standard or Herbie Hancock's "Maiden Voyage" — is to play the root with your left hand while playing a major triad a whole step below the root with your right hand, as in figure 1.

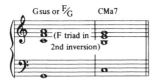

Because G is the root of this sus chord, the triad in your right hand would be F major, a whole step below G. Note that the triad is in second inversion, meaning that the fifth of the triad (C) is on the bottom, instead of the root (F). Triads often sound stronger inverted than in root position, especially so when in second inversion. The **Gsus** chord resolves smoothly to a **CMa7**.

The "sus" refers to the suspended fourth of the chord, in this case the note C. In traditional harmony, this note usually resolves downward a half step, the sus chord becoming a dominant seventh chord (figure 2). In modern music, this note often doesn't resolve, which gives sus chords their "floating" quality.

You might see this same **Gsus** chord notated as **G7sus4, Gsus4, F/G,** or **Dm7/G**. **F/G** describes exactly what's happening in figure 1: an F triad in the right hand over the note G in the left hand. **Dm7/G** describes the *function* of the sus chord, because a sus chord is like a **II-V** progression contained in one chord. The **II-V** progression in the key of C is **Dm7-G7**. In figure 3, your right hand plays a common **Dm7** left hand voicing over a G root, combining **Dm7** and **G7** into a single chord — **Dm7/G,** or **Gsus**.

Two songs recorded in the 1960's did a lot to popularize sus chords among jazz musicians: John Coltrane's "Naima"[1] and Herbie Hancock's

"Maiden Voyage."[2] "Maiden Voyage" consists entirely of sus chords, which made it a revolutionary tune for its time. Hancock's vamp on the first two bars is shown in figure 4. The **Dsus** chord is voiced with a C triad a whole step down from the root, D. One note in the triad has been doubled, and the fifth has been added in the left hand to give the chord more "bottom."

A persistent misconception about sus chords is that the fourth takes the place of the third. Jazz pianists, however, often voice the third with a sus chord, as you can see in the examples in the next figure. Note that in the first five voicings shown, the third is above the fourth. You could play the fourth above the third, as in the last voicing, but the result would be a much more dissonant chord. In a tune like "Maiden Voyage," where each sus chord lasts for four bars, you have a lot more freedom to use dissonance. Let your taste be your guide.

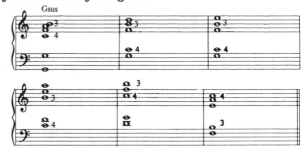

Phrygian chords

A Phrygian chord is a dominant seventh chord with the thirteenth in the bass instead of the root. The next figure shows a **G7** voicing with the root in the bass and the same **G7** voicing with its thirteenth, E, in the bass. You might

see a Phrygian chord notated as **G7/E, Esus♭9,** or **E Phryg** — since there is no single commonly accepted chord symbol for a Phrygian chord.

Continued next page

---

[1]John Coltrane, *Giant Steps,* Atlantic SD-1311.
[2]Herbie Hancock, *Maiden Voyage,* Blue Note 84195.

If you know the major modes, you know that Phrygian is the third mode of the major scale, and that E Phrygian is derived from the third note of the C major scale. The alternate chord symbol **G7/E** gives a clue to what's happening here. Instead of playing G in the bass, you substitute E, the Phrygian note in the key of C. Notice how smoothly it resolves to the **AMa** chord. Even though **G7** is a **V** chord in the key of C, the **V-I** relationship here is between **E** and **A**.

A beautiful example of Phrygian harmony is the **E♭ Phrygian** chord in the intro and the next-to-last chord on the bridge of John Coltrane's "After The Rain" on *Impressions* (MCA-5887).

You can use sus and Phrygian chords effectively to reharmonize standard tunes, as in the accompanying arrangement of "Star Eyes." The original chords are shown above the reharmonized chord symbols. Whenever a sus or Phrygian chord appears, it takes the place of a **II** or **V** chord, or substitutes for the entire **II-V** progression.

The melody has been changed in bar 4 to accommodate the **A♭ Phrygian** chord. There are some other goodies here, too. In particular, note the Duke Ellington-like chords in bars 1 and 3, the McCoy Tyner-like fourth chords in bars 10 and 14, and the Kenny Barron style minor seventh voicing in bar 16. The very last chord is a sus chord in a completely different key. This touch gives an ethereal quality to the ending.

Try your hand at reharmonizing tunes using sus and Phrygian chords. I would suggest "I Didn't Know What Time It Was," "Yesterdays," "Stella By Starlight," and "What Is This Thing Called Love." ●

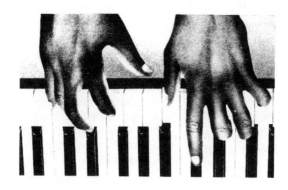

From triads to fourth chords

Subscriber Eric W. Sutz, a professional pianist and teacher from Illinois, wants to know more about quartal harmony. Quartal harmony is based on the interval of a fourth. Let's take this opportunity to review intervals and chords based on thirds, which will lead easily into a discussion of quartal harmony.

Intervals

All music is made up of intervals. An interval is the distance between any two pitches. The pianist can easily see intervals on his or her instrument as the distances between any two keys. Intervals begin with the half step (m2) and whole step (Ma2).

Above are the basic intervals within one octave. Notice that two of them are fourths, the "perfect" fourth (2-1/2 steps in size) and the "augmented" fourth (3 whole steps).

Triads usually contain two superimposed thirds. The thirds may be either major (2 whole steps) or minor (1-1/2 steps). The upper pitch of one third is the lower pitch of the other third in a triad. Here are the four basic triads: diminished, minor, major and augmented.

Seventh chords can be voiced as a stack of three thirds. For example, here are CMa7, C7 and Cm7 all voiced as stacks of thirds.

The C7sus4 chord above is voiced in stacked fourths. Jazz pianists in the 1960's (notably McCoy Tyner and Herbie Hancock) popularized the sound of stacked fourths. The fourths may be perfect or augmented, depending on the chord and the voicing.

To become familiar with fourth chords, play those given in the next figure in your right hand while you strike the given roots with your left.

Notice that the voicings in boxes are more closely related to the chord symbol than the others. The boxed voicings do not contain the suspended fourth; they have the third of the chord instead. They may or may not contain the seventh. These are good alternative voicings for seventh chords.

Applications

Voicing individual chords in fourths opens new possibilities for your playing. You can use them to harmonize a melody in the right hand while the left plays chord roots. Or you can play fourth chords in the left hand to accompany a right hand melody. As accompaniment chords, the fourth chords sound best if middle C falls within their range. Below that they sound muddy, and above that they conflict with the right hand's range.

To encourage you to think, hear and play fourth chords, here are two blues that use them. The first features fourth chords moving chromatically and diatonically. This example shows how big fourth chords sound when they are played in both hands. The next example is a minor blues in the Dorian mode, using stacked fourths with a third on top. This voicing is strongly reminiscent of Bill Evans's voicings.

Let these two blues stimulate more experimentation with fourth chords — both stacked fourths and then the more sophisticated voicings that mix stacked fourths and thirds.●

—Becca Pulliam

Quartal Chords

By Andy LaVerne

One of the most popular harmonic devices used by twentieth century composers is quartal harmony (chords built in fourths). In previous columns we have examined aspects of tertian harmony (chords built in thirds). Tertian harmony, while still widely used today, has its roots in the Classic and Romantic periods. Quartal harmony, with its more contemporary sound, ironically can be traced back to the techniques of medieval polyphony. It can also occur as a result of melodic ornamentation of tertian harmony.

Quartal harmony yields a somewhat harmonically ambiguous sound, because the voices have a less direct relationship to the root or fundamental of the chord. It is often not possible to identify a tonal center with chords built in fourths. Chords built in perfect fourths, like all chords built with equidistant intervals (diminished seventh chords or augmented triads) can have any chord member function as the root. The resultant ambiguity can imply more than one chord quality for a chord built in fourths.

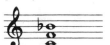

C7sus4; Cm7sus4; BbMa9; Gm7add4; F7sus4; Eb9/6

Three-note chords in fourths — There are three possible intervallic arrangements found in three-note quartal chords. Perfect-perfect, perfect-augmented, and augmented-perfect.

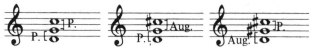

These chords all have two possible inversions.

Fundamental   1st inversion   2nd inversion

By inverting a fourth, the interval of a fifth results. Using the inverted perfect fourth can impart a variety of color to quartal harmony. Using three-note chords in fourths to harmonize a scale or mode can yield some interesting results. Harmonizing a scale or mode using strictly perfect fourths can imply polytonality.

C Major scale   C harmonized in perfect 4ths

Four-note chords in fourths — By adding another fourth to the three-note chord, a more resonant quality results. The added tone forms the consonant interval of a tenth with the bass voice. These four note structures can also be inverted, creating even more variants because of the intervals they contain.

Fundamental

Compound construction (thirds & fourths) brings yet another color to quartal harmony. A third can be added either above or below a three-note chord in fourths. If it is a major third, the chord sounds consonant. A minor third added yields a less consonant sounding chord.

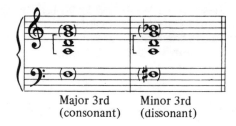

Major 3rd   Minor 3rd
(consonant)   (dissonant)

As chords built in thirds can be arranged in sixths (inverted thirds) chords built in fourths can be arranged in fifths (inverted fourths).

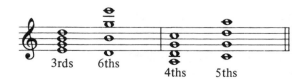

3rds   6ths   4ths   5ths

Multi-note chords in fourths — Fourths may be stacked in groups of five, six or more notes. Twelve different notes may be arranged a perfect fourth apart before one is repeated.

Some of the composers who employ the techniques of quartal harmony are: Debussy, Scriabin, Alban Berg, Leonard Bernstein, Arnold Schoenberg, Igor Stravinsky and Anton Webern. Quartal harmony can also be found in the playing of jazz pianists Chick Corea, Herbie Hancock, and McCoy Tyner. As a composer and performer I find quartal harmonies to be one of my favorite sounds. I leave you with an example of a quartal passage that might appear in one of my improvisations. In this example I am using compound structures (fourths, thirds, seconds) and I am harmonizing modes using quartal harmony.

Cm7   F7   BbMa7

Scriabin's mystic chord

Alexander Scriabin

Classical music has always played an important part in the development of jazz style. In the area of chords and voicings, contemporary pianists such as Herbie Hancock, Chick Corea and the late Bill Evans were heavily influenced by Ravel. Another influential but lesser-known composer was the Russian Alexander Scriabin, a turn-of-the-century visionary, whose music and ideas found many adherents in the counterculture of the 1960's.

Scriabin came up with a harmony he termed the "mystic" chord, and it has many applications for today's jazz player. Here is the original chord.

We can derive many different voicings from this rather thick combination of notes. By selecting some of the pitches we can create **13th, 9th, augmented 11th** and **augmented 5th** chords.

Many of these chord voicings share an interesting quality. They work equally well with either of two roots, a tritone apart.

Here are both applications, presented in descending chromatic (half step) lines.

The fact that we can switch roots with this

voicing is particularly handy in playing a cycle of fifths progression. Here is an example that shows why. Alternating bass notes in the cycle allows us to play an endless progression of **V-I** progressions, simply by moving the voicing down in half-steps!

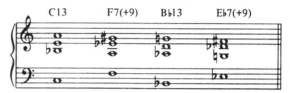

We can accomplish the same feat with the other voicings we selected from our original "mystic" chord.

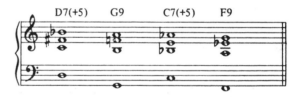

Using these voicings in the left hand while the bass player of the group plays the roots is a common practice among today's performers. Of course, they can also be used in the right hand, sometimes with additional chord tones played in the left — as this last example demonstrates.

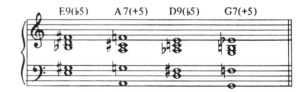

Contemporary harmony, because it makes use of such "altered" chord members as augmented **9ths** or flatted **5ths,** allows for more "shared" tones between different chords. In the case of "tritone substitution" — offered in these examples — the **7th** of one chord becomes the **3rd** of another; the **13th** of one becomes the augmented **9th** of the other, and so on. This makes moving from one chord to another easy.

Scriabin helped lead the way, by discovering his "mystic" harmony.●

-SI

Exploring the sixth diminished scale

by Fiona Bicket with Barry Harris

This is the third, and final, article in a series by Fiona Bicket presenting lessons she learned at Barry Harris' workshops. Bicket came to New York from Australia to study jazz. She has reached the semi-finals in the Thelonious Monk International Piano Competition twice. Currently, she is teaching and performing in New South Wales, Australia. Barry Harris is one of the premiere pianists in jazz — especially bebop — and he has taught piano and theory to students who come to him from all over the US and around the world. This article is the result of a two-step process. Bicket wrote the basic text, and Harris commented on it (in italics), creating variations on Fiona's basic music examples.

Through searching for more and more fundamental ways of looking at harmony, Barry Harris has developed a special scale — the sixth diminished scale. This scale, studied in its major and minor forms, can open up a wealth of possibilities for *movement within a chord*. It can also widen your understanding of harmony in general. After exploring the use of this scale over the past few years, I can see that it has filled quite a gap in my harmonic knowledge and also provided me with unlimited material for creating fresh harmonic ideas.

The major sixth diminished scale is the same as the diatonic major scale, but with an added note between the fifth and sixth degrees of the scale. The minor sixth diminished scale is the same as the ascending form of the melodic minor, but also with an added note between the fifth and sixth.

To get a feel for this scale on the piano, first practice it in thirds, like so —

Notice that you must play G and A together as a third, as the note G# falls between them in the scale. It takes some time to get accustomed to this unusual configuration. Try it in other keys.

Harris says, "The sixth diminished scale should be taught all over the world, in classical music and all others." Here are a couple of other ways of looking at it.

*Put your fingers down on a **C6** chord — C, E, G, and A.*

It's a combination of two things. The C and A are from one sixth diminished chord,

the E and G are from another diminished chord.

*And there's one additional diminished chord that's not in the **C6** chord, the **D°7**.*

Some of the prettiest sounds happen when you play a diminished note — like this A♭ — over a minor chord. The A♭ says "Move me." Diminished notes have a way of saying "Move me somewhere."

You can begin to see the harmonic implications of the scale by building a chord up in thirds from each degree of the scale. The chord generated off the first degree of the scale is **C6**.

And off the second degree, **D** diminished (**D°**) . . .

off the third degree, **C6** in first inversion, and off the fourth degree, **D°** in first inversion (or **F°**).

Carry on up the scale, generating chords off each degree of the scale. You will notice that only two chords are created — **C6** and **D°**. Also do this with C minor sixth diminished scale. You will find that the chords generated are **Cm6** and **D°**.

Now, play the whole chord scale in "short chords."

To hear this a little more clearly, play it also in

"long" chords, by swapping the top and bottom notes of each chord.

Another way to show it — go up the scale switching short and long.

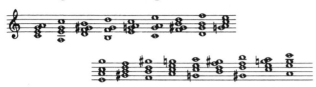

As you can see, what we have here is a way of moving away from a sixth chord and back to the same sixth chord via the associated diminished. See how Barry uses this in the first one and a half bars of his tune "Father Flanagan" (Xanadu Records, 1978), where he moves from B♭m6 to C° and back using the B♭ minor sixth diminished scale.

© Barchris Publishing. Used By Permission.

Now look at this usage of the C major sixth diminished scale to embellish a C6 chord.

The above example shows how the diminished notes of the scale can be used to create *melodic movement within the chord.*

It's so pretty. She uses contrary motion. She could also have played this using parallel motion.

[In the following example] the A and C (from the C6 chord) are held and the G, E, and A move up one degree of the C diminished sixth scale, then back. Next, the voices move up two degrees, then back. In the last example shown, they move up three degrees. You could extend this movement further. You could also move from the Am7 to the D7, as Fiona shows in her next example.

The usage of this scale is not confined to IMa

or Im situations, however. For example, the C major sixth diminished scale can be used for the chord Am7. Here I've used the scale for movement in an Am7 chord as it moves to D7.

You can practice this type of movement by playing the chord scale, but in each chord raise and then resolve one or two of the notes involved. For example, here is the C minor sixth diminished chord scale with the top note raised and then resolved.

Try raising and resolving one or two of the other notes in the chord, and see what interesting sounds can be created. For example, moving the note second from the bottom would give you this:

Try applying some of these sounds to a II - V situation. (The C minor sixth diminished scale can be used for Am7(♭5).)

Try this: move the pattern down one whole step at a time, ending with a run up the keyboard. (See below.) How to execute this run? Divide it between the hands. At first, play it in "clumps." Then, when you play it as a run, the hands stay in shape, but rotate a little, to separate the clumps into absolutely even notes.

Play in hand positions . . . I am a firm believer in not playing with your fingers. A notewise procedure gets you in trouble.

When you begin to use these sounds in their appropriate contexts, you can soon see a real connection between the sixth chords found in the original sheet music of standard tunes and

HARMONY

our modern chord voicings. Now, we often use other bass notes, and we often leave unresolved diminished notes in our chords. **CMa9**, for example, is C6 with two unresolved diminished notes — B and D. But the true sixth sound, if only we could recognize it, is still intact.

You have already seen one example of this — **C6** to **D7**, or **IV** to **V**, in place of **IIm7** to **V**. Another example is **Cm6** to **D7**, or **IVm6** to **V**, in place of **IIm7(♭5)** to **V**. Knowing this can help you find the appropriate sixth diminished scale to generate movement.

For dominant seventh chords, the choice of scale depends on the context (or melody note). For most "altered" dominants, the minor sixth diminished scale found a half step above the root note will work. Play this chord.

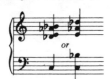

Do you see how this **C7(+5♭9)** is **D♭m6/C?**

Here's an example of Barry's, showing how you can put this knowledge to work, using moving thirds from the scale.

There are many ways of exploring and applying these scales. Above all, let your ear guide you; never be afraid to let your intellect, governed by the logic of this harmonic material, take you into new areas. Many of the questions I've heard uttered in Barry's workshops — "What if we did it backwards?" or "in contrary motion?" "How about moving the left hand instead of the right?" — reflect the playfulness which can be at work in this kind of harmonic exploration.

Contemporary left hand chording

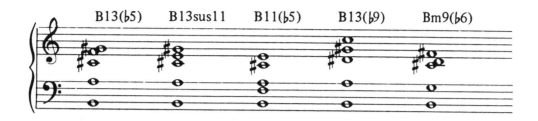

Many contemporary pianists have adapted the Bill Evans style of playing left hand harmonies in the piano's mid-range while soloing with right hand an octave above. But today's harmonies are often quite different from those used by Evans. McCoy Tyner specializes in stacked fourths, while Herbie Hancock and Chick Corea often use clusters or combinations of half-step and wide interval conjunctions in their voicings to create a *misterioso* sound.

That sound need not be so mysterious. Let's survey a few of the chord types used in contemporary jazz harmony. Above are five possible two-handed voicings, all on a B harmony.

Placing these in the left hand alone requires a process of selecting some of the pitches and leaving others out. Your ears will help you decide how to get the desired effect. Here are a few possibilities.

First, here's a left hand voicing for the very first harmony. Notice the placement of the **G#-A** half-step. Most of the voicings used in this style employ a half-step either on the bottom or in the middle, and the root is often left out.

Our **B¹³** can be distilled down to just three notes.

For an unusual **b6** sound (to me it somehow conveys a minor tonality even though the third is missing), try this one.

Using these voicings in a chord progression can take a little practice, but it's not all that difficult. The idea is to keep common pitches if possible, and to move the hand very little; at the same time, use of half-steps and upper members of the harmony — **9, 11, 13** — is essential. Try to think of common tones that will add color to your chords. Here is a short chord progression in which the common tone — **C#** — is first a **9**, then a **13**, before becoming the third in an **A** triad.

Another version of that progression first uses the common tone **C#** (**9** to **13** again), before switching to a common tone of **F#** (**9** to **13** once more, in the new **V** to **I** sequence).

It's even possible to keep the same pitches despite a changing root. Here, an **Em** harmony (with **9** and **13**) turns by the mere switching of roots into an **A** with a dominant **13** sound.

Experiment with these "close" voicings, and your efforts will be rewarded. ●

-SI

Figured Bass

BY ANDY LAVERNE

Given today's emphasis on performance techniques and interpretation, the more theoretical side of music is often overlooked. However, with a deeper understanding of music theory, performance and interpretation can be enhanced. We can gain greater insight into the composer's original intent, as well as a deeper understanding of the period in which a piece was written.

At one time, keyboard players were expected to study harmony, in order to perform music that included "figured bass" parts. This was a practice which began in the days of Couperin, Rameau, Bach and Handel. Figured bass is a method of short-hand notation which uses bass notes and numerals under them as a guide to the harmonic structure of the music.

In the Baroque period, the ever present keyboardist was required to fill in missing parts or reinforce weak ones in various ensembles. Instead of writing out complete parts for the keyboard, composers used the figured bass. Therefore the harmony was prescribed, yet the distribution of notes was left to the performer. This gives much latitude in the placement and voice leading of tones. It is in fact, a form of improvisation, not unlike that of reading a set of chord changes from a piece of pop sheet music today.

Let's take a look at some of the components of figured bass:

1) The bass note indicates the lowest note to be used in the chord voicing.

2) The Arabic numerals name the interval(s) to be played up from the given bass note (this indicates the position [inversion] and quality [Major, minor, etc.] of the chord).

3) Accidentals are used next to the numerals which they are meant to affect. An accidental standing alone signifies that the third above the bass is to receive that sign.

The full figuring of a triad in root position is 8, 3, 5 (Ex. 1). Root position triads are so common that it is assumed that one is meant when no figure appears. Occasionally a 5 or 3 is given to insure that a triad in root position is used.

The first inversion of a triad (third in the bass) is indicated by the numeral 6 (Ex. 2). The third is understood. Har-

monically, this chord has a lighter quality than the same chord in root position. Melodically, the use of the 6 chord often allows the bass to move in steps as well as in larger intervals.

The second inversion of a triad (fifth in bass) is indicated by the symbol $\frac{6}{4}$ (Ex. 3). (The six-four chord is unstable. Its most common use is as a tonic six-four found in cadences (Ex. 4). It can, how-

ever, be used in noncadential passages (as an appoggiatura) and as a passing chord, when the bass is a passing tone between two notes a third apart.)

Next we come to a four-note chord, the dominant seventh chord. In figured bass this usually appears as 7 (full figured $\frac{7}{5}{}_{3}$) (Ex. 5). The first inversion (3rd in bass) is figured $\frac{6}{5}{}_{3}$ (Ex. 6). Since the 3rd is usually understood, this chord is commonly referred to as the dominant six-five ($\frac{6}{5}$).

The second inversion (5th in bass) is called the four-three and is figured $\frac{6}{4}{}_{3}$ (Ex. 7).

The third inversion (7th in bass) is figured $\frac{6}{4}{}_{2}$ (Ex. 8). This time, 6 is again usually omitted as being understood, leaving either $\frac{4}{2}$ or 2. This is a dynamic chord, with a strong tendency to resolve with the bass moving down a step (V2-I6) (Ex. 9).

Paul Halley, the organist and choir master at the Cathedral of St. John The Divine in New York, who is also keyboardist in the Paul Winter Consort, has some thoughts and advice on figured bass and its practical applications today. "In order to recognize what the figures mean quickly, and to gain versatility in voicing the chords in the context of a phrase, it's important to spend time studying and playing the music. Recitatives in operas (by Mozart, for example) are figured. Looking at full string versions of these passages is helpful to see a realized figured bass. Although there are rules, a familiarity with the style will lend a fair amount of freedom for the realization of figured bass.

"Handel — as opposed to Bach — is freer with harmonic progressions and movement, and is generally less dense. Monteverdi and the Italian school use an even greater range for the continuo parts. The main thing is to acquaint yourself with the style of the piece so that you're free to embellish. It is one of the few areas in the classical field where improvisation is possible. To get beyond just playing chords, think of lines and counterpoint within the continuo part. Working first *within* a set of parameters, and then removing them gives your playing a greater depth and richness. Playing figured bass will take you inside the spirit of the time." ∎

Section 3
THE RHYTHM SECTION

Rhythm Workshop

The Songwriter's Guide to Rhythmic Notation Part 1

Why bother about rhythmic notation?

Countless rehearsals and recording sessions have ground to a dead stop because the composer or arranger did not bother to give the player the best possible notation of this or that rhythm pattern. What happens? The player reads the part, plays it wrong, stops the rehearsal, scratches his head, talks to the leader, questions the composer/arrangers, gets things straight, pencils in the correction . . . and *then* resumes the session.

Not many sessions escape this typical scene, even among professionals who ought to know better. But among amateur songwriters, arrangers, copyists, and players, this stop-start scenario is played out again and again, until the rehearsal amounts to little more than an expensive, time-consuming, exhausting, and unproductive editing-and-correction session.

This recurrent problem is completely avoidable if someone (you? your arranger? a copyist?) pays scrupulous attention to the way each rhythm pattern is communicated to the player on the written page. This is not a hit-or-miss operation: good rhythmic notation follows exact guidelines.

A basic principle of good notation

For accurate performance, write each rhythm pattern so that *its beat structure within the meter* is instantly clear. This means that the *visual* appearance of the notated rhythm should neither hide nor confuse the basic structure of the meter of your music.

Meter and time signature

Meter is the way beats are grouped to form a measure. We speak of a "2-beat" meter, a "3-beat" meter, a "5-beat" meter, and so on.

A *time signature* is a number formula that describes a particular kind of beat grouping. Thus a "2-beat" meter may be numerically described by the formula "2/2" or "2/8"; a "5-beat" meter, by "5/4" or "5/16," and so on:

Metric structure: "primary" and "secondary" accents

Every meter has its own basic structure, built on two elements.

Its first element is the *primary accent*, or "downbeat": that is, the initial beat ("ONE") of the measure.

Its second element is the *secondary accent* within the measure. Whereas *all* downbeats are in the same place, regardless of which meter you are working with, the placement of the secondary accent *varies according to each different meter.*

Continued next page

The secondary accent in a balanced meter

"A "balanced" meter is any beat grouping with an *even* number of beats per measure (2, 4, 6, 8, 10, 12, etc.). Thus, such meters as *2/8*, *4/4*, *4/2*, *6/8*, *8/8*, *10/16*, *12/8*, etc., are all balanced beat group-ings. In other words, they are divisible into two equal halves.

Whereas the primary accent kicks off the first half of a balanced measure, the secondary accent begins the second half:

The secondary accent in an unbalanced meter

An "unbalanced" meter is any beat grouping with an *uneven* number of beats per measure (3, 5, 7, 9, 11, etc.). Thus, such meters as *3/4*, *5/8*, *7/16*, *9/2*, *11/4*, etc., are all *un*balanced beat groupings. In other words, they are divisible only into *un*equal parts. Moreover, the unequal parts will vary according to the composer's whim, based on the pulsation of the music.

A very common example of variety within an unbalanced measure is the following setup of a 5/8 measure: In (a), the five beats are divided 3+2; in (b), 2+3; in (c), 4+1:

In even larger beat groupings — such as 7/8, below — there is still greater variety in placing the secondary accents:

[2 + 2 + 3]   [2 + 3 + 2]   [3 + 2 + 2]   [3 + 3 + 1]

But keep in mind that these metric divisions are not arrived at mechanically, as a mathematical exercise! These are rhythmic pulsations, notated to match the flow of the music. Some of the most effective applications of unbalanced meters, with their varying secondary accents, are found in Dave Brubeck's album, *Take Five* — a classic, pioneering adventure in jazz experimentation that breaks away from the traditional 4/4 format.

Exceptional secondary accents in a balanced meter

Although a balanced meter, such as 8/8, traditionally builds each measure in equal halves (4+4), it is possible to deliberately *un*balance the even number of beats if the music stresses an irregular pulsation:

[3 + 3 + 2]   [2 + 3 + 3]

The 3+3+2 construction of the 8/8 meter, by the way, is not confined to jazz experimentation, and is certainly not new in music literature. This subdivision lends enormous vitality and rhythmic excite-ment to any number of driving folk dances of Bulgaria, Rumania, and Hungary — an irregularity equally embraced by such "serious" composers as Béla Bartók and Zoltán Kodály.

Summary of Part 1

The concepts of balanced and unbalanced meters, and of traditional and experimental divisions and subdivisions of beat groupings, are fundamental to our understanding of how rhythm patterns should be notated for clarity and ease of performance.

Everything we do in this mini-series, in future studies, will be based on the simple, basic principles we've covered in Part 1. In fact, your easy grasp of our later work will come out of these preliminary steps, and will be made that much easier if you take the time to review this introduction and relate these ideas to the music you read and play every day.

RH ♩

Rhythm Workshop

The Songwriter's Guide to Rhythmic Notation
Part 2: Misadventures in 4/4

This is the second article in a new mini-series concerned with accurate, professionally competent rhythmic notation. The first article appeared in the Feb. 83 issue.

The first chapter of this Guide stated the single, fundamental rule of good rhythmic notation: that a rhythm pattern — no matter how simple or complicated — should be written *so that it clearly reflects the basic beat structure of the meter* of your piece of music.

If your music is in 4/4, for example, and you want to write a string of 8th notes to fill one bar, then the clearest notation of this pattern is either

Because 4/4 is a *balanced* meter — that is, because it can be divided into equal halves (2 + 2) — then its "secondary" accent falls on Beat 3:

(The "primary" accent of the bar is always on Beat 1, the downbeat; the "secondary" accent in a balanced meter is on the beat that begins the second half of the bar.)

Keeping that structure in mind — strong beat on 1, stress on 3 — you can see that *both* notations of the 8th-note pattern are good: notation A shows all four beats; notation B reflects the equal halves of the balanced meter (four 8ths + four 8ths).

By contrast, it is inaccurate and confusing to notate the same string of 8ths as

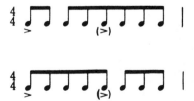

In both examples, the beams (the broad connecting line) confuse the balanced beat structure by *hiding* the secondary accent (Beat 3) in odd places.

Following the same reasoning, the written pattern

also hides the secondary accent. Where is

Beat 3? Obviously *somewhere* near that central quarter note! Beside confusing the balanced beat structure of 4/4, that particular notation adds an extra complication by presenting the performer with two note groups that *look* like triplets but are not.

Continued next page

The clearest notation for that pattern avoids the "lost" Beat 3 simply by showing it:

The *sound* of the two notations is exactly the same . . . but the first will stop a rehearsal while the

player figures out what the composer *really* intended!

And how would like to meet *this* notation in the middle of a long rehearsal?. . .

. . .a classic example of the hidden (in fact, buried) secondary accent on Beat 3. Compared to either

or

— two solutions that sound exactly the same as the terror above — there is no question that now the composer is at least giving the player a fighting chance to play the part accurately. Both solutions

clearly reflect the balanced bar, and are therefore equally acceptable. The first good notation is very common; the second has the added advantage of showing Beat 2 (the tied quarter) as well as Beat 3.

An even fancier, and more frightening, pattern turns up again and again in beginners manuscripts, looking something like this:

Why suffer with it, when

This time we can find only the *downbeat!* Where is Beat 2? Beat 3? Beat 4? They are all there, of course, but totally confused by careless beaming.

(the identical sound) makes immediate sense?

If this concept is clear, try out your solutions to the following rhythm patterns. Our solutions will appear in the next installment of this series.

RH ♩

Rhythm Workshop

The Songwriter's Guide to Rhythmic Notation Part 3: Solutions

This is the third article in our mini-series on professionally accurate and effective rhythmic notation. Earlier articles appeared in our Jan. and Feb. 83 issues.

Last month's cliffhanger ended with three rhythm patterns that were deliberately misnotated to create reading confusion and — if they ever showed up in a rehearsal — a costly, time wasting interruption.

Problem 1, written this way . . .

. . . should be rewritten as:

The poor notation makes only one mistake, but a crucial one: The quarter rest, placed at the exact rhythmic center of the bar, completely hides the secondary accent of the 4/4 meter — that is, Beat 3 of the four-beat bar . . . the beat that begins the second half of this balanced meter.

The solution is simply to break the quarter rest into

two 8th rests. This division immediately shows the player that the bar consists of two equal halves. (The dotted barline should not of course appear in your score. Its sole purpose here is to emphasize the rhythmic separation of the two halves of the bar.) The correct notation shows all four beats of this common pattern.

Problem 2 . . .

. . . can be solved several ways:

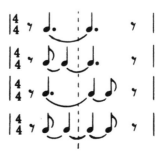

Continued next page

Although the four solutions use different note combinations, they have one feature in common: *Each one divides the dotted half note into tied notes* in order to reveal the hidden secondary accent (Beat 3).

Solution (a) is the simplest of the lot, slicing the dotted half note into two equal parts (two dotted quarters, tied). This creates a perfectly balanced visual picture of a bar divided into equal halves.

Solution (b) and (c) are alike in the way they break down half of the bar into still smaller parts. Solution (b) shows Beat *2*; Solution (c) shows Beat *4*.

Solution (d) has the advantage of revealing all four beats, but the disadvantage of cluttering the bar with an overload of notes and ties. Keep in mind that someone has to *read* your music, and that every added symbol (notes, rests, ties, and so on) means added reading time for the player. The best overall solution is invariably one that is both rhythmically clear and uncluttered.

Which one to choose? Solution (a) does the job efficiently, and is probably the best choice. But using the other solutions — all of them correct — is a matter of personal taste.

Problem 3, in this confusing notation. . .

. . . should be rewritten like this:

This time we are not concerned about a hidden secondary accent, since the equal division of the bar is entirely clear. The 8th-16th patterns occupy the first half of the bar, and the half note occupies the second half.

The confusion in this example centers around a hidden Beat *2*, caused by faulty beaming. At first glance, the incorrect notation *seems* to be reasonable because of the appearance of the familiar pattern

But this is deceptive *because the third note of the bar (the 8th) is actually part of Beat 1*. not Beat 2.

Compare the two notations to see how the beam correction immediately tells the player how the notes are grouped into beats. Once the beaming of Beat 1 is corrected, the notes belonging to Beat 2 can now be beamed together (eliminating that "leftover" 8th note just before the half note).

Why the concern for clear secondary accents and accurate beaming? Simply because the composer or arranger must take the time and trouble to give the player the best possible notation of every rhythm pattern in the score. Ignore this and you unnecessarily complicate a rehearsal, a reading, or a performance that should be devoted to making music, and *not* to decoding your rhythm patterns.

RH ♩

The Songwriter's Guide to Rhythmic Notation
Part 4:
Silence in a Balanced Bar

Beginning songwriters tend to cram each bar full of notes, either in the voice part or in the piano accompaniment. If your next piece looks like this. . .

. . . experiment with a few carefully placed *silences,* to get away from nonstop singing or playing. The addition of rests adds rhythmic variety and bounce, and helps define the phrasing of a musical line by breaking down the line into smaller fragments. If your piece is in 4/4, for example (as in the pattern above), and your pattern contains notes of equal value (such as consecutive quarter notes), then a rest may take the place of any note:

You may also introduce rests of greater value (longer duration) — provided that the rest notation *does not hide the secondary accent of the bar:*

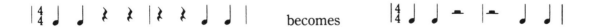

In this example, the substitution of one half rest for two quarter rests does not interfere with the picture of the bar as a *balanced* pattern: both halves of the 4/4 bar stay *visually* clear.

If you want *two* consecutive beats of silence in the *middle* of a 4/4 bar, then write

Continued next page

Although some writers use the half rest this way, it is not as clear as the two quarter rests. The half rest tends to fool the reader's eye, hiding the secondary accent (Beat 3) of the balanced bar; the two quarter rests show the beats in the clearest way.

If you want *three* consecutive beats of silence in a 4/4 bar, follow the same principle (show the eye the balanced bar) by writing either. . .

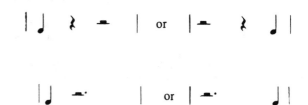

instead of

Rest notation in 6/8 — also a balanced meter (3+3) — follows exactly the same principle:

SHOW THE EYE THE BALANCED BAR! If you want silence in the *first* half of the bar, then

$$|\,{}^6_8\,\gamma\ \gamma\ \gamma\ \,\text{becomes}\,|\,{}^6_8\,\xi\cdot$$

For silence in the *second* half of the bar,

$$|\,{}^6_8\ \gamma\ \gamma\ \gamma\,|\ \text{becomes}\ |\,{}^6_8\ \ \xi\cdot$$

If you want *two* consecutive 8th-note beats of silence in the *middle* of a 6/8 bar, then write

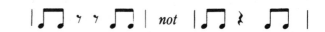

The "wrong" notation is tempting because we see it so often in *3/4* measures. But remember that 6/8 is a balanced meter (3♪ + 3♪), and should maintain a notation that shows those equal halves of the bar.

A bar of 3/4 is *un*balanced (2♪ + 2♪ + 2♪), and therefore needs a different notation. (We'll look at rests in an unbalanced meter in a future article).

If these few basic ideas are clear, try your hand at renotating the following bars. Each one is in a balanced meter. Therefore, each one should help the music reader by using the clearest possible rest notation. (Solutions will appear in the next installment.)

RH

(a) $|\,{}^4_8$ . . .

(b) $|\,{}^4_2$ . . .

(c) $|\,{}^4_{16}$ . . .

(d) $|\,{}^6_{16}$ . . .

94

Rhythm Workshop

The Songwriter's Guide to Rhythmic Notation
Part 5:
Silence in an Unbalanced Bar

Before we launch into new matters, here are the solutions to the notational problems that appeared in our June/July issue. Remember that the best solution for each is a notation that clearly shows the reader *how the balanced bar is balanced!*

PROBLEM   SOLUTION

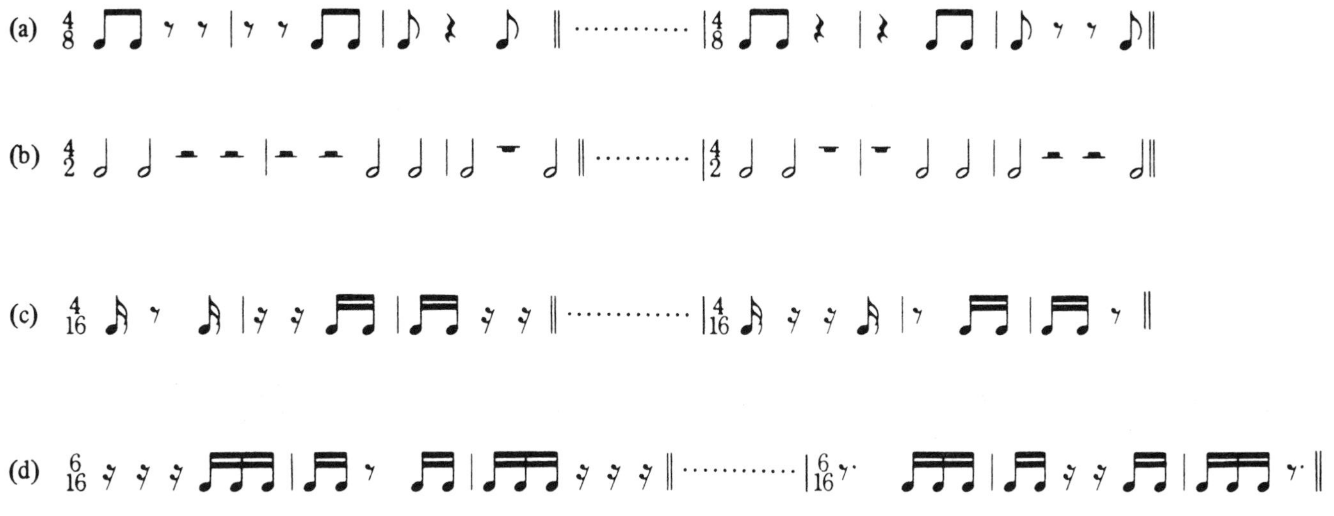

(a) [musical notation]

(b) [musical notation]

(c) [musical notation]

(d) [musical notation]

(To check these and similar notations, you should be able to draw a dotted line through the *exact center* of each bar, with the *simplest possible* notation clearly visible on each side of that line.)

Continued next page

While a balanced bar divides cleanly in half, an *un*balanced bar does not. A bar of 3/4, for example, divides into three parts; a bar of 5/4 usually splits unevenly, as 3+2 or 2+3; a bar of 7/4 (rare in popular music, but commonplace in Eastern folk music and modern concert music) divides unevenly as 3+2+2, 2+3+2, and so on. The dotted lines, below, show these unbalanced divisions at a glance:

Music engravers do not of course fuss with dotted lines to point up the rhythmic stresses of an unbalanced bar! Those uneven splits are suggested in the music itself — either by the composer's phrase marks . . .

. . . by added accent marks . . .

. . . or by the placement of a left-hand chord:

In *8th*-note meters, however, the unbalanced divisions are far clearer, because of the presence of *beams:*

96

Just as the various rests in a balanced bar followed the music's pattern of *balance*. . .

. . . the rests in an *un*balanced bar follow the pattern of *imbalance:*

The same applies to these 5/4 bars (divided 2 + 3)

. . . and to these 7/4 bars (divided 3 + 2 + 2):

In unbalanced *8th*-note meters, the rests again *follow the design of imbalance:*

(although some composers hang onto the second notation)

[3 + 2] *(confusing! 3 + 2? 2 + 3?)*

[2 + 2 + 3] *(appears to be 3 + 4)*

If these general principles seem clear, try your hand at some more cliff-hangers! (Solutions to the incorrect notations will appear in the next installment.)

RH

(a)

[2 + 3]

(b)

[2 + 3 + 2]

(c)

Continued next page

Rhythm Workshop

The Songwriter's Guide to Rhythmic Notation Part 6: Stem Up? Stem Down?

One of the oddities of the music writing business is the matter of which way a note should point. Should the stem—the vertical line attached to the note head—go up or down? Does it matter? Yes, it does if you want your manuscript to have a professional look. It matters if you want a potential publisher of your song or original piano or organ piece to bother looking twice at what you have submitted. Remember that the average publisher receives *piles* of unsolicited manuscripts everyday. Because they are gone through quickly, you need every edge, every immediate advantage, you can get. Face the facts: A good-looking score gets more attention than a sloppy one. A well-written score reflects your caring attitude toward your music. If it is clear that *you* care, then the publisher

might just care a bit more to read through your music.

The matter of stem directions is probably the most neglected item of music writing. Nobody talks about it. Only a handful of books touches on it, and it is rarely taught. This neglect is pointless because the basic rules of correct note-writing—following international engraving standards—are simple to learn and apply to your manuscript.

From here on, we're going to refer constantly to "the middle staff line." In the treble clef, this means the "B" line; in the bass clef, this means the "D" line. Keep in mind that these rules apply to *all* clefs: The "middle staff line" is in the middle, no matter what clef you use!

Rule 1: *Stem directions for single notes*
For a single note *below* the middle staff line, draw the stem going *up*. For a single note *on* the middle staff line *or above*, draw the stem going *down*.

Rule 2: *The length of a stem for a single note*
A stem for a single note should be at least *one octave* long:

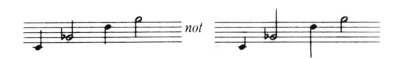

Rule 3: *Stem directions for beamed notes*
(A *beam* is the thick line or lines connecting the stems of eighths, sixteenths, thirty-seconds, etc.)
For two or more beamed notes, the note *farthest*

from the middle staff line dictates *all* stem directions within the beamed group. If, for example, you want to write these two notes

98

as a pair of eighths, then think this way:

(a) "Which note is farthest from the middle staff line?" (Answer: The first note.)

(b) "If that first note were by itself, which way would I draw its stem?" (Answer: The stem would go *up*.)

(c) "Then *both* stems must go up."

The same rule applies no matter how many notes are in the beamed group, and no matter how fast the rhythm is. For instance, if you want to write these four notes as a group of sixteenths, think:

(a) "Which note is farthest from the middle staff line?" (Answer: The third note.)

(b) "If that third note were by itself, which way would I draw its stem?" (Answer: The stem would go *down*.)

(c) "Then all four stems must go down."

(If the farthest notes are equidistant *from the middle staff line, all stems in the beamed group go* DOWN.*)*

Rule 1: *The slant of the beams*

In the old days of metal engraving, all music symbols were either cut or die-punched into a metal plate. This laborious process produced elegant scores but created a basic inking problem. When the finished plate was ink-rolled for the printing press, the liquid would naturally collect in tiny pools wherever two lines crossed each other. One of the messiest pools occurred when a thick beam intersected a thin staff line.

To minimize the problem, engravers established some guidelines:

(a) Don't allow a slanted beam to cross more than one staff line.

(b) Avoid extreme slants of the beam, even if this means that certain stems must be *longer* than an octave in length.

(c) Keeping the above rules in mind, gently slant the beam in the general direction of the note group: *up*, if the pitches ascend: *down*, if the pitches descend; *straight*, if the pitches ascend and descend more or less equally within the beamed group.

Following these guidelines, compare these right and wrong notations:

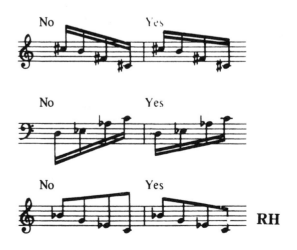

99

The Case Of The Restless Rest

BY ROBERT DUMM

Imagine you are sitting alone at midnight in a large house, reading. Suddenly, there's a soft knock at the back door. You stop, inhale, wait. Was it a knock? Did I imagine it? It's nothing, you decide, and resume your reading. "Knock, knock." This time you stop, your heart thumping. No mistake; there's someone (or some*thing*) there!

What sort of "silence" is this? Is it *rest*-ful? Hardly. It has you frozen, on red alert, your hair perhaps standing on end. An unidentified sound, to our primitive spine, means danger! This "midnight" silence — suspenseful, pregnant with expectation — is the highly charged focus of attention a pianist hopes for and signals when he strides onstage briskly, curtly bows, sits, waits, and slowly raises his hands. He draws on that energy, and echoes it in the rests which occur throughout the piece. Finally, he permits it to surround the last final sound of the music. If he has used the collective energies well — his and yours — even that last silence will seem full of echoes.

For a moment, compare silence — potential for every sound — with the canvas of a painter. Many a painter whitens it first, before he adds other colors, not trusting the linen tint of raw canvas to vivify the colors he will paint upon it. When colors are added, and both stark trees and massive rocks stand in place among the greens, what does he add? The chances are, *more* white — small, special strokes and slants and slits.

In one sense, musicians rely on silences to similarly punctuate sounds. Pauses punctuate speech with the same endless variety. A pause in spoken talk may be a breathing pause, a lapse of memory, an anxious pause to "say it right," or in a larger sense, it may be a pause that *savors* a memory, or a surprise, or a *big* breath that will allow us to dive underwater for a long swim. Think of the sorts of things actually "said" during speech pauses!

The degree of stress felt in musical silences matters as much for the "meaning" of music. Take for one example the opening of Beethoven's Sonata "pathétique" (C min, Op 13) and listen to the distinct question at *:

But the very speaking, or searching effect of that sharp silence itself derives from the full "boom" of the opening chord. Sound "strikes" a silence, just as a rubbed match strikes up a flame. What makes that opening chord *boom*, rather than merely *crash?* A sound in the player's head. It mattered what he heard coming *before* he lifted to play it.

A good musician will first think through the beats of a full bar of silence, in just the tempo of the movement, often with a slight *crescendo* in intensity of those "thought" beats, as if to collect and compact the silence. NO silences in music are slack, and very few of them "rest" or repose. All of them must be charged with the player's *specific* intention.

After sampling the genesis of sounds *from* silences, consider how a piece may end (return to silence). It can stop dead, as many a grand finale intends that it should:

Chopin, *Valse,* E Minor, Op posth 72

Or it can be allowed to "sink" into the silence, as a submarine settles into seabottom ooze:

Chopin, *Prelude,* E Minor, Op 28, no 4

But take another Chopin Prelude, No 9 in E Major, where the composer, by his modulating sequence, crescendo, and fixation on the active B (the fifth of the chord rather than its root), intends it to go on forever, defy "silence," like a choral swell:

The trick here is to crescendo very late (so there seems "more to come"), and lift both hands and pedal after the last chord has had its massive effect, but *before* it has begun to die away.

What if the composer prefers, as Beethoven often does, to "sell you short" a little, just as you were rolling along on an unstoppable rhythm, as here:

Beethoven, *"Pathetique" Sonata*

The fermata over that end barline is the most active rest imaginable, like Beethoven's fist, raised in defiance they say, during a thunderclap at the moment of his death. A similar end cut-off can have a funny effect, as Haydn often does:

Haydn, *Sonata,* A Flat, Finale/Presto, Hob XVI, no 46

To be continued . . . ■

The Case Of The Restless Rest

Part II

BY ROBERT DUMM

"There's no end to what rests can 'say' — musicians spend their lives aiming for this or that inflection."

A *vital* silence awakens a resonance in your mind, in the same way your hands clapped over your eyes after looking at the sun will cause you to "see" a brilliant black globe. It is this left over energy that caused Alfred Brendel in a recent all-Liszt recital to lift his left forearm after producing big bell sounds from the bass, then let it drift absently sideways as the silence kept "resonating."

From that fairly strong silence, let's turn to some everyday low-keyed silences that do their duty to articulate the music. Take "rhythmic" rests, those off- or weak-beat rests that subtly prod along the motor pulses of a piece: (*)

Schumann: *Soldier's March,* Op. 68

Or those tiny, needlepoint silences that separate even notes in Baroque style, or group notes according to their musical sense: (*)

Rameau: *Menuet,* from *Pièces de claveçin*

Or sharpen the accent by cutting it off: (*)

Pachelbel: *Canon*

Closely related to the rest that performs such simple motor functions is that which indicates "dead" time; time has, in fact, stopped. Schumann uses that sort of rest here with spellbinding effect, which, though it interrupts his waltz again and again, does not become assimilated, but remains a disturbing question: (*)

Schumann: *Vogel als Prophet* (The Prophet Bird)

Of course a rest can become a "rupture": (*)

Brahms: *Capriccio,* Op. 116, No. 7, D minor

An operatic composer like Mozart can ring a whole series of changes in repeated pauses:

Mozart: *Fantasy,* D Minor, K. 397

Continued next page

101

Or a grand silence can be rolled into sound like an iron curtain as it rivets attention:

Chopin: *Ballade* No. 4, F Minor

The musical effect of any rest derives primarily from its place among the beats of its bar. For example, take this bass that "waltzes":

Schubert: *Impromptu,* A Flat, Op. 90, No. 4

After you've played that through, over and over, insert a rest for beat three, like this: (*)

That particular rest will sound light because it replaces a very weak beat in the bar. Now what if a composer replaces his *down*beat — a strong beat — with a rest as here: (*)

Schumann: *Waltz,* A Minor, Op. 124, No. 4

It will certainly sound "strong"; even strong as a kick or blow, depending upon the verve and clean cutting-off of what comes *before* it.

There's no end to what these un-silent rests can "say," and musicians spend their lives aiming for this or that inflection. It is never enough merely to register a rest. You must feel it with the exact degree of punctuation, surprise, sigh, or breath that helps or dramatizes your musical narrative. ■

Using The Metronome

- *To Understand Time Signatures*
- *To Build Technique*
- *To Put Steadiness In Your Playing*

By Douglas Riva

A metronome sits on top of virtually every piano in homes and studios throughout the world. Almost every pianist, student or professional acknowledges that the metronome is an important part of music study. Nevertheless, the metronome, which is one of the most valuable tools available to us, is widely misunderstood. Many people, while believing that it is indeed important, do not have any practical idea of how to use one, and still others proclaim that it is a nuisance or worse, useless.

The question of tempo is one of the favorite topics among musicians and listeners. Even the most casual listener can not help noticing wide differences in tempo in performances by different players. This difference is not really surprising when you consider that the appropriate tempo for a composition is indicated by a handful of Italian words which are descriptive but vague: largo (broad), lento (slow), adagio (slow, literally, at ease), andante (walking), allegretto (quick, cheerful), allegro (fast), presto (very fast) and prestissimo (as fast as possible). These indications are very helpful in determining what the correct tempo should be, but they are not very precise in indicating exactly what are the composer's intentions. After all — How fast is fast? Everyone is bound to have a slightly different answer.

As early as the 16th Century, musicians realized that it would be beneficial to have a tool for measuring the varying speeds of music. Galileo conducted early experiments in an attempt to develop a device to measure musical motion using a simple pendulum. Later Gottfreid Weber developed a simple pendulum on a cord with knots placed at varying intervals from which the cord could be hung, making it possible for the pendulum to swing at different speeds, marking faster or slower tempos depending on the length. However, this device was not particularly successful nor practical, since the pendulum required a cord 40 inches long.

The idea of developing a "musical chronometer" attracted the attention of Beethoven's friend Johann Nepomuk Mälzel. Mälzel

The metronome is a guideline to help you *learn to feel the tempo within yourself.*

102

Metronome

was a colorful figure who might be described as half Thomas Edison and half P. T. Barnum. He was an inventor and succeeded in having himself appointed "Court Mechanician" to the Austrian Emperor in Vienna. Beethoven became acquainted with Mälzel because the latter made 4 ear trumpets which helped the composer maintain some aural contact with the world before he became totally deaf.

Beethoven believed that tempo must be felt, but he acknowledged the need for a measuring rod to substitute for "absurd" descriptive terms (i.e., allegro, andante, etc.) He said that Mälzel's "metronome affords the best opportunity for doing so." With Beethoven's endorsement Mälzel's success was insured.

How can the device best be used? A metronome divides a minute into equal parts, usually on a scale of 40-208. A setting of 88, for example, provides a click, or sound, marking each one of 88 divisions of a minute. Other settings are faster or slower. Composers indicate the desired speed by placing "M.M." (an abbreviation for Mälzel's Metronome) or simply "M." followed by the appropriate setting, in their music. The indication might be further simplified by placing, for example, " ♩ = 120" (or depending on the composer – "M.M. ♩ = 120," or "M. ♩ = 120"). This setting would apply to any piece in 2/4, 3/4, 4/4, 5/4, 6/4, etc. or to any time signature (or meter) where the ♩ represents one beat. In this case you would play each quarter note at the rate of 120 per minute. Consequently, a half note (♩) would be held for two clicks, a dotted half note (♩.) for 3, etc.

Eighth notes (♫) would indicate that you sub-divide each click into two equal parts.

Time signatures with a 2 as the bottom number, such as 2/2, 3/2, or 4/2, indicate that each half note (♩) receives one beat. Consequently the metronome setting would be indicated as (for example) ♩ = 72. Since each half note contains two quarter notes – which move twice as fast as half notes – you could also set the metronome at 144 and have a click for each quarter note, achieving the same tempo.

Time signatures with an 8 as the bottom number, such as 6/8, indicate that each eighth note (♪) receives one beat. In other words, each measure contains, in the case of 6/8, 6 eighth notes or their equivalent. Bear in mind that 6/8, 9/8, and 12/8 are also "compound" time signatures, meaning that in some cases 3 eighth notes are grouped together to form one unit (a ♩.), which is felt as the beat. In this case the composer might provide a metronome marking such as ♩. = 100.

If you follow the instructions for a piece such as this Czerny Etude, you will see that you are to set the metronome between 72 and 84 and time each quarter note to coincide with each click of the metronome.

complete control over each note. If even the slowest tempo indicated seems too fast, pick one that is slower and gradually work up to the tempo indicated. However, you may be able to play faster than the top speed given. Fine – but ask yourself, "Does the piece sound good at that tempo?" Having the facility to play at a fast tempo is an excellent pianistic attribute, but always let the musical effect determine what the correct tempo should be. Playing fast is not its own reward, as it is in typing.

After careful practice with the metronome to insure that you can play accurately in tempo, neither rushing nor slowing down, you *MUST* turn off the metronome. The tempo of any piece must be felt internally by you, not dictated by a machine. The metronome is a guideline, a standard against which to measure the tempo, but in the final analysis you must feel the tempo within yourself.

When asked about the metronome markings he put in the score to his Requiem, Brahms wrote, "I think . . . that the metronome is of no value . . . everybody has, sooner or later, withdrawn his metronome marks." Perhaps so, but other composers have felt quite differently.

Verdi, for example, in describing his Te Deum, said, "This entire piece ought to be performed in one tempo as indicated by the metronome. This notwithstanding, it will be appropriate to broaden or accelerate in certain spots for reasons of expression and nuance, coming back, however, always to the first tempo." Verdi's two sentences "express the essentials of all music making" according to noted conductor Eric Leinsdorf.

Whether you have a wind-up pendulum model metronome, or an electronic- or battery-operated transistor model, listen carefully to check that the beats are evenly spaced. Once dropped, metronomes may not be reliable. In order to check the accuracy of a given setting, count the number of beats during 3 minutes and divide the number of beats counted by 3. The answer will tell you how many beats, on the average, your metronome gives per minute at that setting. Your metronome may provide evenly spaced beats but may not be accurate to its own scale.

A final word of advice – manufacturers are experts in making fine metronomes but they may or may not be expert musicians. Ignore the scales of tempos shown on metronomes such as Allegro = 84-144, or Andante = 56-88. Let the composer and his music tell you what the correct tempo is. ⌒

Metronome markings indicating a *range* of tempo are intended as a guide. One tempo within the range may be too slow and another too fast. You should play the piece through at several different tempos within the range given, and select one which is fast enough to be challenging but slow enough for you to have

Pop Rhythms
Unravelled!

Pop rhythms are easy enough to remember and perform once you have the sound in your ears. But often the sheet music for these bouncy syncopations look impossibly complicated, like a roadmap to somewhere you don't want to visit. So, here is a three-step procedure for figuring out how to play what's on the page, without coming down with a migraine headache.

1) *Look for the shortest note value in the melody, and think of the whole phrase in terms of that note value.* For example, in a tune like Burt Bacharach's *Always Something There To Remind Me*, there are many phrases that mix eighth notes with quarter notes — sometimes in offbeat combinations:

It becomes easier to count out the rhythms of these phrases by seeing the dotted quarter notes as a quarter tied to an eighth, and by converting the quarter notes which appear on the second half of a beat into two tied eighth notes. In other words, we can see these phrases as being based on an eighth note count:

2) Now that everything is clearly based on the shortest note value we have to count, the next step is to *remove the ties*. Now the rhythms aren't complicated at all! You can practice all of this at a slow tempo, to help make things crystal clear.

3) After practicing the phrases without any ties, look at the tied version once more. Play the phrases with an accent on the first note of each tied group, and hum the second tied note instead of playing it.

After you've run through this routine, you can bring the whole thing up to tempo. Voila! That back roads map has gotten you to the right place after all.　♩ SI

Rolled Eighths

By Champ Champagne

Sometimes you see the symbol ♪♪ = ♩³♪ or even ♪ ♪ = ♩³♪ situated on top of the first measure of a song. Most often it follows the indication of style such as (swing ♪ ♪ = ♩³♪) (boogie-woogie ♪♪ = ♩³♪), big band, rock-a-ballad, funky, shuffle, slow blues, back-beat, be-bop, dixieland, twelve-eight feel, jazz-waltz, nanigo (salsa), jig, Charleston, bunny hop, Mexican hat dance, tarantella, African, Tijuana, soft-shoe, bolero, barrel house, country, country-waltz, gospel-waltz, bounce, medium jump, or groove tempo.

These eighth-notes are sometimes called rolled eighths. (Not to be confused with rolled oats).

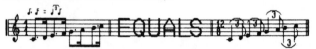

If you have a rhythm machine handy, set it to swing, rock-ballad, whatever. Make sure your beat-box has a setting that goes (1-2-3, 2-2-3, 3-2-3, 4-2-3) or a variation of that beat. Set the tempo to 82 (Andante). Once you have mastered that tempo, just increase the tempo.

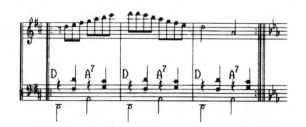

Keep ascending by a half-step. Then increase the tempo.

I bet you're wondering when the composer wants you to play straight eighth notes. Watch the signs in this example:

You may eyeglass the changes if you like.

Of course when there are both dotted eighths and sixteenths, regular eighth notes are played straight.

About the eyeglasses: It is the custom with some professional musicians to use them to point out some surprises in the music, such as sudden key changes, difficult passage, time signature changes, etc. You simply  it ⌢

RHYTHM

How To Play Compound Time

If you take two bars of ⅜ time and put them together you can make a bar of ⁶⁄₈ time, and if you put together two bars of ¾ time you can make a bar of ⁶⁄₄ time. There is not much difference between:

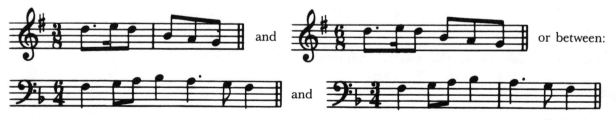

and   or between:

and

Continued on next page

How To Play Compound Time *Continued from previous page*

If the music is slow we count three eighth notes in $\frac{3}{8}$ and six eighth notes in $\frac{6}{8}$. But when the music goes more quickly we count one in a bar in $\frac{3}{8}$ and two in a bar in $\frac{6}{8}$. Let's concentrate for a moment on $\frac{6}{8}$.

Look at this piece:

Don't play it but think it and count it. There are six eighths in a bar, and you should count with an accent on ONE and FOUR.

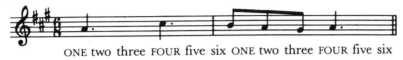

ONE two three FOUR five six ONE two three FOUR five six

Now take it faster, too fast to count eighths, and count dotted quarters instead.

ONE   TWO   ONE - n - n TWO

Now clap that.

What happens here is that the beat is a dotted quarter and when it divides it does so into three parts. That is what compound time is: a time in which the beat divides into three parts instead of two. Whenever you see **6** as the top figure in a time-signature count two, and whenever you see **9** count three, and whenever you see **12** count four.

But, you may ask; if I'm to count two or three or four in these bars, why not put **2** or **3** or **4** at the top of the time-signature? The answer is that many musicians would like to do this, but the other method has been going on for so long that it is difficult to alter it immediately. And so compound time will continue to be shown in most music as **6** or **9** or **12**, and whenever you see those figures (unless the music is very slow) think two, three, or four beats in a bar.

There are two very common rhythms in compound time. In $\frac{6}{8}$ they are ♩ ♪ and ♪.♪♪ , and you should learn them by heart as quickly as you can.

Here are three exercises to give you practice in these rhythms. Play this one several times:

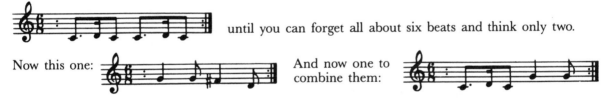

until you can forget all about six beats and think only two.

Now this one: And now one to combine them:

The next exercises should help to make you familiar with the commonest rhythms in compound time. $\frac{6}{8}$ time is much easier to read than $\frac{6}{4}$, because the joining of the eighths helps you to see the groups (♪.♪♪ ♪♪). ♩ ♩ ♩ ♩. ♪♩ is not so easy to grasp.

Right Hand   **Left Hand**

Creating an improvised line

Stuart Isacoff

Jazz rhythm has evolved in the same way concepts of harmony and melody have changed over the years. But its basis has always been a kind of ragged, shifting pulse which acts as a steady backdrop or foundation for everything else. This rhythmic underpinning has its roots in folk music, of which the following African percussion music is a good example.

The overall impression is one of complex syncopations, although each musician is playing a simple pattern. The repetition of these lines added a flavor to the music of pioneer jazz pianists such as Meade Lux Lewis and Jimmy Yancey, who employed repetitive bass figures such as these.

A repetitive underpinning helped shape melodic phrasing too. Early jazz artists would "rag" their eighths. (European classical artists of the Baroque era did the same, by the way. They called their version notes inegales, meaning "unequal notes.")

Later, in the bebop era, musicians changed articulation from note to note, slightly stressing particular eighth notes rather than taking the

> **"Rhythmic diversity is an essential element in jazz performance."**

more obvious dotted figure approach. Many bebop musicians played lines consisting solely of eighth notes and occasional triplets.

These observations about the history of jazz underscore the fact that rhythm is all important. Rhythmic diversity is an essential element in jazz performance.

Adding interesting jazz rhythms to your own improvised lines requires the ability to feel the rhythmic patterns that underlie contemporary styles. Jazzing up a phrase today (as opposed to in Jimmy Yancey's day, for example) might involve the use of anticipation, a type of syncopation in which an accented note is played earlier than expected.

On the other hand, we might use the opposite approach: a kind of delay tactic (especially on ballads).

In both cases, the improviser is performing a sort of dance around the normal pulse. Practicing these will give you one type of "jazz feel."

Another approach that will help you inject more of a jazz flavor in your phrases is to turn to typical big band swing figures — the kind you've heard every group, from the Count Basie Orchestra to the Mel Lewis Big Band, use all the time. These employ syncopation to create a "swing" effect. Try tapping these out on a table top.

108

These rhythms could easily be excerpts from various African ensemble performances, pared down for use with a few dominant sounding chords.

Here, for example, is a simple bluesy scale-like pattern.

Applying the big band figures to any series of notes will create a more interesting melody.

It really comes to life with an injection of rhythmic swing.

Next time: melodic/harmonic color. ●

■■■

RHYTHM

Advanced Cuban rhythms

Isabelle Leymarie

In recent years Latin jazz has become increasingly sophisticated and diversified. In the late 1940's, when Dizzy Gillespie and then Laurindo Almeida, Stan Getz and others popularized the *samba* and the *bossa nova* in the United States, jazz musicians started to incorporate these Brazilian rhythms into their playing. Such numbers as ''Girl from Ipanema,'' ''One Note Samba'' and ''Blue Bossa,'' for example, have become jazz standards. Today we hear a high degree of syncretism both in Latin jazz and in the more commercial brand of music known as fusion, and the different Latin rhythms blur. Argentinian pianist Jorge Dalto, for one, has written pieces that mix the *tango* with *salsa;* and Jay Hoggard's composition ''Sao Pablo'' is a samba that segues into salsa *montunos.* As this cross-pollination continues to occur, pianists interested in Latin jazz and fusion might want to master a wide variety of Latin rhythms. Even in a more straight-ahead jazz context, occasional Latin touches can add color and an element of surprise.

We saw in previous articles that *tumbaos* are figures that rhythmically anchor Cuban music. Let us start with examples of tumbaos that are slightly more complex than the ones we studied before. Again, I would like to stress that these tumbaos can be played with the left hand while the right hand improvises. The purpose of this is to develop independence between the hands. The following tumbao (normally played by the bass)

can fit the type of *rumba* known as *guaguanco.* Tap the *clave* with your foot.

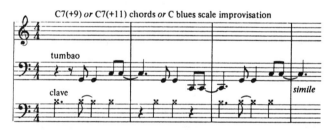

The clave (basic rhythm pattern) of the guaguanco is actually slightly different from the clave generally used in salsa. There is a slight *ritard* occurring on the fourth beat of the first bar, as follows.

The conga tumbao that goes with this clave is as shown below. Remember that the conga drums are tuned in fourths. If a *conguero* is not available to practice with you, a bass player could play this tumbao.

Continued next page

In the more traditional guaguanco, the tumbao and the clave used to fall together in the following way:

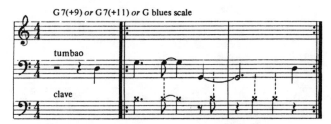

But in recent years this formula has changed, and the tumbao falls in a less obvious relation to the clave.

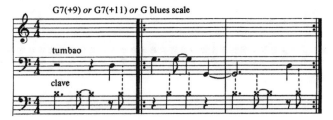

Piano players who are not used to playing with a full Latin rhythm section can easily lose the downbeat when faced with five or six different percussionists, all playing different rhythms. It can be a very disconcerting experience! But what it takes is experience. And pianists called upon to play guaguancos should be familiar with both of the above formulas.

Another more difficult tumbao is the one invented by Cuban bassist "Cachaito" Lopez, which he dubbed "Sandunga, mandinga, mondongo." (In Spanish, "sandunga" means "grace," "mandinga" refers to the Mandinka — an African ethnic group, and "mondongo" is a Cuban stew.) Here is the "Sandunga, mandinga, mondongo."

I have added chords in the right hand to give this tumbao the feel of a *mambo* figure. Of course the left hand can also be played by itself. I have heard the Cuban pianist Frank Emilio play marvelous solos while keeping this tumbao in his left hand. It's very difficult.

Merengue

Finally, the *merengue,* which comes from the Dominican Republic, is very popular now and it's also cropped up in Latin jazz. Saxophonist Mario Rivera, for one, often plays jazz based on the merengue. In the fast section of the merengue (it's also a dance step), called *jaleo,* the piano plays figures called *guajeos* that build up excitement. They also build muscle power! If you play in a merengue band, chances are you'll play this and similar figures at a fast tempo all night long.

Other merengue recording artists are trumpeter Wilfrido Vargas and the singer Johnny Ventura.

I'll be back in a future issue with a discussion of rhythmic displacement and polymeters. ●

Latin montunos

Isabelle Leymarie

Latin devices started gaining currency in jazz with the advent of "Cubop" (Cuba + bebop) in the late 1940's and early 1950's. The term "Latin jazz" has now replaced Cubop as Latin rhythms other than the Cuban ones have found their way into this musical genre. Latin jazz combines jazz harmonies and improvisational techniques with Latin rhythms.

Afro-Cuban rhythms are still fundamental. They also constitute the mainstay of the dance music known as salsa. These rhythms are based on a pattern called clave (pronounced KLAH-vay). This first pattern is known as the 3/2 clave.
FIGURE 1.

The clave can be reversed and is then known as the 2/3 clave.

FIGURE 2.

Some rhythms call for the 3/2 clave, others for the 2/3 clave.

One variation of the clave is the so-called guaguanco clave. The guaguanco is a traditional form of rhumba that comes from Cuba. It is now finding its way into Latin jazz. This clave has a slightly different syncopation at the end of the first bar.
FIGURE 3.

The clave easily fits many bebop tunes. This can explain why Charlie Parker soloed so fluent-

110

ly with Machito's Afro-Cuban Orchestra on the recordings he did with this band around 1949-1950.[1] Try singing Parker's "Donna Lee," for example, and clapping the clave at the same time. Practicing this way will give you a good bebop feeling and help put your phrasing* in place.

Latin pianists often play two-handed rhythmic figures or "vamps" known as montunos or guajeos behind soloists. They provide very effective rhythmic support for improvisation. These montunos have to be based on the clave. One finds many examples of these Latin vamps in jazz. A case in point is this introduction to "Star Eyes."[2]

The clave fits well under the entire song. Try singing "Star Eyes" while you clap your hands or tap your foot to the clave.

Here is a commonly used montuno based on the G minor chord.

These montunos are played in unison with both hands. Make each attack staccato. By this I mean not only that the notes should be short and separated, but that you need a percussive touch. Don't forget that the piano is a percussion instrument, and in Latin and Afro-American music it's played even more percussively.

Practice this montuno slowly with metronomic regularity and without rushing. One good way to practice is to sing the montuno and clap on the upbeats (beats 2 and 4). Gradually play the montuno faster, yet in a relaxed way. Too many inex-perienced Latin pianists tend to come on the downbeat (beat 1) too soon. One of the best ways to practice montunos in rhythm is to play them along with a conga or bass player. Some salsa pianists mark the clave with their foot while playing montunos. This develops coordination and independence.

At the bottom of the page is a more complex eight-bar variation on the previous Gm7 montuno.

As opposed to jazz, Latin rhythms are very precise. Each instrument of the Latin rhythm section has a definite role to play. Each part is played very evenly and precisely, even at fast tempos. I suggest you listen to pianist Eddie Palmieri.[3] He is an excellent montuno player. Kenny Barron and Cedar Walton are two jazz pianists who occasionally use montunos as alternatives to chords to "comp" (accompany) on Latin-tinged tunes.

With experience, you will soon learn to create your own montunos based on chord changes. I'll close with a short one which resembles "Tea for Two." In a future article, we'll continue with more montunos that connect chord changes. ●

The "Tea for Two" Montuno

Here is a more complex eight-bar variation on the previous Gm7 montuno for you to practice.

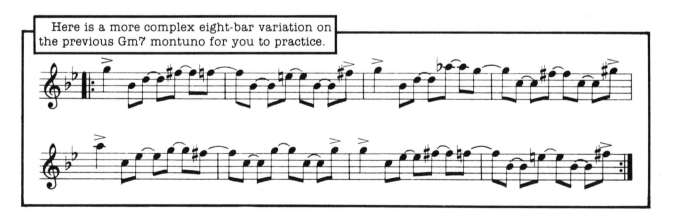

[1]Charlie Parker with Machito (Verve 8174451).

[2]Available on the Charlie Parker album Swedish Schnapps (Verve UMV 2030) or Charlie Parker Verve Years 1950-51 (VE2 2512). Parker first recorded this introduction on January 17, 1951. Thanks to historian Phil Schaap for this information. — Ed.

[3]A recent Palmieri album is Palo Pa' Rumba (Musica Latina MS 56).

Isabelle Leymarie has a Ph.D. in Ethnomusicology from Columbia University, and she is Assistant Professor in the Department of Music and Afro-American Studies at Yale. She studied with Mary Lou Williams and Cedar Walton and led her own ensemble, Tropics, in New York before moving to New Haven. Leymarie contributed a chapter on Salsa and Latin jazz to the book Hot Sauces edited by Billy Bergman, published by Quill, 1985.

Montunos and mambos — more Latin rhythmic devices

Isabelle Leymarie

In JKW vol. 1, no. 2, we became acquainted with <u>montunos</u>, the counterpoint figures used in salsa and Latin jazz. The primary purpose of montunos in Latin music is to provide rhythmic figures behind the soloists. In fact, the part of the Afro-Cuban song form during which the pianist plays the montuno and the soloist (saxophone or trumpet for example) plays the solo is called the <u>montuno section</u>. The montuno section generally follows the theme.

Montunos themselves are usually played over specific chord progressions. The rhythmic efficiency derives from the fact that the montunos

---

> "... the part of the Afro-Cuban song form during which the pianist plays the montuno and the soloist plays the solo is called the montuno section."

---

are repeated over and over behind the soloist. The following montuno is commonly used by the string and flute bands known as <u>charangas</u>. It also can be used as an accompaniment for the famous song "Guajira Guantanamera," popularized by Pete Seeger in the 1960's.

A variation of this montuno is found on Eddie Palmieri's hit of the early 1970's, "Vamonos Pa'l Monte."

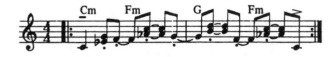

Isabelle Leymarie is writing books about popular Cuban music and Senegalese music.

The bass figure played against these montunos is known as the <u>tumbao</u>. It too is based on the <u>clave</u> rhythm.

ᴠ *means lift your hand*

This tumbao fits the two previous montunos. It is a good idea to start practicing a montuno in the right hand and a tumbao in the left to see how the figures fall together.

It is also excellent to practice improvising with the right hand while keeping a tumbao in the left hand. The tumbao will anchor the right hand and assure that the solo stays "in clave." Playing in clave is a rhythmic consideration. You learn its meaning through hours and hours of listening to <u>salsa</u> music, just as you learn the meaning of "swinging" from long listening to jazz. On the bandstand, however, montunos are played with both hands in unison, or with a slight counterpoint in the left hand, as the bass plays the tumbao.

The percussion section

The percussion instruments in the salsa rhythm section include <u>timbales</u> and the <u>conga</u>. The timbales (a set of two drums mounted on one stand) play rhythms that fit very precisely with those of the piano and the bass. The left hand gives the clave; the right plays figures (known as <u>cascaras</u>) such as this one.

The conga drummer plays a complementary pattern. One of the patterns most frequently used in salsa is the following one.

B = *bass tone*, S = *slap*, T = *tone*
L = *left hand*, R = *right hand*

This pattern will change if the rhythm played is a songo, a guaguanco, a yambu, etc., and the piano will have to change accordingly. Just as it is extremely valuable to practice with a bassist, it is also useful to practice montunos with a timbalero and a conguero to see exactly how the piano fits in the rhythm section.

Rumbas

Chordal comping can be used in place of montunos, especially in the musical forms known as rumbas. Open voicings are usually preferred for rumbas. 13th chords with +11s are particularly good, as in the boxed example below.

Chordal comping is also used in cha cha cha rhythms, and in the sections known as mambos. Earlier I noted that the montuno section follows the theme in a salsa number. The mambo section follows the montuno section and consists of a short riff (usually four bars) that signals the end of each solo. The last figure below is an example of a mambo riff. Both hands would play this figure in unison.

"The mambo section follows the montuno section and consists of a short riff that signals the end of each solo."

There are many other types of montunos and rhythmic devices in Latin music. We'll get to more in our next installment. In the meantime the pianists Hilton Ruiz and Kenny Kirkland play montunos on their recordings. I especially recommend the song "Sao Pablo" featuring Kirkland on the album Rain Forest (Contemporary 14007), led by vibraphonist Jay Hoggard.●

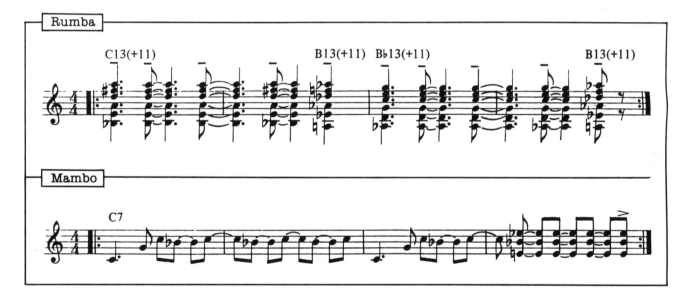

MONTUNO OF THE MONTH

Here's an example of a montuno that fits a descending chord progression. Try it, and then try some variations on it. For example, reverse the rhythmic values of the first two notes. Another variation is to play the left hand an octave lower than written.

The Charleston And The Clavé

The best way to start developing a feeling for jazz is to study jazz rhythm, not only for its own sake but because it's the fun, physical side of this music.

Early jazz rhythm used an element called the Hornpipe. This consists of a dotted eighth note followed by a sixteenth note. Here's an example of the Hornpipe, using the C scale.

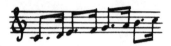

You may be familiar with a sound called the "shuffle rhythm," a favorite among blues players. This uses the dotted rhythm as well. Blues musicians use it in a chordal pattern, as shown.

A popular dance step of the "roaring twenties" was the Charleston, based on a song with this rhythm in the melody.

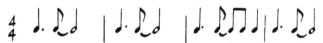

The Charleston rhythm is a variation on the Hornpipe. Our original Hornpipe consisted of a dotted eighth note followed by a sixteenth note. ♫ In the Charleston, the rhythm is stretched out so that it takes twice as much time: a dotted quarter is followed by a dotted eighth.

Playing The Charleston

On the piano, the Charleston rhythm can be played in the right hand against a steady quarter note rhythm in the left. This rhythm is typical of the kind of figures that the brass played in the big bands of the swing era. To complicate things a little, the dotted quarter is silent in this example. Nevertheless, the syncopated feeling of putting an accent on the "and" of a beat is still very much present.

"Charleston"

Now, look at some other rhythms that were typical of those swing era brass sections.

"Charleston"

Look at each measure separately. In the first measure there are notes on one and four. The second measure has a syncopated figure on two and three, with the accent on the "and" of two. ♫♫ And, as in measure 1, there are notes on one and four. Bar 3 is like bar 1. Bar 4 is the Charleston rhythm.

These rhythms are difficult to read and play if they are unfamiliar. If you are having trouble playing them, try clapping the rhythms along with a metronome. Then, still using the metronome to keep time, play the rhythms on a single note.

The Clavé

Just after World War II, Latin rhythm and percussion instruments became popular in jazz. The clavés are two wooden sticks that have a penetrating sound when hit together. In traditional Afro-Cuban music, they play the rhythmic pattern:

Notice how the first measure of the Clavé rhythm is similar to the Charleston.

The Clavé can also be reversed.

Practice the Clavé away from the keyboard by clapping your hands or snapping your fingers to the Clavé pattern while you're counting out loud "one, two, three, four" or while you're walking "left, right, left, right." Once that comes naturally, practice the reverse Clavé. When you're ready, you can learn the Brazilian Clavé. It's slightly different from the Cuban.

Play the Clavés on the keyboard in octaves with both hands. In due time, you can learn to play a straight four in the left hand, and the Clavé in the right.

114

LATIN RHYTHM GUIDE
(Tango)

To fully understand the unique quality of Latin Rhythms, we would do well to start at the origin of all rhythms.

The BEAT itself!

Students sometimes disregard the fact that the beat must conclude a full cycle, much like a bouncing ball. We will work with the quarter note as representing 1 beat, although other note values are used for this purpose. Thus, the quarter note would be counted ONE-AND, TWO-AND; "one" representing the DOWNBEAT, and "two," the UP, or AFTERBEAT.

Like this:

1 and 2 and, etc.

As you see, the elements that establish rhythm are missing.

The ACCENTED note (or beat) can provide to some degree, one of the important elements.

Like this:

A BAR line before each accented note establishes the time signature 3/4. The rhythm: WALTZ. Accents can be applied at greater intervals, depending upon the "pulse," or rhythm desired. As in our first rhythm - TANGO:

In the tango rhythm, the first and **fourth** beats are heavily accented, unlike the usual 4/4 pattern, in which the first and third beats are accented.

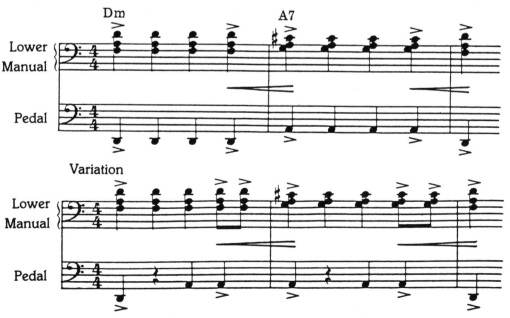

115

Continued next page

LATIN RHYTHM GUIDE
(Cha Cha)

The Cha, Cha, like the Tango, deals with ACCENTED DOWNBEATS.

Please refer to the illustration extracted from the arrangement of "Sweet And Gentle."
The Pedal/Bass pattern consists of 4 equal beats. The 2nd beat, denoted by a quarter rest, is silent, or "empty".
The resulting effect of this pattern is the basis for many Latin rhythms.
The Left Hand must perform figurations more complex.
The left "side," meaning the Pedals and Left Hand, should be practiced together as a team; since here lies the rhythmic support for the Right Hand. It is after this aspect has been mastered accurately, in tempo, that automated rhythm (if desired) may be applied with some assurance it will coordinate with the activities of the Pedal and Left Hand.

116

LATIN RHYTHM GUIDE
(Bossa Nova)

This extremely popular Latin rhythm is very "versatile" and lends itself to many forms of music in the popular and Jazz idiom. The bass (or pedal) line is most important. See Below:

I to V Bass progression

Pedal

Left Hand

Left Hand

Pedal

VARIATION*   *This rhythm produced by automated unit.
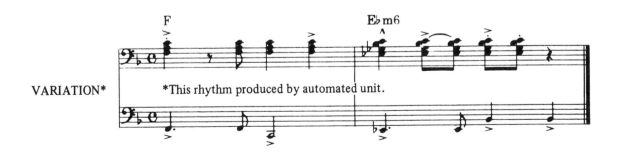

Continued next page

LATIN RHYTHM GUIDE
(Rhumba - Beguine)

RHUMBA: The rhumba is another example of how we can produce a completely different rhythmic effect by altering the accent pattern of the four beats. In this rhythm, beat 1 is emphasized slightly, there is a rest for beat 2, and 3rd and 4th beats are accented more heavily than the first.

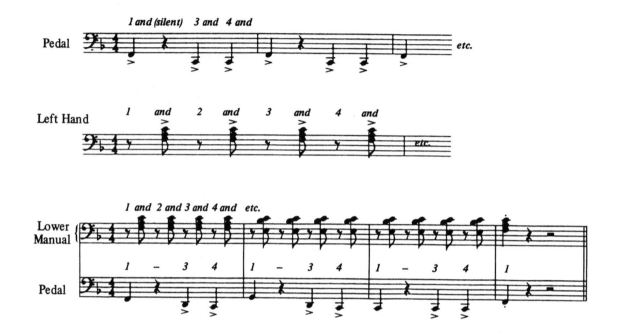

BEGUINE: The beguine is not unlike the rhumba in accent pattern. However, please note the "AND 2" in each bar. It is a quarter note and frequently can be of slightly longer duration. Also, the second beat is **not** silent in the pedal, but is consolidated with the first beat.

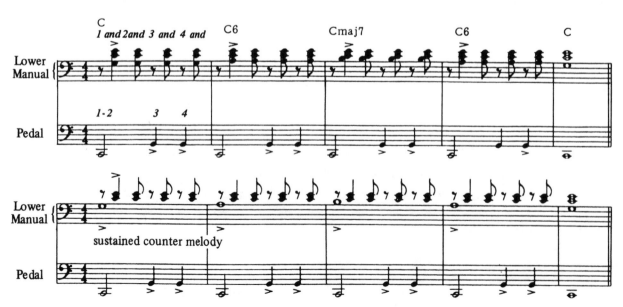

LATIN RHYTHM GUIDE
(Mambo)

The Mambo is played at a very bright and lively tempo. Below are some of the various Pedal patterns.

Accents on beats 1 and 3.

Accents on beats 1 - 3 and 4

Stationary

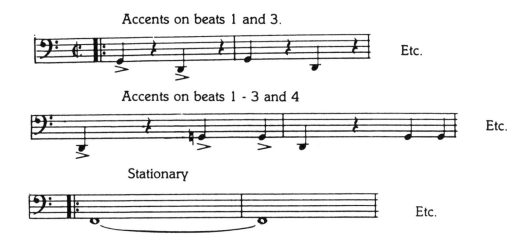

RHYTHM ACCOMPANIMENTS:

Melody and Accompaniment - I

Both Hands
Upper

Melody and Accompaniment.

CHORD RHYTHM:

Continued next page

LATIN RHYTHM GUIDE
(Samba)

1. PEDAL or BASS pattern: The heavily accented 2nd beat.
2. LEFT HAND: The "anticipated" beat preceding the 1st beat of each bar.

INTRO:

*Observe accent on 2nd beat throughout.

The anticipated beat is accomplished by placing the accent on the weak or second ("and") half of the beat cycle. This often involves the "borrowing" of time value from one beat and giving it to another.

ML

120

Polymeters

Isabelle Leymarie

Here are two **polymeters.**

Such polymeters as 3 against 4, or 6 against 4, are often used in Latin jazz. They can be practiced at the keyboard or away from it. Let's start away from it.

Sit in a straight chair with your feet on the floor. Keeping a steady pulse (a metronome will help), tap a foot on the quarter notes at a tempo of approximately ♩ = 80. This pulse can be counted either "1-2-3-4-5-6-1-2-3-4-5-6" etc., or "1-2-3-4-1-2-3-4" etc. You're going to do both, putting one meter in the right hand, one in the left! Clap your hands against your thighs on the downbeats (the "1's"). The right hand is in $\frac{6}{4}$, the left hand is in $\frac{4}{4}$. The foot taps the pulse. The result is

Once you've established this pattern, speed it up. At a certain speed, you won't be able to tap your foot on every quarter note beat; you'll have to tap on only 1 and 3. A variation that emphasizes the "backbeat" is to tap on 2 and 4. With the polymetric pattern firmly in your mind, it won't be long before your foot can't keep up at all. Finally, when you've mastered this exercise, reverse the roles of the hands.

The other polymeter also establishes a 12-beat pattern. Here the right hand is in 3 and the left in 4.

You'll find these very polyrhythms in Latin jazz occurring between two instruments when the conga is in 4 and the piano in 3, for example. Or the pianist may play polyrhythms between the two hands. Use octaves or some simple harmony and put the polymetric pattern on the keyboard, just as you've been slapping the pattern on your thighs.

Rhythmic displacement of a phrase

Another device frequently used in Cuban music is the displacement of a rhythmic figure over several bars. This device may give the impression that the line is being "pulled away" from the ground beat, and it can momentarily disorient the musician who has not established a strong pulse. Here are two examples of rhythmic displacement of a figure.

Begin very slowly, tapping the *clave* with your foot over and over until it's very steady and second-nature to you. Then add the hands. The coordination is no easy feat, and you'll need patience and persistence (and maybe help — can a friend clap the clave for you?), but it's fun when you get the hang of it.

The final exercise is in sixteenth notes. The rhythmic figure is

in both hands, one octave apart. After you're very comfortable with it, you can sequence it up and down the keyboard. Play any notes; keep the rhythm exact.●

Swing It!

By Champ Champagne

A few issues ago we discussed the concept of "rolled eighths" (♫ = ♩♪). This technique is essential to the art of swing phrasing because swing gives the feeling of a side to side motion, as opposed to 2/4 marches, most forms of rock, and Latin music, which move up and down.

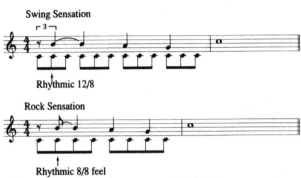

In a syncopated passage, weak beats become strong. The usual strong beats in 4/4 time are the downbeats of 1 and 3. Beats 1 and 2 of the following example are syncopated because of the emphasis on the up beat of 1:

Push beats occur on weak beats and are *always* accented:

Keeping the above principle in mind, here's an example of swing phrasing:

The rhythmic figure ♪ ♩ ♪ is useful for jazz waltzes or tunes in 5/4 time. Why don't you play this 5/4 rhythm using rolled eighths as in the swing feel? If you were to write this phrase out, it would be in 15/8 time. It's much simpler to just roll the eighths:

Another rhythmic figure you might encounter in swing style is:

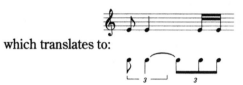

which translates to:

Finally, a word about quarter note triplets. I get a feeling of falling backwards from my chair. It's so natural in swing phrasing.

Fancy that... it's the same thing! ∩

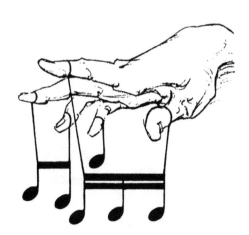

122

Section 4
ARRANGING SKILLS

Harmony at the Keyboard

An Introduction To Keyboard Arrangement

In the last issue we showed how to construct the chords for the first four bars of *The Twelve Days of Christmas*. We arrived at a very basic keyboard arrangement, with simple block chords in the left hand and the melody in the right. The chords were derived from chord symbols, which are shown here between the staves.

The same chords can be arranged in much more interesting ways. The notes making up the chords will stay the same, but they will be distributed around the keyboard in various configurations. To begin, we might use the left hand to play only the chord roots, and add chord tones in the right hand, underneath the melody. (Notice that on the second beat of the third bar the melody itself provides both the F and the D of the G7 chord.)

It is also possible to divide the chord tones more evenly so that there are two "voices" in the right hand and two in the left. This gives a fuller, more resonant sound, and exploits the various ranges of the keyboard.

A more rhythmic effect can be achieved by having the left hand play the chord roots in a low register on the strong beats, and then play chords in the middle register on the weak beats. This works out well for the first two bars, but in bars three and four the harmony changes too quickly to allow for up-beat chords, so it is necessary to put the chord tones into the right hand.

125

Continued next page

Another kind of arrangement makes use of what are called "broken chords." Here the notes of a chord are played in succession, rather than all at once. Usually the sustaining pedal is used to combine them. In our example the broken chords are played by the left hand, forming an accompaniment that gives a lyrical, flowing quality to the music.

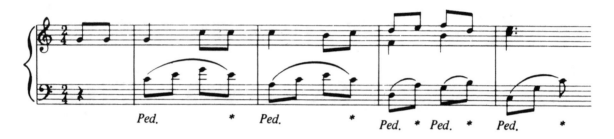

Of course there are many ways in which broken-chord figures can be arranged. The next example—utilizing exactly the same chords—shows a more widely spaced pattern. Now the effect is more sonorous, and in keeping with this the right-hand part has been thickened by the addition of chord tones.

In all our examples the harmonies have remained unchanged, but the notes of the chords have been arranged and rearranged to form a variety of musical textures. And we have only scratched the surface. The possibilities for keyboard arrangements of a given tune are virtually endless. It is often amazing to see how many ways a resourceful musician can find to play the same melody and chords. In future issues we will discuss some more complicated, elaborate forms of arrangement.

RC ♩

Harmony at the Keyboard

Harmonizing A Melody

In the previous issue we began to discuss the harmonization of melodies. We saw that in any key there are three primary chords, built on the first, fourth, and fifth notes of the scale. In a major key I and IV are major, while V may be major or a dominant seventh.

Let us work out the harmonization for the familiar tune *Auld Lang Syne* in the key of F major.

In the key of F major the three primary chords are F, B flat, and C7. All three of these are needed in the first four bars of the tune. In the first bar the notes F and A suggest an F chord. And, in fact, the "I" chord is usually present at the beginning of a melody. In the second bar the main note is G, which forms part of the C7 chord. In the third bar the melody spells out the F chord. And the D in bar four is part of the B—flat chord.

The second half of the tune is a bit more problematical. In bar five the melody spells out an F chord. Bar six is the same as the second bar, and C7 is again a good harmonization. The last three notes of the tune, beginning with the second half of bar seven, suggest the progression B flat-C7-F. But what harmony is right for the first half of the seventh bar?

Let us consider the alternatives. The F at the beginning of bar seven could, of course, be accompanied by an F-major chord ("a" in our next example). But this seems a little dull, and we really don't want to arrive at the F major until the eighth bar. The note F also forms part of the B-flat major chord (b), but it would be better to reserve this chord for the second half of bar seven. So we must look beyond the primary chords. The note F is also part of the D-minor chord (c), and if you try this harmony in the seventh bar, you will find that it sounds just right.

127

Continued next page

Now we can complete the harmonization of the second half of *Auld Lang Syne*, with a D-minor chord in the seventh bar. This chord is built on the sixth note of the scale. Because it is a minor chord it introduces a new, interesting sound. Another improvement would be to use an inversion of the F chord, with A in the bass, at the start of bar five.

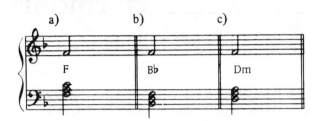

There is a system to be followed here. Begin the harmonization of a tune with the expectation that the three primary chords will play an important part. The tune often starts with the "I" chord, and almost always ends with it. When you come to a problem spot, try various chords that contain the main melody note. Once you hit on the best solution you will usually know immediately: your ear will tell you that it is right.

RC

A "Funky" Voicing

By Joan Stiles

Did you ever wonder how jazz and rock musicians get that down-and-dirty flavor in their harmonies? One way is through the use of the colorful augmented ninth chord — its essential members are the third (3), dominant seventh (b7) and augmented ninth (#9 — often spelled as a minor third above the root).

Jazz musicians often use it in left hand voicings when playing the blues:

The "clash between the major and minor thirds (Eb and E) is what gives this chord its "funky," bluesy quality. Notice that the root (C) is omitted in the left hand.

Rock star Jimi Hendrix popularized the sound of the #9 in the 1960s with pieces like "Foxey Lady" and "Purple Haze." The next example is a rock riff derived from Hendrix's innovative guitar style:

C minor: V7#9   I   C major: V 7#9   I

Practice these voicings up and down the keyboard chromatically to make this "foxey" chord a part of your vocabulary. Here are some drills to give you a head start:

F minor: V7#9   I   G minor: V7#9   I

In a ballad, the #9 is usually not "left hanging" in mid-air. Instead it resolves by moving down a whole step to the flatted ninth (b9) and then down another half step to the fifth of the I chord. In this example, even more tension and color are provided by adding the augmented fifth (#5):

128

pop piano

Christmas Carol Creations

There is a long history of pop performers using classical themes as jumping-off points for their own hit songs; old favorites such as *Strangers In Paradise* originated in the classical world, and even contemporary musicians like Barry Manilow have found the classical repertoire fertile ground for their creative endeavors.

In addition to culling the classical literature for tunes, it is also worthwhile to look at the way classical masters dealt with the "popular"

materials of their day. Often, we can find some fresh ideas that might lend themselves to contemporary arrangements. One musical source that never becomes dated is the Christmas Carol, and many of the masters offered their own versions of the carols which we still play and enjoy today.

A case in point is *In Dulci Jubilo* (*Good Christian Men Rejoice* in this issue). Here is the traditional four-part arrangement:

Franz Liszt produced this version, which makes use of a repeating figure in the bass:

Bach came up with a very different arrangement. The theme starts in the top voice, and then begins again a measure later in the bass, to pro-

duce a canon! Meanwhile, another countermelody plays along as an accompaniment, and it too is set up in canonic imitation:

129

Continued next page

We can learn from these composers, and go on to produce a new arrangement for ourselves. Let's look at Liszt's idea in the key of F:

We could create any number of similar patterns: the device is common enough. But we can also take Liszt's music as a starting point. One approach that springs to mind is to add harmony to the bass pattern—keeping the basic chords of the song intact, and adding a second line:

We can also add our own harmonies to the same pattern that Bach set up. First, let's create a canon with the melody, just as Bach did:

Now, let's play the countermelody in thirds.

When we place it all together, we will be left with something completely new — and perhaps not totally satisfying. Here is where we rely on our own ears and imagination; after all, we are using the older models only for inspiration.

When using harmony and counterpoint in this way, there will surely be times when we want to make changes or take certain liberties in order to produce a more satisfactory sound. That last E note in the second full measure, for example, will clash with the F in the melody; so, we can change it to an F. We may want to double some of the notes of the countermelody (in octaves). We might even add little bits of the countermelody in new places (see the top voice at the end of the second measure below):

In this way, we can take ideas from the masters and make them completely our own. Whenever you can, glance through the classical collections, and try to spot a phrase or technique that will come in handy. There is a treasure trove of material out there, and half the fun is in the finding! **SI**

Down And Dirty

by Joan Stiles

When choosing left-hand voicings, it isn't always necessary to use complete chords. Modern players frequently leave out the root and play only the most "essential" notes. This works especially well when playing the blues.

The dominant seventh is the basic blues chord, and the two notes of this chord which best express its dominant seventh quality are the 3rd and 7th. For example, for a G7 chord, try playing F and B. for a C7, play E and Bb; for D7, F♯ and C. You have just played the three chords used in 12 bar blues, dominant sevenths built on I, IV and V, in the key of G. Notice how this voicing allows the individual notes of one chord to move smoothly by half or whole step to members of any other chord in the progression, creating good voice leading.

To show you how to use these voicings, I have written them out in 12 bar blues form with the melody of W.C. Handy's "St. Louis Blues." Version 1 uses just the essential 3rds and 7ths. At first, just play these voicings *in time*, adding the melody when you feel secure:

Version 2 incorporates more "color tones," 9ths and 13ths, on top of these basic voicings, as well as some chromatic motion to add interest. Try this version alone first, and then with the melody: ⌢

The Art Of The Intro

"I've told everyone who has ever taken a lesson from me," says pianist/organist Jane Jarvis, "that there are two very important things to remember when you are going to perform professionally. The first is to dress well and to present yourself nicely. The second is to play a good introduction to every song."

Here are two introductions that can serve as models for slow tunes. The first, by Lou Stein, was written originally as an intro to the song *Here's That Rainy Day,* but it is useful with any slow tune (it's presented here in the key of G).

Notice that Lou keeps a G *pedal point* in the bass throughout. The harmony first moves from G to C, then back to G before venturing a little further away from the key center: in the second half of the intro the notes of an Ab Major 7th (one half step up from G) create tension above the G bass, but resolve down to a G Major 7th in the end.

The second intro example is one by Jane Jarvis. This was written for her arrangement of *The Party's Over,* but once again we are left with a wonderful model. This one makes use of the cycle of fifths with "altered" jazz harmonies for a truly contemporary sound.

Jane's introduction is a perfect lead-in for any slow song in Eb. Try transposing it to different keys and you will gain both a greater understanding of how it works, and more flexibility in its use.

131

Intros And Endings
Part I: Endings

While you can memorize set intros and endings, learning the musical theory and chord structures behind them will allow you to create your own, based on standard chord progressions and harmonic principles. Here are some ideas to help you along.

Example 1 is a deceptive cadence, or delayed ending—an ending where the tonic chord is momentarily avoided and substituted with other chords before returning to the tonic. The following series of progressions are for deceptive cadences.

In the key of F, a G^9 chord and a C^9 will bring the piece to the final F. If this were a typical ending, the F^6 would follow directly after the C^9 chord. However, you can delay the F^6 chord by first hitting the chord exactly one whole tone lower, an E^{b6} chord, then going to the F^6 chord.

Try to transpose this to at least one other standard key, ie: C, B^b, G, E^b.

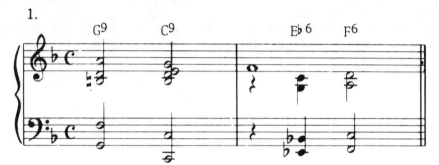

Not only can the F^6 chord be delayed by going to a tone a whole tone below, it is also possible to go a tone above the F^6. The G^{b6} chord is exactly one half tone above the F^6 chord. This technique uses "neighboring tones" (tones which neighbor the tonic).

Transpose this exercise to the key of C, plus one other standard key.

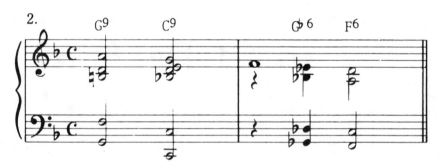

This example takes both chords in the previous two examples (the E^{b6} and the G^{b6}) and uses them in connection with each other, to create a deceptive cadence. Through these examples you are learning some standard simple endings, but you are also learning the thought processes behind them, such as how to use neighboring tones. In order to become thoroughly comfortable with these concepts, though, continue to practice transpositions of intros and endings. This will increase your ability to play them in other keys.

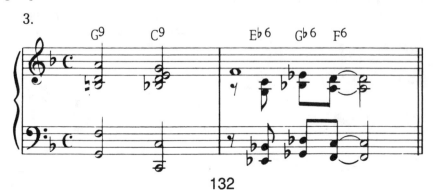

132

This is an example of another neighboring tone, the one exactly one half tone below the tonic. The last measure in example 4 shows an E^6 chord going to an F^6 chord. In example 1, the neighboring tone is a whole tone below the F^6 chord for the deceptive cadence. This time it is only a half tone below the F^6 chord. Play the entire progression and then transpose it to the key of B^b.

Example 5 uses all the neighboring tones previously discussed in this article (E^{b6}, G^{b6}, E^6) and puts them together in one deceptive cadence. If you can play this ending in the standard keys of C, G, B^b as well as F, and memorize it, you will be well on your way to being able to use it in your playing (in place of the uninspiring endings found in conventional sheet music).

Example 6 moves from the sixth chords we have been dealing with so far, to the major seventh chord. To create a major seventh chord, delete the sixth tone of the chord and put in the major seventh. For example, for an E^{bmaj7} chord, substitute a D for the C. In a G^{bmaj7} chord, substitute an F for the E. The major seventh chord is a jazzier, more modern sound. Transpose the major seventh chord progression to several familiar standard keys.

This example is also a deceptive ending, but instead of going to a neighboring tone on the last note, it goes to a tone a major third below the tonic chord. This ending could go directly from the D^9 chord to the G^9 chord to the C^9 chord, but instead goes to the chord a major third lower — an A^b chord — and from there to a D^{bmaj7} chord, before winding up at the C^{maj7} chord. This is the basic harmony of the deceptive cadence. Most pianists will arpeggiate or put runs in on the last three chords. Try playing this progression with some arpeggiated notes. It is a good ending to use when a singer is ending on the tonic note. In C, let the singer hit the C while you play the A^b. It is a dramatic effect.

Continued next page

133

7. Key of C

The next to the last measure in this example is a neighboring tone chord, a half tone above the C: a D♭maj7. This can be used in an up-tempo song such as "Lady Is A Tramp."

8. Key of C

In this example the second measure should have been an E♭ chord, going from Fm7 to E7 to E♭maj9 to the end of the song. Instead, a chord which is exactly an augmented fourth above has been inserted. This is an Am7 chord with an E♭ in it. This technique is used by pianists, arrangers and composers as an effective ending when the tonic note is the melody note—the E♭ in this case. All you need do from here is to take every tone in the Am7♭5 chord and lower it. If you analyze the seven chords from the Am7 to the E♭maj9, you will see they are basically a chromatic progression downward until the final chord is reached.

This progression is used often and you should learn it in as many keys as you can. Once you learn the progression well, you can improvise on it by simply rolling some of the chords, or by playing neighboring notes within the chord.

9. Key of E♭

Part II: Introductions

This exercise uses the same chord progression as example 9. Once you have learned it, it can be effectively used as an introduction. You can write any melody over it while playing the progression with your left hand.

10. Key of E♭
Same progression as Intro:

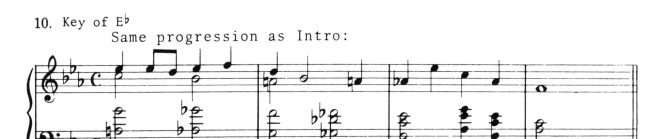

Example 11 is an intro which uses the III chord (in the key of C, the III chord is an Em based chord with D as the seventh) and progresses chromatically downward until you reach the C chord. The first chord is a minor chord. The second chord, while it can be a minor chord, is usually a dominant seventh, i.e. an E♭7, B♭7, D♭7. Play this exercise with two hands and play the chords over and over until you are very familiar with them.

The right side is a variation on the basic chords. It is a good finger exercise and can be used as either an intro, an ending or a fill. Play the arpeggiated variation slowly with two hands to begin with and work up to speed. Move on to the keys of F, B♭, E♭, A♭ and G and play both the chords and the variation with both hands. Your left hand should not be neglected in any exercise. Remember that the first and third chords are minor sevenths and the second and fourth chords are dominant seventh chords.

11.

IIIm7 ♭III7 IIm7 ♭II7   VARIATION

Continued next page

The original sheet music ending in example 12 is dull. Substitute example 12a which uses the chord progression you have been practicing. Although it has a slightly different voicing than you have been practicing, it is essentially the same progression. 12b can be used as well, and is closer to what you have been practicing.

12. Original ending:

12a. Delayed ending:

12b. Or...

Example 13 is a II-V chord progression. In the key of C, a Dm^7 chord would move to a G^7 chord, which would normally progress to the I chord, C (not written in your example).

Variation I: this uses a Dm^9 chord (an E on top), instead of the Dm^7 chord, which lends a more modern sound to the II chord.

In the next example, which is in the key of F, the II chord is a Gm^9 (A on top).

Look at the first measure of each of these examples, and learn the II chord for a few different keys.

Go back to variation I. A Dm^9 progresses to a G^{13}. Learn this chord progression (the minor ninth chord to the thirteenth) and memorize it in each key. This is a good way of playing the II-V-I progression rather than in using the simple triad or the seventh chord. Now play this progression in the keys of B^b, E^b, A^b and G. Write them out yourself in the space provided.

Variation II is a more modern sound than variation I, although the first chord is exactly the same. In the key of C, the B in the G^{13} chord in variation I becomes a C in the G chord in variation II. It looks like an F^{maj7} in the right hand over a G. This is often the way you will see the chord written in modern music. Learn variation II in every key and memorize it.

We are now getting into a very modern sound that will take your piano into another dimension of contemporary music. Try to play these variations in some kind of rhythm, not just half notes, or alternate between keys, perhaps from the key of B♭ to the key of E♭.

You can create many different kinds of intros with ninth and thirteenth chords. Another good way to use these chords is to skip around from one key to another and then return to the key that you are going to play your song in.

In the last example, the first two measures are in the key of C. This key is established with a II chord, going to the V chord. The second half of the second measure has a chromatic chord progression up to the key of E♭. In the third and fourth measures the II chord of E♭ (an Fm chord) going to the V chord (a B♭ chord) establishes the key of E♭ momentarily,

while the fifth and sixth measures reestablish the key of C with the II-V progression. The final two measures have the III chord descending to the flatted III, to the II, to the flatted II. These elements are what make up this intro.

Now that you understand the theory behind creating intros like this, you can do them in many keys for many songs, instead of imitating this one note for note. The key to success is to reread this article and redo the exercises until the theory and principles become a part of your playing.

13.

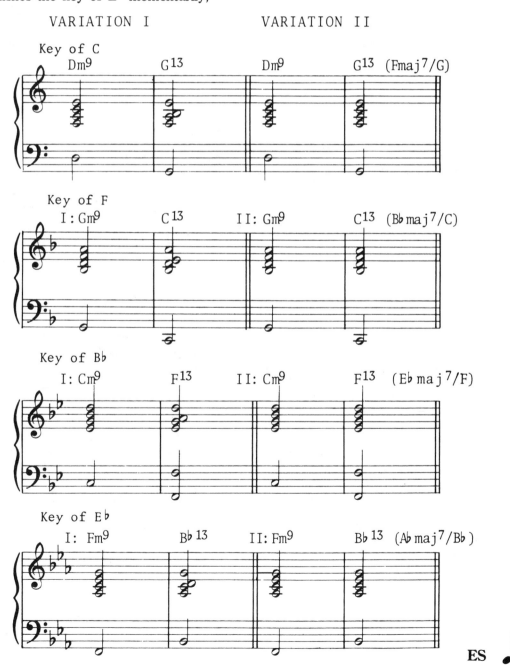

Endings

Here's a way to improvise a song ending using a slash chord and a Tatum-inspired run.

Does the song end on a C major chord? Then, play a D triad over a C major seventh and turn that D triad into a four-note phrase.

Transpose this into any major key, using the neighboring triad in the right hand. For example,

Extend the run, as in the example below where it begins on the highest note of the keyboard and drops steeply over six octaves!

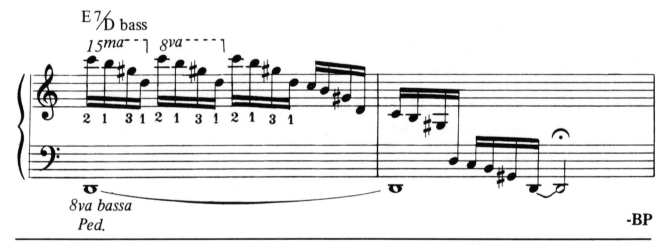

-BP

The Whole Tone Sound

In our second ending, three chords descend in whole steps toward a major seventh chord. As you play this example slowly, listen for the whole step drop between each of the first three chords. Play one ''voice'' at a time, as though it were written for soprano, alto, tenor, and bass singers. Become familiar with that ''whole tone'' sound in each voice and in the voiced chords.

Here's the whole tone ending in three keys.

-BP

More endings

A *cadence* is a harmonic progression that brings a musical passage to its conclusion. The simple "Amen" cadence (IV-I) that concludes hymns underlies the Gospel sound. By stretching the cadence out and syncopating it, you can create a Gospel-style ending. For example,

A *deceptive cadence* alters the formula by making chord additions or substitutions in the traditional cadence. For example, insert a chord a half step above or below the chord of resolution just before the last chord.

The chromatic feeling can be stretched across a larger interval. The progression below is basically a ii-V-I in Bb with the cadence between V and I progressing downward in half steps. Notice the chord qualities (minor, dominant, diminished, etc.) and transpose the progression into other keys.

Finally, here are a few trick endings, beginning with the "Basie tag."

Another tag using contrary motion — right hand descending, left hand ascending — is this one.

And the reverse . . .

Can you hear how well the clave fits with this tag?

Happy endings! ●

-ME

pop piano

Finish your songs with flair

Let's continue our catalog of well-known "fills" with a look at some stock endings. There you are, at the finish of a song. The last chord is coming up. You have a choice: play the final chord and move on to the next tune; or, add a little something extra to go out with a bang, or with a stylish flourish.

Many musicians use "tag" endings, in which they repeat the last musical phrase over three times before stopping. The following "cliché" endings work on a similar principle: they use a chord progression which begins and ends on the same chord, so they can be "tagged" on to the song you are playing.

Here is a familiar progression which can be used as an extra "tag" to finish off a fast, bouncy tune ending in B♭:

Here's a variation with a dixieland feel:

To spruce this up even more, try adding *another* little fill onto the ending of the last example:

140

Let's look at another chord progression used for dixieland and swing endings:

Adding rhythmic variety to this produces a fun variant:

Here is a full-blown arrangement of this progression:

For more variety, try this substitute in the second measure:

or this in the last measure:

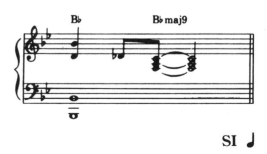

SI ♩

141

Happy Endings
Adding The Right Finish To Your Arrangements

Part I

by Michael Esterowitz

Sometimes it can be a little tricky to end a tune, especially since so many contemporary pop recordings end with a "fade out." In such situations, sometimes a *"ritard"* (slowing down) will help bring a sense of finality to the last chords. Here we demonstrate such an ending in D (using a cadence reminiscent of gospel music), which starts on the IV chord and "walks down" to the final chord.

When professional pianists play standards, they often use certain harmonic figures for the ending to give it more flair and style than it would otherwise have. Many of these formulas are called "deceptive cadences." A cadence is a resting point in music. In a deceptive cadence, you expect to hear a final, resolved I chord, but some other chord is used as a substitute, delaying the final resolution. There are a number of different deceptive cadences that can be used as slick, stylish endings. One such cadence uses chords that are built on neighbor notes to the tonic — a semi-tone above or below (the VII 7 or bII 7). For instance, if we were ending a song in G, we could delay the final chord with an Ab or F# chord, or a combination of both. As demonstrated below, these endings generally work best in tunes that do not use simple triads, but contain richer harmonies (major and minor sixths, sevenths, etc.).

Besides using a major seventh chord as our neighbor deceptive cadence chord, we can use a major sixth or a dominant seventh chord (bII6, bII7, VII6, VII7). The effect is similar, but we should choose a chord type to accommodate particular notes

Professional pianists use certain harmonic figures for ending with more flair.

that are repeated or sustained, or one that will mirror a particular melodic figure. (In our example, there is an A held in the last bar, and the chords used [B7, A6] also contain that note.)

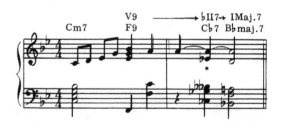

Next time we'll look at more deceptive cadences, and some more sophisticated endings using the same principles outlined here. See you then!

To be continued . . .

Michael Esterowitz is the author of How To Play From A Fake Book.

Happy Endings
Adding The Right Finish To Your Arrangements
Part II

By Michael Esterowitz

[th]ere are many other good deceptive cadence chords besides those we looked [at] last time which lie a semi-tone away from the tonic. These also may be used [in] combinations or by themselves. A major chord built a full tone below the I [(the] *b*VII chord in a major key) is often used, sometimes "walking up" chromatically [to] the I, or skipping up to the II before the final chord resolves.

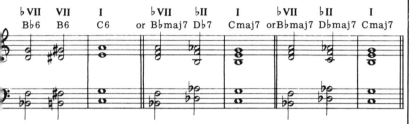

Also possible is the *b*VI, a major chord built a major third below the I. This [de]ceptive cadence is especially effective with a sustained note at the end when [th]at note is a common tone for both the *b*VI and the I chord. (For instance, the [no]te C held for the final note of a song in C is part of both the deceptive A*b* [m]ajor chord and the final C major chord.) The *b*VI can have a subtle effect when [com]bined with other passing chords, but when used along with the *b*VII, also [cr]eates a big climactic ending (as shown below).

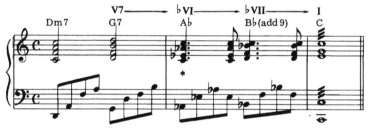

There are several longer and more sophisticated chord progressions that work [eq]ually well as deceptive endings or as introductions. We can't go into all of them, [bu]t one frequently used progression starts on a half-diminished chord built an [au]gmented fourth (diminished 5th) above the I chord and then descends [ch]romatically. Here is an example of this progression in B*b*; work it out in other [ke]ys as well. In this pattern, the chromatic bass line is the key element, while [th]e specific chord type (major, minor, diminished, sixth, seventh, or ninth) can [oft]en be altered without much difference in effect.

[B]efore we finish our discussion of endings, we would be remiss if we did not [me]ntion a few favorite "cliché" tags that are used — often with humorous intent [—] to end a tune . . . particularly light-hearted, peppy numbers. We'll look at those [ne]xt time. ⌒

To be continued . . .

Happy Endings
Adding the Right Finish To Your Arrangements
Part III

By Michael Esterowitz

We can conclude our discussion of well-worn endings by mentioning the "cliché" tags that are used in a light-hearted fashion — often with humorous intent. Practice transposing them so you can use them spontaneously in any key. The first one is the famous "Basie tag," often heard in big band swing arrangements.

Another common tag line is based on the contrary motion of treble and bass voices.

The figure above can be filled-in harmonically for a "fatter" sound.

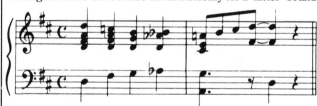

Another way to vary this is to switch the voices, so they move apart rather than together. Here we do this in F with a dotted rhythm.

Last but not least, here is the "Shave And A Haircut" tag, always good for a chuckle from your listeners!

These are just a few ideas among infinite possibilities for endings. Listen to what other keyboardists do, and try always to be creative and invent your own! ⌒

143

Stock Endings

by Champ Champagne

Now that you've experimented with creating your own endings, it's time to add some stock endings to your repertoire. These endings are the ones you've always heard. They will fit many different tunes.

The Soft-Shoe ending:

You might prefer the "Hard-sock" ending (with contrary motion):

Here's a typical "Dixie" ending:

Here's a "Dixie" ending with the right hand and bass reversed:

Here's a "Ragtime" ending:

The "Shave And Haircut" ending:

It must be "J-E-L-L-O" 'cause jam don't shake like that!!!

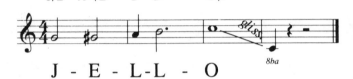

J - E - L - L - O

The "Barbershop" ending:

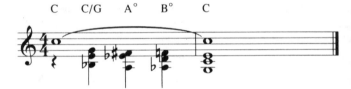

The "Blues" ending:

The "Good Evening Friends" ending can be added to the "Blues" or the "Barbershop" ending:

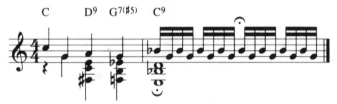

Und now ze big "Theatre" ending (to be played with full chords):

144

The "Hymn" ending:

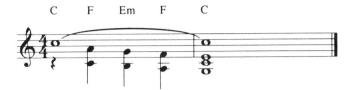

The "Waltz Hymn" ending:

The "Standard Slow Rock Ballad" ending:

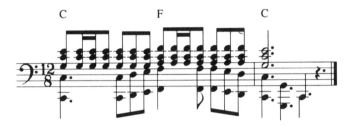

The "Latin" ending:

The "Tango" ending:

The minor "Tango" ending:

145

Section 5
RUNNING WILD!: MELODIC TRICKS OF THE TRADE

Ornaments

When today's song stylists ornament a melody with a grace note here or a trill there they are continuing a tradition that goes back to the beginnings of music as we know it. These little touches add polish to any performance, and for hundreds of years musicians have been writing down just how to use them. Of course, our idea of ornamentation is a bit different from that of Bach's, but the principle is pretty much the same. Some of Bach's ornaments, in fact, can still be used by contemporary keyboard players!

Let's begin to look at ornamental embellishments using the tune "Lazy River." One type of embellishment, a rhythmic device known in the Baroque era as "Notes Inegales," is already written into the music. In French music of the Baroque period, eighth-note passages were often played as dotted rhythms, and Hoagy Carmichael has dotted the opening phrase of the song. (See Example 1)

This device can be applied to other songs, of course; dotted rhythms are often used to give melodies a raggy or jazzy quality. The dotted eighth-sixteenth sound is most closely associated with ragtime and early jazz; a triplet feel comes closer to today's jazz sound. (See Example 2)

Among other Baroque ornaments we can adapt for our own purposes are the *trill* and the *grace note*. The trill was often used to give color (and in the case of the harpsichord, to sustain the note) to a pitch of long duration. (See Example 3)

This can easily be applied to "Lazy River." Imagine a honking saxophone playing the descending quarter notes. (See Example 4)

The grace note was originally performed as a note of fairly long duration; it shared the time given the main note of a melody. (See Example 5)

But by the Classical era, it had become a note that just sort of slides into the main note. And that is how it is used today.

To give a jazzy sound to a melody, try a grace note a half-step below the note you are aiming for. (See Example 6)

For a country-flavor grace, musicians use these slides. (See Example 7)

There are many more complicated ornaments, and they can lead a performer toward longer "improvisatory" approaches to playing a melody. For more material on this aspect of playing, see the new publication, *Jazz & Keyboard Workshop,* available through Sheet Music Magazine's Paramus, NJ address.

EXAMPLE 1

EXAMPLE 2

EXAMPLE 3

EXAMPLE 4

EXAMPLE 5

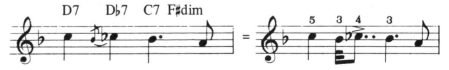

EXAMPLE 6

EXAMPLE 7

-SI

Tricks of the Trade
Fancy Runs To Spruce Up An Ending

There was a time when young musicians would learn their craft by gathering around the piano and watching the dancing fingers of an old pro. If they were really lucky, their teacher might repeat a passage over and over while his audience sat wide-eyed in hushed silence, struggling to memorize every musical gesture. (Eubie Blake learned to play in this way.) Others placed their fingers over the moving keys of player pianos, taking their lessons by proxy.

In our "Tricks of the Trade" department, we're going to continue this tradition. The examples below illustrate noted jazz pianist Lou Stein's method of adding runs to the ending of a tune. You can play the "bare bones" versions first (in both cases, they follow the standard II-V-I progression). Then try the spruced up "professional" stylings with elegant runs.

Note the fingering Lou suggests: there is a heavy concentration on fingers 1,2 and 3 (a trademark of Art Tatum and many jazz players). After you've mastered these examples, try transposing them to all twelve keys. Soon you'll be adept at ending any song like a pro.

Bare Versions Without Runs

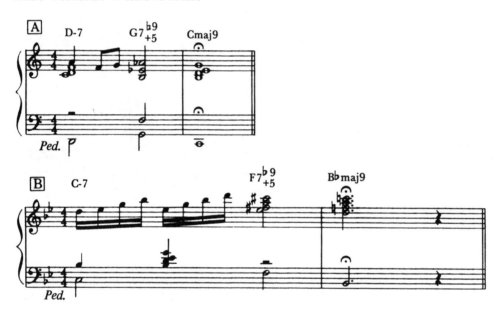

The Same Endings With Runs Added

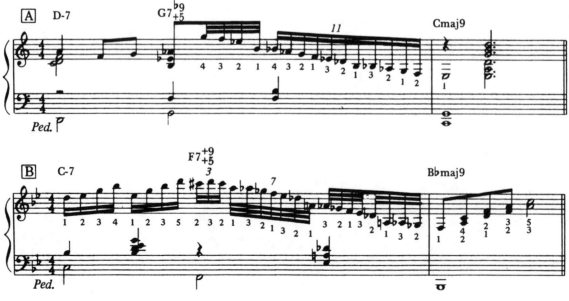

-LS

150

Breaking Up Is Easy To Do

Tasteful arpeggios never seem out of place, and it is hard to imagine playing a contemporary pop ballad without them. Here are some ideas on approaching arpeggiation; the examples below use a chord progression similar to that of "What Are You Doing The Rest Of Your Life."

One simple way to decide on the pitches to use in your arpeggios is to pick out the harmony at any given point, and play it one note at a time. Keeping the arpeggio within a one-octave range is often a good idea; you may wish to establish a particular shape (up, down, up, down), and then add variations to it for increased excitement (up, up, up):

An arpeggio of sixteenth notes would also work well here. Notice that the points at which a "down" or "up" movement turns around occur at changes in the harmony. The transition is ac-complished in a variety of ways: repetition of the same note; continuation of the chord arpeggio; or a smooth step-wise connection.

Placing the accents in an arpeggio on unexpected parts of the bar can make the accompaniment even more interesting. This technique brings to mind the guitar finger-picking patterns which add so much to the sound of country music.

Finally, arpeggio patterns can be pulled out of the nonstop motorific environment in which they are normally found, and placed here and there as melodic fragments. This will create a more sensitive, romantic effect.

SI

151

pop piano

Fill 'er Up!

A catalog of musical "hooks"

One of the fun things about pop music is that there are little phrases — intros, endings, and fills — that can be used all the time, but which don't become boring. In fact, such pop "clichés" are expected — they're a regular part of the style — and never fail to bring a smile to those listeners within earshot of the piano or organ.

With this column, we're going to begin a catalog of great pop "one liners." Use them wherever, and as often, as you like.

There are hundreds. For example, think of those little figures played at ball games, or at the race track. Then there are silent movie themes, and Irish, Hawaiian, Jewish, bluesy, country, rock, and Oriental gimmicks, too.

Here's a typical honky-tonk introduction:

Ex. 1

You'll notice that it leads into a song beginning on a C chord. Suppose the song we're leading into is not quite so exuberant. Here's a variation of the last three measures:

Ex. 2

Part of the enjoyment of these little phrases is that there is always one to fit just the mood you are looking for. Here's an often-used ending on C:

Ex. 3

If Lawrence Welk were playing, the ending might come out more like this:

Ex. 4

If a blues player were performing, we might hear this ending to a tune:

Ex. 5

Or, perhaps we would hear this slightly more sophisticated approach:

Ex. 6

The Three-Two-One Romp

By Champ Champagne

Here's a run that was devised by a showman keyboardist who wanted to show off the big diamond ring on his little finger.

Although it's a six-note run, it uses only five different pitches . . . the C must be repeated.

We can break it into groups of three.

Did I forget to mention that you use fingers 3-2-1 in the right hand? That's why it's called a three-fingered run. And besides, what better way to highlight that pinky ring!

The five notes in our romp form these chords:

Play this:

Now the notes take on a different aspect. This run is part of an Eb13 chord. It works even though the seventh (Db) and the root of the Ab chord are both missing. Here's another application:

You can even use it for your Bossa Nova (fading out in the sunset):

There you have it. By now you know me. I can't leave well enough alone. Let's eliminate another note. We've proved you don't need all the elements of a chord for the run to be effective.

This adds more possibilities:

Try the 3-2-1 romp with any chord that these notes will fit: Abl3, Gbmaj7#11, Dbma9, Fml1 . . .where will it all end?

153

RUNS AND FILLS FOR RIGHT HAND

Have you ever sat and listened to a professional pianist and said to yourself, "What was that wonderful run he just played? Wish I could do that?" If you ever got up the courage to ask, (and pianists *love* to be asked, by the way) you would probably discover that the fill or run was truly based on a very basic concept, such as an arpeggio, or a major scale. One of the tricks, however, is that the scale or arpeggio he or she used is not exactly the most obvious. For example, the left hand might play a G7 chord, while the right hand plays a D♭ scale.

As our first example, we will play the very last chord of a song in the key of C with one final flourish: an arpeggio ascending. You have heard pianists use this, but may never have known exactly what it was.

The left hand changes the C Major sound to a C dominant 7th sound, but the right hand plays a D7 chord ascending. To transpose this run to other keys simply change the tonic chord, the final chord, to a dominant 7th (by lowering the 7th), play it with the left hand. And then arpeggiate with the right hand a dominant 7th chord whose root is a whole tone higher than the left hand chord. In the key of F, for example, the left hand would play an F7, and the right hand would arpeggiate a G7. Learn this ending in several keys by transposing it yourself.

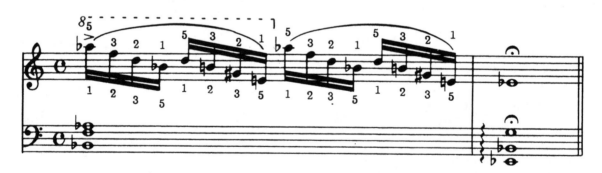

In this example two arpeggios are being used. The left hand chord is a B♭7, and the right hand alternates between a B♭7 arpeggio and an E7 arpeggio descending. Once you have mastered this run, you can use it in connection with the first example to create a very fancy ending for a hundred songs. See example 3.

In order to transpose this run to other keys, let's analyze the method used: Example 2 uses a B♭7 in the left hand which is the V chord in the key of E♭. If we were to transpose this to the key of C, the left hand would play a V7 or G7 chord. The right hand starts on a B♭7 arpeggio, or a V7 arpeggio, and it begins the arpeggio on A♭ (the 7th of the chord). Therefore, in the new key of C we must also start on the V7 chord, the G7, and begin the descending arpeggio on the 7th of the chord, an F. The second arpeggio used by the right hand in Example 2 is an E7. This is one half-tone higher than the Tonic E♭

(called a raised tonic or lowered 2nd). And it also begins on the 7th of the E7 chord. In the new key of C, the chord which is one half-tone higher than the Tonic (C) is D♭ (or C#). The second arpeggio, therefore, in the new key is a D♭7. And we start the new arpeggio on the 7th of the chord, a C♭, or B. You should continue to transpose these runs and fills by analyzing them in this manner, and playing them in those keys in which they feel comfortable. There are many keys where this and other runs do not fit the hand. Don't force the issue in these cases. Play the runs in those keys where they are comfortable.

(Key of C using both runs)

The example above can be used wherever you think it fits. Trial and error is the only way you can decide what is appropriate. Starting on a B♭ as it does, it can be played over a 1) D♭7 resolving to a C chord, 2) a G7 resolving to a C chord, 3) a G♭7 resolving to an F chord, 4) a C7 resolving to an F chord.

This is essentially the same run starting, however, on an E♭. It can be played over a 1) G♭7 resolving to an F chord, 2) a C7 resolving to an F chord, 3) a B7 or F7 resolving to a B♭ chord.

(Use Same Fingering)

The above starts on an A♭ and can be used over a B7 or F7 resolving to a B♭ chord, or over a B♭7 or E7 resolving to an E♭ chord.

155

Continued next page

Starting on a D♭ this can be played over a B♭7 or E7 resolving to an E♭, or over an E♭7 or A7 resolving to A♭.

The above can be played over an E♭7 or A7 resolving to A♭, or over an A♭7 or D7 resolving to D♭.

You can make this run as long as you want simply by always going to the next black note with your second finger:

etc.

Now that you have learned and mastered this run, a good sounding variation is to go up a major third from each black note as follows:

etc.

Our next run is a scale variation and can be used as a fill with a C7 chord or a C7♭9. Be patient and practice these slowly. Once you master them, you will use them all the time.

This same run can be used with an Ab7 chord as follows:

Here is the same run transposed to an F7 chord, which can also be played over a Db7 chord:

Here is a great two-handed "white key" exercise which will do wonders for your finger technique and becomes a very impressive fill when you need it. It can be used as a one or two-handed run on any "white note" chord such as C, G7, Dm7, Am7, Em7, and sometimes an F or FMaj7.

If you wish to play this same run in the key of F, simply remember to flat all the B's:

Continued next page

The following example is once again a great finger exercise and a marvelous run that's been used by everyone from Frederic Chopin, to Art Tatum, to Errol Garner. It will take a great deal of slow practice for the right hand to be accurate with the thumb under when you wish to play it at a good speed. Play over a G Major chord, or G7.

Here is the same run over an F chord:

USE THESE RUNS
AS EXERCISES

Most people hate to practice finger exercises. Well here's a new method, and a new outlook: use these runs and fills as your exercises by playing them with two hands (to help keep the left hand active) and by practicing them very slowly to get evenness of tone and finger strength. The fun part of this kind of exercise is that you are mastering a stylized run or fill while improving your technique as well. Use the left hand fingering indicated below the notes, so that you may practice the right hand run with two hands.

Add these runs to your favorite arrangements, and before long someone will ask: "What was that fill you just played? Wish I could do that!" **ES**

158

JAZZ RUNS FOR THE RIGHT HAND

Jazz runs are used in a variety of ways. They can form a catalog of sounds for a jazz or pop musician improvising on a song, and can be used as endings, intros or fillers. They can also help in modulating from one key to another.

Runs come in a wide variety of forms based on scales, arpeggiated chords, sequences (patterns which repeat on different notes), weaving lines and harmonic progressions. This article will examine all of these varieties and how they are used over single chords or with chord progressions. Once you have learned the entire range of runs, as well as the theory behind creating them, you will be able to apply this to any music you play.

We will begin with scales. There are many different types of scales, the most common of which is the major scale. This can be used simply by inserting it as a run or fill over a simple major chord.

The scale can be varied in a number of ways. It can be broken into patterns of three notes at a time to create a simple sequence, as in example 1. Play the run in example 1 descending. Be sure to watch your fingering very carefully. Try playing this example in a few different keys.

Ex. 1

Example 2 is a sequence pattern which ascends first, then descends. The fingering is similar to the fingering of the simple major scale. To play this, keep a relaxed hand and begin by playing it very slowly.

Ex. 2

Example 3 is a slightly more sophisticated sequence.

Ex. 3

Example 4 is another scale passage which goes over a C major chord. The only member of this scale foreign to the C major scale is the D# which acts as a leading tone into the E note. Begin by playing this slowly and practice the fingering very carefully.

Ex. 4

Example 5 is another simple scale passage. It is written over a C chord.

159

Continued next page

Simple sequences in scale passages can be made into weaving lines, as in example 6. This run is based on the E♭ major scale, used with a B♭⁷ chord. This is a simple arpeggiated pattern. Note that if this pattern were broken up it would be the weaving line shown in example 6a.

If this pattern is divided into groups of four, in the beginning of the pattern, the rise to the next member of the scale occurs on the first note of each group of four. By the end of the passage, the rise is on the second note in each group of four. This shift in accent keeps the pattern interesting.

Ex. 6

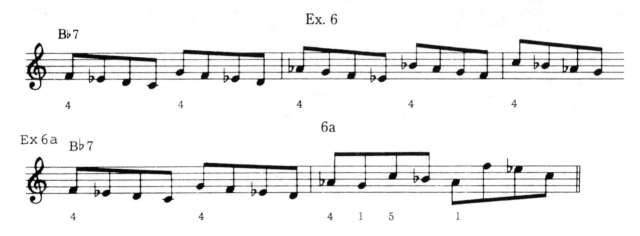

Example 7 uses a weaving effect. Practice this exercise with the fingering indicated until you are comfortable with it.

Ex. 7

Example 8 is another example using the notes derived from a scale in order to create a weaving pattern.

Ex. 8

Example 9 makes use of the C major scale to create a weaving motion. Example 9a is another run based on the concept of using a scale to create a run or a sequence. Try creating your own pattern based on this idea.

9a

While the patterns previously mentioned in this article can be played over one chord, the pattern in example 10 can be played over a II-V-I progression. (In the key of C this would be over Dm^7 to a G^7 to a C.)

Ex. 10

Another scale that can be used is the blues scale shown in example 11. Blues notes often contrast with the notes normally found in a major scale. Patterns can be built using the blues scale in the same way that they were built using the major scale.

Ex. 11

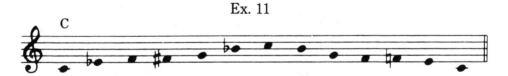

Play example 12 until you are familiar with it.

Ex. 12

Example 13 is a "whole tone" scale, so called because there is a whole tone between each of its members.

Continued next page

Ex. 13

Example 14 is a typical pattern built on a whole tone scale.

Ex. 14

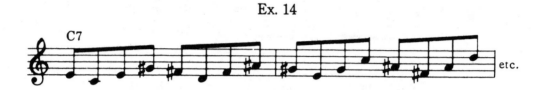

Example 15 features the half tone/whole tone scale, alternating from a half step between notes to a whole step. The scale in this example can be played over a Bb7 chord. Try transposing it to different keys and chords.

Example 16 uses the half tone/whole tone scale in a sequential pattern.

Ex. 16

Example 17 combines the scale pattern in example 11 with a pattern based on the half tone/whole tone scale.

Ex. 17

Example 18 shows the chromatic scale made up of half steps in a series.

Ex. 18

Example 19 is a pattern based on the chromatic scale.

Ex. 19

etc.

1 3 1 2 1   2 3 1 2 1 3 2 3 1

Example 20 makes use of chromatic movement over a C⁷ chord.

1   2   4 3 2 1 4   3   2   1 4 3 1   2

Example 21 shows a series of fourths played in chromatic ascending movement.

Ex. 21

Example 22 shows chromatic motion used in a series of grace notes.

Example 23 shows a chromatic run that jazz great Art Tatum used over a C chord.

163

Continued next page

As patterns increase in length they should have dramatic rises and falls to make them interesting. Example 24 shows a typical question and answer type pattern.

Arpeggiating harmonies is another way to create runs. Example 25 shows a C^maj7 chord arpeggiated in a pattern.

More interesting arpeggios involve jazz harmonies. Instead of playing a simple C^7 in example 26, play a C^7 with an eleventh and a thirteenth.

Example 26

The C^7 with an eleventh and a thirteenth can also be formed into a scale passage, as in example 26a.

Example 26a

Example 27 shows another variation of the C^7 harmony.

Example 27

Example 28

Example 28 shows a minor harmony.

164

Example 29 uses fourths.

Example 29

Here's some more information about using fourths. We began our C⁷ arpeggio using fourths on the 6th of the chord. We could have also started on the 3rd, or the 2nd: E, A, D or D, G, C. Take a number of different chords and try playing three-note arpeggios built in fourths by starting on the 6th, 3rd, or 2nd of the chord. This can be a very beautiful color for your sound canvass. You may also want to try these arpeggios with major seventh chords.

Example 30 shows some variations on a B♭⁷ harmony.

Ex 30

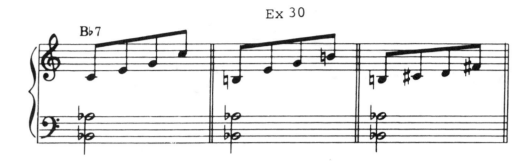

Example 31 shows a harmony on a D⁷ chord which rises and then falls. Experiment with different harmonies on different chords and create patterns using them.

Example 31

Example 32 is based on a B♭ major harmony. Practice this example very slowly. The whole hand shifts and then shifts again. Now try playing it descending and then play it both ascending and descending.

Example 32

Example 33 uses an alteration of two harmonies over the same chord: First a C harmony, then the harmony a tri-tone away (based on F♯). Then back to the C and again to the F♯. Harmonies based a tri-tone apart are often used as substitutes for each other in jazz playing.

Example 33

C7

1   1   1   1

165

Continued next page

Example 39 is a sequence pattern built over a B^7 chord. 39a is the same pattern built over a C chord. Take the time now to build this pattern over an F chord.

Example 39

Example 39a

Example 40 follows the cycle of fifths from a C^7 chord to an F^7 chord to a B^b chord to an E^b chord. At the end of each of the groupings the hand must be lifted up and placed down again. Practice this with prolonged separations between each of the groupings.

Example 40

Example 41 is the last sequence example. This pattern is based on repeating the same pattern on the 1, 3 and +5 of the chord. You must shift the entire hand for each grouping. The fourth finger is very important in this exercise.

Example 41

Example 34 was created by Charlie Parker and goes over a V-I progression; in the key of C this is a G⁷ chord to a C chord.

Example 34

Example 35 was used by Art Tatum. This is an arpeggiated harmony.

Example 35

Example 36 uses the pentatonic scale which works well over the progression I-VI-II-V-I.

Example 36

Example 37 is a sequence that can be used over a G⁷ chord.

The above patterns can be designed to fit over any chord progressions.

Example 37

Example 38 uses the cycle of fifths. Play it a few times until you are familiar with it and then get it up to speed.

Example 38

167

Continued next page

CHORDAL RIFFS

Example 42 is a very simple chord riff.

Example 42

Example 43 is more difficult. When playing this riff allow the hand to move from side to side so that it remains relaxed. Play it slowly, concentrating on this motion. Example 43a is a variation of this riff.

Example 43

Example 43a

Play examples 44, 45 and 46 slowly until you are comfortable with them and can get them up to speed.

Example 44

Example 45

Example 46

Example 47 is played over an F⁷ chord. This pattern can also be arpeggiated or broken up.

Example 47

Example 48 can be played over a I-V-I chord progression.

Example 48

Practice example 49 which is another chord riff.

Example 49

As these runs become second nature to you, you'll be able to string them together into longer solos or insert them in your music whenever you feel you would like to. Practice these runs in every key until they become a part of your own style. And, of course, don't be afraid to try your own variations.

SI♩

A lick for dominant chords

Every stylistic era in jazz has been marked by a few "riffs" or melodic phrases that musicians of the time seem to turn to in solo after solo. These phrases help to define the style itself. The term "bebop," for instance, originated in the sound drummer Kenny Clarke produced with a simple rhythmic riff he was fond of using.

Getting the right kind of riffs under your fingers is a great help in learning to play in a particular style. Here is a bebop-sounding phrase that is used quite often today.

There are several obvious ways in which this melodic fragment can be harmonized, and some less obvious ways as well. Jazz — like any music that is based on dominant-sounding harmonies — is extremely flexible when it comes to chord substitutions. Phrases that work with a **Bb7** chord, for example, will almost always work with an **E7** — the harmony a tritone* away. (One of the reasons for this is that the third of the **Bb7** is the seventh of the **E7** chord, and the seventh of the **Bb7** is the third of the **E7**.)

So, our original riff can be used in this harmonic context . . .

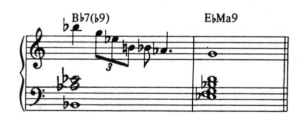

But also in this one . . .

*Remember that a tritone is the interval of a flatted fifth, or raised fourth.

But there's more. I remember telling bassist Chuck Israels once that the music of Bela Bartok is often based on the idea that any chord can be substituted by another chord that belongs to the same diminished seventh harmony (**Bb** can be replaced by **Db, Fb (E),** and **Abb (G)**). He replied, "Any jazz player knows that." And indeed, we can place our riff in these additional harmonic settings.

(In the last example we resolved to **C** instead of **Gb** just to demonstrate another possible chord movement in the tritone substitution game.)

Let's not stop there. Suppose we tried ending the riff on the thirteenth of some chord. Here's what would happen.

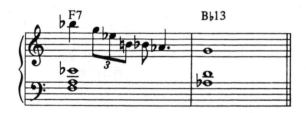

Or, we could end it on the major seventh of a chord.

Is there any harmony that won't work with this useful riff? Be sure to let me know!● -SI

Diminished scales and runs

Many of the lightning-fast and jagged runs that you hear in contemporary jazz are based on the diminished scale. It's simple in design, and it's as versatile as your imagination and fingers permit.

The design of the diminished scale is alternating whole steps with half steps. Beginning on any key, then, there are two diminished scales available. One begins with a whole step, followed by a half step. The other begins with a half step, followed by a whole step. Find each, beginning on the key of C.

Notice that an arpeggio played on every other note of either C diminished scale outlines a Cdim7 chord. The remaining notes outline another diminished chord. No wonder the diminished scale is harmonically exciting!

Once you have these two scales under your fingers and in your ears, you have mastered 2/3 of all the diminished scales on the keyboard. Here is the third. It contains no C, so we'll begin it on Db.

To recapitulate, even though there are twelve pitches and two scales available on each pitch, there are only three different diminished scales on the keyboard. Convince yourself of this with lots of practice, beginning on every note and playing the whole step-half step diminished scale, then the half step-whole step diminished scale.

Patterns

Many exercises can be created from the notes of a diminished scale. The exercises take advantage of the simple musical design of the scale to create patterns up and down the keyboard. First, run up the scale using a series of descending steps.

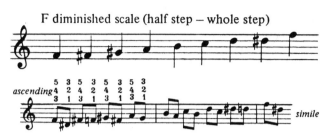

Then run down the scale using a series of ascending steps.

Notice that the three sets of alternative fingerings make these runs into true finger exercises. The same fingerings (3-5, 2-4, 1-3) are appropriate for the left hand.

Here's another pattern running up the scale in a sequence of descending steps, then down the scale in a sequence of ascending steps. These patterns can be repeated over several octaves.

Although the patterns lend themselves to speed, they can be played slowly and with different rhythms. For example,

Finally, take this figure based on the first four notes of a descending diminished scale, and run it down the keys.

We'll have more diminished "licks" next time. ●

171

Two Hands Are Better Than One!

By Champ Champagne

Champ Champagne has been a legendary figure in the world of keyboard music for many years. He is a noted composer with two books, MUSICAL MANEUVERS 1 and 2, to his credit.

As musical director and performing artist on station CJOH in Ottawa, Canada, he appeared in many shows. He was also Music Director on the GALLOPING GOURMET cooking show with Graham Kerr, which was seen on 145 television stations both in Canada and the USA.

Champ became known for his lively and challenging workshops at the Home Organists Adventures and Home Organ Fes-

tival at Asilomar. He has had his own orchestra, owned a piano and organ studio, was a finalist judge for the Yamaha Electone Festivals and for many years wrote a popular instructional feature for KEYBOARD WORLD Magazine.

Now recovering from a massive stroke, Champ is utilizing all his resources to regain his motor skills, and is progressing slowly but surely. His musical talents have remained intact and through the pages of this magazine we will once again be enjoying and learning from this gentleman, who is indeed a CHAMP.

Champ Champagne

Arpeggios can be a great effect for adding splash to intros and endings, or to use as a flourish for dressing up a melody. The word "arpeggio" means "harp-like," and, basically, an arpeggio is a chord that is "broken" or played one note at a time. We've all seen terrific players use arpeggios as they glide across the keys with seemingly no effort at all. Fortunately for those of us who don't have a lot of technique (me included), there's a way to play arpeggios using *both* hands!

You must play the notes *evenly:* two notes with the left hand (stems down) and three with the right (stems up).

Learning is the perception of patterns. Try some chords with the same pattern:

It is not necessary for the arpeggios to have each and every component of a chord. It is customary to omit the eleventh in the thirteenth chord, for example. The most important notes in a chord are its *root, third, seventh* and the *thirteenth.*

A further explanation is offered on page 14 of my book, *Musical Maneuvers, Volume 1*. Once you get the hang of it, it is truly easy!

Which arp sounds the best?
Which is easier to play?

Three-Fingered Runs

by Champ Champagne

"Doesn't that look artistic? The fingers seem to be dancing on the keys!" What am I talking about? Well, play this, using fingers 2-4-2-1 of the right hand:

Welcome to the world of the three-fingered run. I dedicate these runs to all those cartoon characters who have only three fingers on each hand.

Unless you are one of them, use the 2-4-2-1 fingering as you frolic your way down the keyboard. Whereas harmony is used to support melody, these runs can be said to embellish or enhance the feeling of color conveyed by each chord.

Let's analyze the run. It consists of four notes played in a broken fashion. This one run can be used with any of the following chords:

ROOT-3rd-5th-6th   ROOT-5th-7th-3rd   3rd-7th-9th-5th   #11th-6th-7th-9th

It is not necessary to play each note of every chord. Just plunk down a chord, and the sound will carry over till you plunk down the next chord. Here are some more harmonies the run will fit:

5th-9th-11th-7th   5th-7th-Root-#9th   3rd-5th-13th-Root   7th-b9th-#9th-#11th

Of course, you've already noticed that the second and fourth digits press the black keys, while the thumb stirs the coffee. The thumb is really the pivot on the white keys.

If you've followed thus far, check the following runs, which will decorate the chords indicated:

Ab, Fm7, Dbmaj9, Gbmaj13+11, Bbm11, F7+9, Ab13, D7alt.

Abm6, Db9, D13+11b9, G7b9, Fm7b5, Bb7b9sus.

There you have it. You may have a number of three-fingered runs of your own. Use these as a starting point, and have fun till next time!

With A Little Help From Chopin

Chopin with a student, 1844

by Joan Stiles

While preparing for a restaurant "gig," I was playing through some Broadway show tunes which were likely to be requested. Later that day, after listening to a recording of the Chopin *Preludes* and marveling at the beauty of the left hand accompanimental melodies, I began to experiment at the piano. I found I could adapt the left hand part of the Op.28, No.13 *Prelude* and combine it with various pop melodies for a new approach to often overly-played songs.

Here is Chopin's left hand pattern:

Now here is my adaptation of that pattern. It goes well with the melody to the song "Memory" from *Cats*. Try it, then see if you can create similar accompaniments for your favorite ballads.

173

Section 6
HOW TO STYLE YOUR KEYBOARD SOUNDS

Sounds of the '50s
(Doo-wop-Doo-wop)

By Joan Stiles

Early rock and roll piano styles are easy and fun to play. Music of the 1950s simplified the more complicated rhythms of 1940s blues and boogie-woogie, and made them more accessible.

To get you started on playing in this style, I've combined an introduction (which can be repeated as a vamp) with an 8-bar section. The chords of the intro are built on the first (I), sixth (vi), fourth (IV) and fifth (V) degrees of the C major scale. Many songs of the '50s such as "Silhouettes on the Shade" and "The Book of Love" use just these chords in the same I-vi-IV-V-I progression. The next section is based on an 8-bar blues and uses only three chords — I, IV and V. "Blueberry Hill," popularized by "Fats" Domino, is an example of this type of tune.

Notice how smoothly the chords change. This is accomplished by keeping the "common tone" of C in the pinky of the right hand whenever possible. Also notice that the real "action" is in the bass line which should be brought out in your performance. In the 8-bar section, the left hand arpeggiates the chords of the right hand. After you can play this model, work it out in other keys such as Bb, F and G major.

Next time we'll talk about how to add bluesy devices to the right hand part.

177

"Rock and Roll Is Here To Stay"

Sounds of the 50s Part II

By Joan Stiles

Many of the "hard-driving" rock and roll tunes of the 1950s, like "At the Hop" or "Johnny Be Good" are based on the 12 bar blues. Once you know a few simple ideas that work over these chords, you are well on your way to playing authentic 50s style piano.

First learn a basic left-hand pattern of steady quarter notes in which the thumb plays fifths, sixths and sevenths while the fifth finger retains the root of each chord:

When that feels comfortable, try adding the right hand figures of examples 2, 3 and 4. To help you concentrate on the rhythm and the left hand, I've only used notes that can be repeated through the entire 12 bar form. Example 2 has octaves on G; try it with repeated D's (Example 3). Listen to the clash (dissonance) that occurs at different points as the chords change. That tension is an essential part of the blues.

Next, play fourths, D and G, in the same eighth-note rhythm. Try the bluesy device of "crushing" the lower note by sliding from C-sharp to D using the second finger (Example 4). When that feels good, change the rhythm of the right hand part as in Example 5.

At first, practice these combined parts slowly. Gradually increase the tempo while maintaining a steady beat. If you really want to "Rock Around the Clock," play these patterns while singing "At the Hop" or "Rock and Roll is Here to Stay."

Example 2   Example 3   Example 4

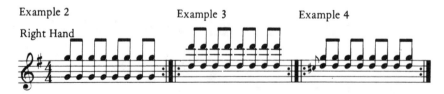

Example 5

1 & 2   3 & a 4 - & a

COUNTRY-STYLE AT THE KEYBOARD

The popularity of country music has grown so swiftly over the past few years that almost every musical style has been influenced by it in some way. Pop and rock artists often record in Nashville, and the little slides and fills which grew in the green hills of "Opry" country have now worked their way into urban music centers with pleasant insistence and rewarding results. While the elements of this style spring from the way certain instruments, notably the guitar, are played by country musicians, these techniques are easily transferred to the piano.

Let's look at some of the phrases and "frills" you can add to pieces to give them a country flavor, beginning with basic accompaniment patterns. Country back-up rhythms are usually very simple and straight-forward (like down-home country people!):

Ex. 1

Depending on the particular song, the accompaniment may have less movement in the left hand, and more in the right:

Ex. 2 & 3

Notice the bit of *walking bass* used in switching from the C chord to the F. Other forms of this movement occuring in country-style piano include the use of a *drone* note above:

Ex. 4

or parallel 3rds or 10ths:

Ex. 5

or triplets which arpeggiate or break up the individual harmonies:

Ex. 6

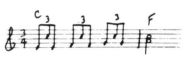

The walking line can move down, as well as up.

Ex. 7

Ornaments play a big role in this music and many of them duplicate sounds characteristic of the guitar. For example, guitarists sometimes "hammer on" notes, by striking a vibrating string down against the fingerboard; or they "pull off" notes by plucking a string with their fingering hand. The equivalent sounds on piano are these:

Ex.'s 8, 9, & 10

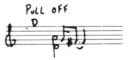

179

Continued next page

Floyd Cramer is famous for using these devices. The moving note always ends up on the third of the chord, starting from the second or the fourth.

Those *drone* notes can be used in many situations, and they often are:

Ex. 11

Other country sounds are the *tremelo* (used in slow songs very effectively):

Ex. 12

the quick chord *arpeggio* (like a guitar strum):

Ex. 13

and guitar-like "picking patterns":

Ex. 14

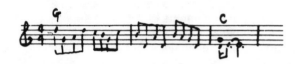

Applying these country "flavorings" to a song is simply a matter of looking for places to plug into the chord progression one or several of the "riffs" we've explored. It's important not to over-do it, but filling in with these sounds can be great fun:

Ex. 15

SI ♩

180

pop piano

Country Piano-Picking

A couple of years ago, we featured a column on country-style keyboard playing (October '80). As you'll recall, that introduction to country style contained several ornaments and guitarlike fills (made famous by Floyd Cramer and other Nashville artists).

Let's take another look at country playing, this time concentrating on "finger-picking" patterns. Standard country accompaniments to songs like *"Green, Green Grass of Home,"* may consist of just a simple chord arpeggiation like the one in example 1:

Note the bass line. It moves back and forth between the root and fifth of the chord; just before the chord changes from Bb to Eb, it moves up to the third of the chord, for smooth voice-leading to

the Eb. This bass line can be made a little more animated through dotted rhythms and scale notes leading into the new chord:

Using these simple bass lines the right hand can be freed for even more energetic accompaniment patterns. Guitarists have a catalogue filled with different strum patterns, and keyboard players can

easily adapt some of these. For instance, a favorite finger-picking routine of country guitarists is to play a chord arpeggio that is broken up into a series of 3 + 3 + 2:

It is easy to make up your own patterns, too. Take any chord and find a nice-sounding way to

arpeggiate it; after a few repetitions, change the pattern, and you're all set:

181

Continued next page

It's not necessary to stick only to the notes of the chord, though. Remember this country ornament, similar to the "hammer on" technique of guitarists?

Strum patterns can make use of those notes which are extraneous to the chord, as long as they move into the chord tones, the way the "hammer on" pattern does:

By combining different patterns and breaking up the eighth notes into irregular groups of three and two, you'll produce "finger-pickin' " good sounds, perfect for backing up your favorite country tunes.

SI ♩

182

Blues Sounds For Pianists

"The Blues" is a term which has been used to describe both a particular form in music, and a kind of sound which can color any piece, at the whim of a performer. Here is the form of a "12 bar blues."

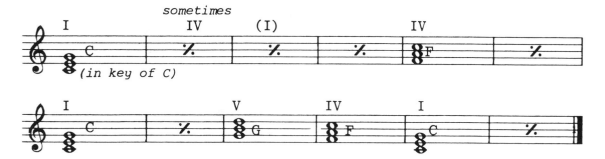

Most often, musicians use dominant seventh chords instead of the simple triads indicated above. The characteristic sound of the blues results from these dominant sevenths, and from so-called "blue notes." (We'll cover the blues scale shortly.) It is also closely tied to the "gospel" cadence (see below).

The best place to begin in describing the blues *flavor* is with the cadence IV-I. It is known by various names: the *plagal cadence* and the *gospel cadence* are both terms used to describe it.

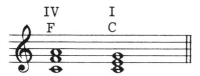

It will certainly sound familiar as the basis of the "shuffle" pattern used in many blues and pop songs:

The IV-I cadence also serves as the foundation of many blues phrases and fills — those little professional "touches" added to an arrangement by blues musicians:

183

Continued next page

The switch from I to IV and back again will sometimes even occur over a steady harmony, as this shuffle study indicates:

There are other elements to the blues sound, however, and certain characteristic approaches for both the right hand and left hand in keyboard technique.

Left Hand Patterns

Many of the left hand blues patterns were adopted by early rock and roll performers. Try each of the following, and then apply them to the 12 bar blues pattern you saw earlier.

Right Hand Patterns

Over the rock-steady foundation of the left hand patterns above, blues players often insert little "fills" which are based on a few simple principles. Sometimes these fills are just arpeggiated chords or tremelos, played in repeating patterns.

These fills also make use of chromatic notes, especially the b3 and b5 of the chord being played.

These phrases can be practiced by going through the circle of fifths:

The b3 and b5 are prominent members of what is known as the "blues scale."

185

The blue notes found in this scale stand out because of the contrast between the notes of the normal major scale, and these alterations. Therefore, many blues phrases move back and forth between, for example, the major third of a chord and the minor third:

Right hand phrases will also employ the IV-I cadence, as well as chromatic movement (cited above):

Advanced Harmonies

Contemporary, jazzy versions of the blues use advanced harmonies, such as the ones below:

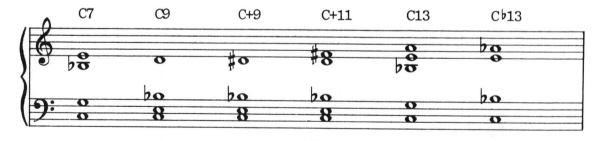

Note the left hand voicings in the following examples; modern pianists often omit the root of the chord. These sophisticated harmonies were unknown to the original blues players.

Ornaments

One final technique is all you need to start playing blues sounds: grace notes. When a series of ornamental notes are played in blues style, a single finger is often used to slide across two or more. Try the following examples, and slide across the grace notes as smoothly as possible.

SI♪

POP-PIANO   Do I Hear A Waltz?

It's hard to imagine a more charming or "civilized" dance than the elegant waltz, with its soft rhythmic "sighs" and bright, swirling energy. In the early nineteenth century, though, it was considered scandalous: critics labeled it "indecent," and it was forbidden at the Prussian Court. Composer Richard Wagner called it "a more powerful drug than alcohol."

Times do change, however, and the waltz finally gained general acceptance — and evolved into new forms as well. The lovely *Christmas Waltz* by Jule Styne and Sammy Cahn gives us an opportunity to explore a few of the many approaches to playing music in 3/4 time.

Many people are most familiar with the simple oom-pah-pah approach to waltz music. Think of a German brass band at Oktoberfest, and you'll get the effect straight off.

The Viennese version of the waltz is less rigid. The characteristic feature of this approach is the slight breath before the chord on the third beat.

Contemporary jazz-waltzes are even trickier.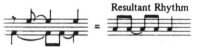

Play these jazz waltzes (the first example is for two handed accompaniment; the second uses the right hand for the melody) with a bouncy, energetic spirit.

Finally, there is a romantic, low-keyed approach which makes use of arpeggios and inner-voice melody.

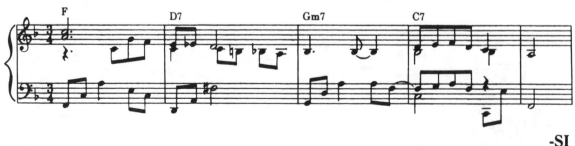

-SI

188

POP-PIANO

A Polish Bossa Nova

Long before the legendry of Poland centered on the courage of its people, before the Polish ham, the Polish sausage, and the Polish pickle — even before the Polish joke — there was the magnificent artistry of Frederic Chopin, Poland's musical shining light. Chopin's influence is so great that we can find it not only in classical works, but also in contemporary pop music, including songs of Barry Manilow ("Could This Be Magic"), McCarthy and Carroll ("I'm Always Chasing Rainbows"), and (!) Antonio Carlos Jobim ("How Insensitive").

The connection between Jobim's song and Chopin's *Prelude #4* in E minor is astonishing. The melody is practically the same for a good part of the tune, and the harmony also bears many similarities. Notice how Chopin moves through the harmonies of his *Prelude* by changing only one note at a time; the shifting of harmonies could not be accomplished more smoothly! See example 1.

Jobim's song can be given similar treatment. Here, Chopin's harmonic motion is duplicated, with a rhythm-guitar-like strum pattern in the left hand. See example 2.

Other tunes can be similarly arranged. Below is Jobim's "Quiet Nights Of Quiet Stars" with a chromatically descending bass line. Try your hand at using Chopin's subtle technique in changing from one chord to another. Any time you find a song in which the melodic phrases repeat or move very slowly you can assume that it is a candidate for the "Polish" treatment! See example 3. ■

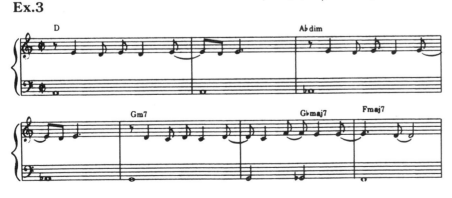

-SI

POP-PIANO — Slidin' and Stridin'

The difference between a left hand pattern for a march or two-step and that of a jazz stride piece is often ever so slight. Sometimes the difference seems to be a matter of some elusive magic that, in the hands of a jazz artist, mysteriously breathes fire into the simple oom-pah oom-pah rhythm which lies at the heart of both styles.

One *tangible* aspect of stride style, though, is a kind of "sliding around"—the use of chromatic movement—which can help bring that professional touch to your playing. Using "Honeysuckle Rose" as our example, let's look at the way various pianists mix slidin' with their stridin'.

Art Tatum was a phenomenal musician, and might play hundreds of variations on any given approach, but we can use some simple Tatum techniques in looking at stride "slides." A straight stride pattern might look something like example 1.

Example 1

But Tatum would likely add a little chromatic slide to lead into any of the chords. See example 2.

Example 2

This kind of movement would be used especially in measure four, where the harmonic progression aims toward the F major chord in measure five. Example 3 shows the way the sheet music indicates the chord changes.

Example 3

But example 4 is one way in which Tatum might play it.

Example 4

Of course, there are many possibilities. For another typical Tatum solution, see example 5.

Example 5

Fats Waller might use either of the approaches of examples 6 or 7 in his left hand pattern for measure four.

Example 6

Example 7

An interesting version of the first eight measures of the piece, as played by another up-and-coming pianist named **Ed Shanaphy** may be found in example 8. Note the use of various harmonic "slides." The right hand styling is a swinging, joyful improvisation on the original melody (the original is indicated in "cue" notes).

Example 8

Finally, example 9 is a more modern version of "Honeysuckle Rose," as played by **George Shearing.** The stride is gone, but the slide—as can be seen from the chromatic "stroll" taken by the bass notes— is alive and jumpin'!

Example 9

-SI

"I Found A New Baby" In Stride

O.K. You're the musical director of a stride concert in New York City which features six of the best stride players in the world. You have the brilliant idea to close the show with all six playing on three pianos at the same time. Hmm . . . No time to rehearse. What tune will everyone already know, enjoy, and be able to play coherently with ten other hands striding away simultaneously? Dick Hyman, the musical director for the 92nd Street Y's "Jazz in July" chose "I Found a New Baby" for just this situation with wonderful results.

Long a favorite among jazz musicians, "I Found a New Baby" is especially well suited for stride piano. Its chord changes and structure make it an easy improvisational vehicle and fun "riff" tune. (Certain songs have chord changes that easily adapt to "riffs" – repeated figures that musicians can play in unison as rhythmic background for a soloist.)

Exercises 1 and 2 are bass patterns that can be used in the first four measures of the tune or anywhere that a Dm is played. Practice these until you can play them well before you try the right hand exercises.

It's always best to learn the left hand first when practicing stride. Because the left hand is both your time-keeper and rhythm section, you must know it solidly so your time won't slip when you add your right hand.

Exercise 1

Exercise 2

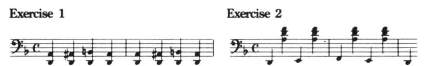

Exercise 3

Exercise 4

Exercise 3 is a right hand figure that works well with the bass patterns in exercises 1 and 2. In addition, a well-known jazz riff is illustrated in exercise 4. Again, practice the left hand first before you add the right.

Experiment. Invent your own riffs with the rhythm illustrated in exercise 4. Or play the notes in exercise 3 with a different rhythm.

Listen to the melodies that run through your head as you play. Learn the piece well so you *can* listen to your ideas and try to play them. When you stop searching for notes, improvisations do come to you. They may seem simplistic at first, but as you learn to listen more carefully your ideas *will* grow and your creativity blossom.

And just think — next time you're in a room with three pianos and five stride players, you'll not only be creatively alive and ready to play — you'll know what tune to suggest!

-JC

191

POP-PIANO — Fit For A King

CAROLE KING has been an important songwriter, and an influential pop pianist as well. Many of the features of her style can be used to good effect in most pop and soft rock music; here, in a nutshell, are ways to use the King sound in your own playing.

Harmonically, Carole King makes good use of a couple of techniques we've discussed before in this column. One of these is *pedal point*; when a progression begins and ends on the same chord, King keeps the root of that chord in the bass throughout the progression. For example, if a tune were to use the chord progression C-G-F-C, she might play it this way:

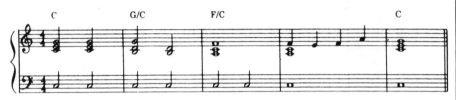

Here is an example from *It's Going To Take Some Time*.

The harmonies that result from this device often contain major sevenths and elevenths and thirteenths: elements Carole King brings to the chords of her songs even when pedal point is not appropriate.

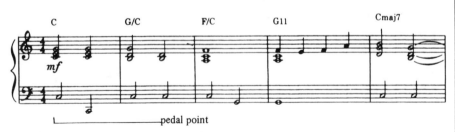

Rhythmically, King makes extensive use of syncopation: the technique of interrupting or contradicting the regular accents in a measure.

One way to use syncopation is in creating "hooks" which act as fills or endings:

Another form of syncopation, called *anticipation*, is used extensively in her music. Simply put, this device involves playing a note which falls squarely on the beat slightly early:

The melody of *It's Going To Take Some Time*, for example, is played with anticipation:

rather than in a straight, on-the-beat manner:

One way of extending this device beyond applying it just to the notes of a melody is to incorporate it in arpeggio patterns used for a song's accompaniment. This pattern, for instance:

192

may be played this way: This pattern: may be played this way:

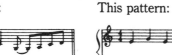 

(This is a good way to produce musical "hooks" for your own arrangements!)

Here's a short tune made up of syncopated arpeggios. After you've practiced it for a while you'll be ready to sound like a pro—if not like a King! ⌢

Jason

Stuart Isacoff

-SI

POP-PIANO　Walkin' The Left Hand

Just You, Just Me

Creating a pulse (the beat) with the left hand has always been a challenge for the solo piano player. I find that one method of swinging the beat is "walking" the left hand.

In Example **A**, the tune of *Just You, Just Me* is played mostly with half notes in the left hand, and a harmonization of the melody in the right hand. This is fine, but you need more movement in the left hand to feel the beat coming through.

In Example **B**, the left hand is written without the right hand. Practice this and memorize it. In the second bar, notice the dotted eighth note followed by a sixteenth note; this gives the beat an extra push. Also, in bar 7, the sixteenth grace notes leading into each down beat help firm up the beat.

Now you're ready for Example **C**. Give yourself a good count off to set up your tempo, and just let it fly!

-LS

Example A

Example B

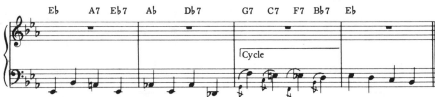

Make sure to give each bass note its full value.

Example C

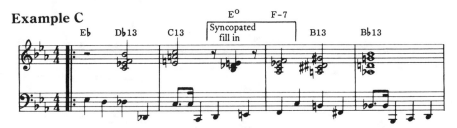

Repeat as many times as you like, but keep the beat rolling.

194

POP STUDIO
Swingin' the Melody

How many times have you wished you could give more life to a tune by adding just a few touches of jazz pizzazz? You can do it!

"Fills," which have been discussed in a previous Jazzercise column, are one way of adding zip to a passage. Syncopation of the melody is another technique that will give a song some swing.

First, take a look at Exercise I. This is an excerpt from *Pagan Love Song*, with no frills added.

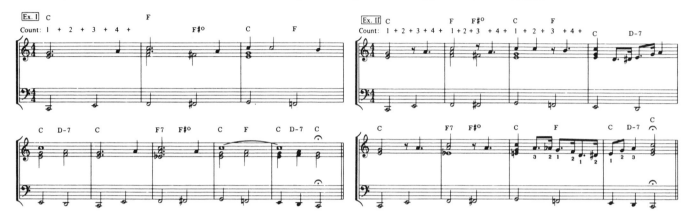

When you can play Exercise I comfortably, move on to Exercise II. Note the syncopation in bars 1, 2 and 3. Be sure to give the right hand dotted quarter notes their full value. Take it slowly, and count out loud until you can "feel" the syncopation. Now, note the fills in bars 4, 7 and 8; they add another extra touch.

And there you have it! With just a shot of syncopation and a dash or two of fills, you're swingin' the melody.

—LS

"Hey, Mac, Give Us A 4 Bar Intro!"

Whenever a group of musicians get together to play a few swing songs, there is invariably somebody who says to the piano player, "Hey, Mac, give us a 4 bar intro!" This can be a frustrating experience if you are not prepared to deal with the situation.

If you ever find yourself in a spot like this, here are two 4 bar intros which lead into the downbeat of the tune. Both use a III, VI, II, V, I harmonic pattern. First, take a look at the pattern:

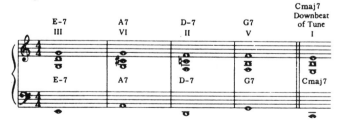

Exercises 2 and 3 are both intros which will get you in and out of the chorus, using the root and the 7th in the left hand:

When these exercises feel comfortable, try creating intros in other keys, using the III, VI, II, V, I harmonic patterns. And, remember, the intro sets the rhythm of the piece.

"All right, Mac, let's hear it!"

—LS

Mastering Stride Piano

By Judy Carmichael

The swinging, stride sound of early jazz pianists like Fats Waller and James P. Johnson is undergoing a newfound popularity. Suddenly, everyone wants to play and hear this bouncy style again. So here are some exercises to help you get in the stride groove. Remember, when playing stride you should not be thinking about lightning-fast tricks or an amazing left hand, but rather a *steady* left hand and an all-around relaxed feeling.

Exercise No. 1

Exercise No. 2

Exercise No. 3

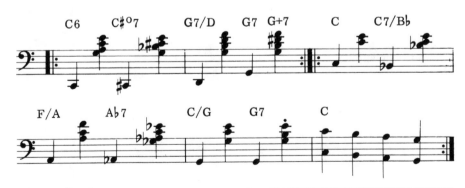

Judy Carmichael is the author of Judy Carmichael's Complete Book of Stride Piano.

Keyboard Workshop

Stride and Rhythm Style
At the Keyboard: Part I

Would you describe your playing as being "stuck in a rut?" Whether you are a pianist or organist, learning the stride or rhythm style can change your whole outlook on playing. Even if you never become a good stride player, working at it can add a lot of zip to your own style and get you out of that rut. The truth is that stride players seem to have more fun. So let's give it a whirl . . .

The best way to get started is to get the left hand going in some of the patterns that are found in stride. For organists, it is a combination pedal and left-hand drill. For pianists, it's all left hand . . . and it isn't as impossible as it first seems if you practice these drills very S-L-O-W-L-Y.

The left-hand rhythm is established by alternating bass notes, triads, and ascending and descending bass lines. See the 4th, 6th, and 9th measures of our drills for ascending and descending bass lines.

Learn these four drills in the "easy" keys as shown. Again, play them as S-L-O-W-L-Y as you can, gradually picking up speed when you have mastered the slow tempo. Your hands (and feet) are learning something new. Be patient with them. (You are free to move on to harder keys once you've mastered these.)

Note: Organists should play all the single notes on pedal. The ascending and descending lines may be doubled in the left hand if you wish.

Get these down pat before our next issue because we are going to add some right-hand licks . . . and you don't want to be thinking about the left hand. It should play almost automatically. Good luck. Remember to keep it S-L-O-W!

197

Continued next page

Stride and Rhythm Style
At the Keyboard
(Part II)

Now that we have established a left-hand pattern via the four drills (January '84), it's time to superimpose some typical right hand patterns over them. The overall purpose of these exercises is to create the *feeling* of the stride style, not only in your head, but in your muscles. Keep it light. Try not to be tense and bangy. The music does not have to be played fast to be effective. And it should not be loud. Strive for the *light and easy* feeling as well as sound.

These drills constitute typical treatments of pop harmonies used in the stride style. Write out the right hand part for the other two keys practiced in the last article (G and Bb), and see if you can't create some simple variations or alterations on the original. This will be your first attempt at creating a stride arrangement.

ES

198

RAGTIME RIFFS

In the introduction to his *Etudes,* Scott Joplin lashed out at those who threw bricks at "hateful ragtime," and announced with some pride that it is a music of often painful difficulty. He created his set of ragtime lessons, as he wrote, "to assist amateur players in giving the 'Joplin Rags' that weird and intoxicating effect intended by the composer."

Keyboardists who attempt ragtime rhythms are more likely to face confusion than intoxication, but with a little practice the weirdness of the music will seem no more jarring than falling down a flight of stairs. A good way to begin is to examine the music to see what the shortest note value is. If a sixteenth note is the shortest, count the entire measure in sixteenth notes.

Ex. 1

Using the sixteenth notes as a basis, the tricky rhythms that contradict the natural accents in each measure become less of a problem. Usually the left hand keeps up a steady, even pulse (although it will at times play a raggy countermelody).

The right hand riffs of ragtime will most often fall into a few rhythmic combinations, all based on the syncopated feeling of example 1. These combinations place the "syncope" either before or after an even group of eighth or sixteenth notes; one of the key features of ragtime is the contrast set up between the syncopated figures and the "straight" figures surrounding them.

Ex. 2a

Ex. 2b

These combinations become a little more complicated through the use of ties.

Ex. 3a

Ex. 3b

Ex. 3c

Ex 3d

- or -

Ex. 3e

Again, the way to practice these is by counting them in sixteenth note divisions. Go through all the combinations above and then make up some additional ones yourself. After practicing each of the rhythmic possibilities, you'll be set to tackle any ragtime piece.

SI ♩

Boogie woogie

Forty years after the boogie woogie craze, in classroom presentations to young people who hadn't lived through it, Mary Lou Williams would say, "Boogie woogie was a rhythmic thing." That statement wasn't a dismissal; it was an explanation.

Boogie woogie was a piano variation of the blues, carried forward by a rhythmic, assertive, even pounding left hand pattern. Three champions of the form were Albert Ammons and Meade Lux Lewis of Chicago and Pete Johnson of Kansas City. At the 1938 Carnegie Hall Spirituals to Swing concert — a tremendous milestone in the presentation of jazz — these three pianists raised the roof with a six-fisted, three-piano performance of boogie woogie.

In the fifties, boogie woogie fired the playing of early rock and roll through its piano proponents, Little Richard and Jerry Lee Lewis.

Both played a hammering left hand and interspersed their sung phrases with sharply articulated right hand responses.

Today, boogie woogie has value as a rhythm stabilizer, a left hand builder, a blues lesson, and an exhilarating workout. Here is an example.

Recommended listening

Besides the four artists mentioned above — Ammons, Johnson, Lewis, and Williams — look for recordings from the thirties by Pinetop Smith and Freddie Slack. Orchestrated boogie woogie hits were "Maxixe" by Bob Crosby (Joe Sullivan, pianist) and "Chips' Boogie Woogie" by Woody Herman (Tommy Linehan, pianist). Count Basie played fine boogie woogie. A contemporary boogie woogie artist in Cincinnati is Big Joe Duskin. ●

Boogie woogie on the blues

pop piano

The Sound of Soft Rock

Today's pop sounds are a hybrid of many musical styles. Music that once appealed to only limited numbers of people — such as rock and country — have taken their place alongside more traditional elements of the pop "melting pot." Now, more than ever, the pop musician must be familiar with the whole range of contemporary styles.

One modern style in common use is often labeled "soft rock." Contemporary ballads are almost always backed up with a strong, steady beat, and slightly syncopated rhythm—trademarks of the popular "soft" sound. Keyboard players who want to practice this style can do so with a tune like "We've Only Just Begun."

The bass is important in all pop music, and soft rock bass rhythms really help to set the right mood. Often, the rhythm is a simple repeating pattern based on a dotted quarter followed by an eighth:

Try this using the "We've Only Just Begun" chord progression:

This pattern can be spruced up at times by adding little connecting scales from one root to the next:

or by using "anticipation," the practice of hitting a main note earlier than expected:

The right hand can also play a basic pattern, which simply arpeggiates the notes of the chord being played:

To add more of a "kick" to the sound, this chord arpeggiation can be made more interesting through a bit of rhythmic "play." Practice this pattern for a while, and you'll have a basic "rock" approach that can be used over and over in countless songs:

Continued next page

Want to get even fancier? Try adding these six-teenth-note arpeggios every once in a while:

Now, let's put the whole package together, using the first few measures of our chord progression:

The only thing left to do is integrate these patterns with the melody of the song. Just keep in mind that you don't want to cover up the melody, so you'll want to save the fancy or busy background figures for times when the melody is static or silent:

Keyboard Workshop

Playing Rock . . .
What a Feeling!

Do you ever hear a great hit on the radio, go out to buy the sheet music for it, and wonder how the written version could possibly share the same title as the recording? This happens frequently in contemporary music because the "sound" produced in the recording studio is dependent on very stylized playing by some of today's top artists; the "bare bones" version of a song, as printed in the sheet music version, is always going to be a far cry from what you hear in the actual performance.

This is especially true in rock. For example, the standard sheet music version of "Flashdance . . . What A Feeling" doesn't convey the energy and excitement of the original soundtrack. One way to overcome this is to study some of the keyboard patterns studio musicians use to back up rock singers.

The basic approach used in playing this kind of contemporary song can be described in two steps: 1) keep a fast eighth-note feel going all the time; and 2) divide the rhythmic patterns between your right and left hands so that they take turns playing the accented notes. This leads to an occasional "surprise" in the sound, when the listener expects a strong bass note and hears a treble chord instead!

Here are four typical rhythm patterns for a funky rock keyboard sound. Try playing each one separately — slowly at first. You might want to tap your hands on a tabletop at the beginning, just to get the rhythms straight.

When you feel comfortable with all four of these examples, play them in order without stopping.

Then, try your hand at "Flashdance . . . What A Feeling," using similar patterns. You might try the next example to start:

Before long, you'll have friends asking, "Where can I get the music?" Imagine their disappointment when they find a copy!

SI

203

pop piano

A Happy Marriage

It's no longer easy to classify a piece of music as simply "rock," or "pop," or "country," since in today's music world a whole rainbow of stylistic traits finds its way into almost every recording or performance. One very common mixture of musical influences can be found in songs like "Sweetheart" by the Brothers Gibb: a marriage of Nashville country-pop and urban soft-rock.

Here are some examples to help you with the "frills" and professional touches in this hybrid style. First, the country flavor: In previous articles, we've covered some of the elements of country playing. These include the "hammer-on" ornament (the second of the chord resolving to the root):

Chord arpeggio "fills" are also used. Most commonly, they will include the major chord tones, the sixth of the chord, and the second of the chord. In "Sweetheart," there are many possible places to insert arpeggios. Here are a couple of examples:

Our country-style embellishments can also be formed into short repeating patterns as an alternative to the arpeggio fills. In the example below we switch from a G chord to a D chord, then back to G (I-V-I) in order to produce the pattern on a G harmony:

There are a number of simple devices we can take from the sounds of soft rock to add yet another dimension to this song. One such device is the use of "pedal point." Find a section of the song which begins and ends on the same chord, and hold the root of that chord in the bass, even while other chords pass over it:

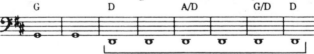

Try playing the song with this pedal point on D, and get that soft-rock flavor developed by artists such as Carole King.

One more rock element to keep in mind is the use of "anticipation." This means playing the downbeat of a measure (the strong, accented "1") slightly early:

Putting all of these devices together, we can come up with a rhythmic, country-swinging, down-home, rockabilly version of "Sweetheart" that will have everyone in the room jumping. Here's a sample starting at the fifth measure of the song:

SI ♩

204

Section 7
JAZZ IMPROVISATION

Keyboard Workshop

PLAYING JAZZ—
More tricks of the trade

Improvisation is like composing, except that it is done spontaneously. So, improvisors have to contend with the same musical problems that face composers. There must be enough variety in what is produced to keep things interesting; at the same time, there has to be a unified feeling, so that the music holds together. Then, there are different structural layers that should be kept in mind:

small-scale issues involve what notes to choose or what rhythm to play in any particular moment; but there are also large-scale aspects to consider, like how one phrase relates to another.

In this column, we'll look at one way to create order and balance in an improvised solo: it's called *sequence*.

Suppose we were improvising a solo using the song *Mona Lisa* . The opening chord is E♭. Here are the notes in that chord:

If we take those notes as our "melody" or basic material to embellish, we might add notes between the chord tones, or above them, or below them:

But we want some kind of form to emerge — a musical gesture that makes sense, that gives direction, and that satisfies. One such gesture can be constructed by repeating an idea:

Continued next page

If we take this idea and repeat it starting on different *pitches*, the result is called "sequence:"

Sequences can be extended over changing harmonies:

The improvisor who comes up with a spontaneous melodic idea can use the technique of sequence to extend that idea, and create a cohesive form within the solo.

SI

Keyboard Workshop

Improvising with Jazz Rhythms

Applying "jazzy" rhythms to standard melodies is not only a good way to pep up your old arrangements, it's actually the first step in building the ability to create jazz solos. "It don't mean a thing if it ain't got that swing," said Duke Ellington. Jazz rhythms give whatever you're playing that essential ingredient of "swing."

Let's look at some typical rhythms. One of the most common is the "charleston" effect, created by a dotted quarter nòte followed by an eighth note which is *accented*. Accenting a note which is normally unaccented is the secret behind all jazz rhythms. Example 1 starts with the "charleston" rhythm, and continues with a few more "off beat" phrases.

Ex 1

We can take a simple melody and *jazz* it up by applying these rhythms to it. Here is a melody, followed by a version that "anticipates" one of the notes; that is, it accents a note earlier than expected.

Ex. 2

Another way to jazz up that melody would be to delay the arrival of some of the notes, instead of playing them early. In each of these cases, we are sort of dancing around the normal pulse.

Ex 3

209

Continued next page

We can take the same approach with any tune we wish. Here is an example to try on a well-known melody. You can extend these ideas by toying with the rest of the song on your own. Next time, we'll apply these rhythms to improvised melodies based on the chords of common pop songs.

Keyboard Workshop

Jazz Improvisation: Melody and Rhythm

Last time we looked at how jazz rhythms can be used to add "swing" to standard melodies. Before that we created improvised melodies by adding notes to chord intervals. This month, let's combine our jazzy rhythms with those improvised lines.

Here are some of the rhythms. Notice that they make use of *syncopation;* that is, they place accents in unexpected places.

Ex. 1

Any series of notes can be made more interesting by keeping these peppy rhythms in mind. Suppose you want to play a *bluesy* scale:

Ex. 2

Used as a fill, this line is pleasant enough. But, it really comes to life when we add the "feel" of those syncopated figures:

Ex. 3

Earlier, we explored the idea of using *sequence* — repeating a musical idea on different pitches — to give direction to an improvisation.

Ex. 4

Continued next page

Watch what happens when we add rhythmic flair to those sequences. The change in accents balances out the sameness of the idea. The result is musically more exciting!

Ex. 5

Practice tapping or singing these rhythms, and they will naturally become a part of your playing. Once they are familiar enough, you'll be able to use just snatches here and there, so that even your improvised melodies will gain a flexibility and freedom that always sounds fresh. Look at the difference between the first sequence example above, and this possible end result:

Ex. 6

SI

212

An Outline of Jazz Techniques

Jazz grew out of the cotton fields of Mississippi and the pleasure houses of St. Louis, through piano rolls and wandering brass bands, to smoky Harlem night clubs where player challenged player into the early hours of the morning. It is a music filled with tradition and bursting with excitement.

There are many different styles of playing jazz that have developed over its long history. Jazz masters play a very complex and difficult type of music. This article is going to outline very basic approaches to beginning jazz improvisation, in order to give you the tools and background to move ahead on your own.

Rhythm

The best place to start in developing a feeling for jazz is to study jazz rhythm. Early jazz rhythm used an element called the Hornpipe. This consists of a dotted eighth note followed by a sixteenth note, as in example 1, using the C Scale.

You may be familiar with a sound called the "shuffle rhythm," a favorite among blues players. This uses the dotted rhythm as well. Blues musicians use it in a chordal pattern as shown in example 2.

Ex. 2

An early jazz style piece that uses this dotted rhythm is shown in example 3.

213

Continued next page

The modern jazz feel, however, does *not* use the dotted rhythm; instead it uses more of a triplet feeling. Often though, as in the eighth note passage in example 4, the triplet feeling, which is very exaggerated, is replaced by the use of stress put on certain notes. In any group of two notes, the stress usually goes on the first.

Ex. 4

Sometimes the stress is reversed, as in example 5. When this happens, we have a feeling that something is not quite balanced. The result is called syncopation — stress on a normally weak note. Often, that stress will be turned back around to fall on the normally strong note. This happens in the second measure of example 5.

Ex. 5

The feeling of syncopation often occurs in jazz in a form of "anticipation." Example 6 has anticipation at the very end. The final E gets an accent that it ordinarily would not have.

Ex. 6

Exercise 7 shows other forms of anticipation. Some of these anticipatory or syncopated rhythms make up what is known as the "swing style." The following examples cover swing, or the big band era phrases.

Ex. 7

Example 8 uses syncopation quite a bit. Use a metronome to keep count as you try to play these complicated rhythms. Play this exercise several times until you are very familiar with these rhythms. If you are having trouble, eliminate the tie and try to play them as a series of eighth notes. When you are comfortable enough, put the ties back in.

214

Play example 9 with a metronome several times.

Ex. 9

Example 10 is a typical jazz run. Place the accents on the first note of every group of two, and note the anticipation on the very final note of the phrase.

Ex. 10

Example 11 is another typical jazz phrase which uses stress accents, but without any anticipation. Notice how important the use of stress is to bring out the flavor of the phrase.

Ex. 11

Example 12 is a simple tune. Play it straight the first time, then use anticipation (12b). 12c shows the same tune, but this time, instead of anticipation, it features a slight delay.

Each of these approaches is just a way of loosening up the rhythm so that it does not sound stiff. The result is known as "swing."

Ex. 12

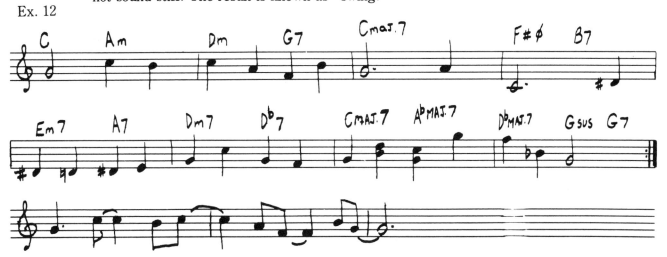

Continued next page

Swing Rhythms

Turn your attention once again to a rhythm that places an accent on the weak beat in a very deliberate manner. One common rhythm that does this is shown in example 13, the "Charleston" rhythm. The Charleston rhythm is played in the right hand against a steady quarter note rhythm in the left. This rhythm is typical of the kind of figures that the brass played in the big bands of the swing era.

Example 13, the "Charleston" sounding rhythm, is a variation on the Hornpipe. Our original Hornpipe consisted of a dotted eighth note followed by a sixteenth note. Here, we have stretched out the rhythm so that it takes twice as much time: a dotted quarter is followed by an eighth. To complicate things a little more, the dotted quarter is silent in this example. But the syncopated feel is still very much present.

Ex. 13

Now look at some other rhythms that were typical of those brass sections. Example 14 shows a number of these rhythms. Look at each measure separately. In the first measure there are notes on one and four. The second measure is in a syncopated rhythm. The third measure is again on one and four. The Charleston rhythm follows. Now put the first four measures together.

These rhythms are difficult to read and play if they are unfamiliar. Use your metronome and play the rhythms on a single note. If you are having trouble playing these rhythms, try clapping them along with the metronome.

Move on to the next line. This line begins with the Charleston rhythm but it is tied over onto the next eighth note so it becomes even more complicated. Try the first two measures with the metronome. Then the next two measures, and repeat.

Play the last measure several times with the metronome to get a steady Charleston rhythm. Now play the entire phrase, both lines, with the metronome.

Ex. 14

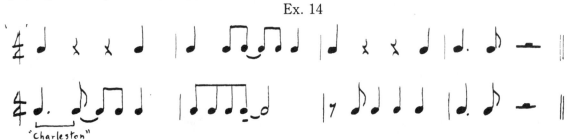

Next is a series of patterns from the swing era. Look at the entire line and use the metronome while playing it. Repeat it over and over until you get the right feeling. Remember, rhythm is the key to good-sounding improvised lines.

Ex. 15

216

Selecting The Right Notes

We can now move on to selecting the notes in making up a jazz improvisation. Let's use a well-known tune as our basis. Example 16 is a well known song called "Worried Man's Blues."

First we'll use variation in the rhythms of the original. Example 17 is a rhythmic alteration of the opening line using anticipation.

Here are some of the swing rhythms you've practiced, applied to the melody. We are now beginning to form an improvisation, although the same notes are maintained. In the second measure of example 18, some notes are repeated in order to accommodate the rhythm. Try this with the metronome.

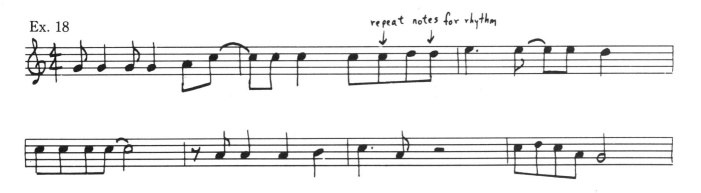

217

Continued next page

Look at the next phrase. If you clap these rhythms you will recognize them from the earlier swing exercises, numbers 14 and 15. Now play the third phrase. Put them all together, keeping the notes of the tune, yet altering the rhythm.

Sometimes, taking things out can be as important as putting them in. You might decide to leave most of the third measure out, for example, in order to bring in more of a resting balance with the activity of the eighth notes. Play example 18b.

Ex. 18b

Until now we have just been altering the rhythms. It's time to look at how to add notes of your own. Jazz improvisation is just a form of spontaneous composition, and as jazz musicians we should start composing while playing at the keyboard.

In order to find a way to embellish what's already on the page, it is possible to go as far back as the sixteenth century in Italian music when embellishment was very commonplace. At that time musicians were expected to add notes to what was on the written page.

Example 19 shows an interval, the note G and the note A, and three ways of embellishing that interval. Play each one. The three different kinds of embellishments that can be added to any interval are: adding notes which lie above the interval, in this case any note above the A; adding notes that lie below the interval, in this case any note below G; and adding notes that lie in between the two original notes, in this case, a $G^{\#}$ or an A^{b}.

Ex. 19

Example 20 retains the original tune, yet notes have been added both above and below the intervals that occur within the tune. The passage begins with a G note and the next note of the tune is another G. A note above or below that G can be added. In this case, a note above has been added. Once you add a note higher than the interval, you might consider

adding a note lower than the next interval in order to create a weaving motion. This alternation between higher and lower notes (and those in between) will create an interesting melodic effect. In the following examples the H indicates a note higher than the interval, the L indicates a note lower, and the B indicates a note in between.

Ex. 20

Some of the notes of the melody have not been retained in example 21. Often jazz musicians will ignore the original melody all together when they are taking a solo and base an improvisation on the chords which underlie the melody. Notes from the original melody are circled.

Ex. 21

Now we're going to use a similar approach to improvise on the chord structure of the tune. Take a C^6 chord and arpeggiate it. You can look at it as if it were the original melody. If you just add the swing rhythm without changing any of the notes in the C^6 harmony, you could end up with the phrase in example 22.

Ex. 22

Example 23 shows the introduction of a C scale which adds more notes to choose from.

Ex. 23

Example 24 shows what happens if notes lower than the intervals and higher than the intervals in the C^6 chord are used. The circled notes, the C, E, G and A are all part of the C^6 chord.

Ex. 24

Choosing non-chord notes is really a matter of developing a personal style. It's important to use your ear to listen for the sounds you like. For example, rather than choosing the $D^\#$ at the beginning of example 24, a $C^\#$ could have been inserted. The key is to experiment as much as possible. See what happens if you add notes very close to the melody notes. Then try wide skips. Try several notes in a row that are higher than the melody notes, or several that are below them. Ideally, of course, you want to create melodic interest.

One way to organize your melodic improvisations so that you don't become repetitive is to think in terms of form. For example, your phrases can be shaped as questions and answers.

Example 25 shows this question and answer technique.

219

Continued next page

Ex. 25

Example 26 uses the original melody at times, and switches off to lines built from the harmonies.

Ex. 26

Example 27 shows an eighth note pattern used by Charlie Parker, who was one of the founders of the modern school of jazz. It shows a Gm^7 chord going to a C^7 chord. The notes that belong to the chords have been circled. Analyze which notes inserted in addition to the chord harmonies lie above the intervals and which notes lie below.

Ex. 27

Patterns

Example 28 shows a pattern that takes you through the cycle of fifths. It is in the form of a *sequence*, a melodic idea that repeats over and over, beginning on a new pitch each time. Continue the sequence through the cycle of fifths.

Ex. 28

A rhythmic sequence can also be used, as is shown in example 29. Here, the rhythmic idea repeats.

Ex. 29

Once you know how to create sequences and are familiar with all the chord harmonies, you have a large palette of colors and shapes to choose from in your solos.

More Jazz Pattern Examples

Example 30 uses some swing rhythms described earlier in combination with eighth note patterns which revolve around the chord tones.

Ex. 30

Example 31 uses scaler passages and then creates a weaving effect.

Ex. 31

Examine both examples 32 and 33 very carefully; circle the chord harmonies and analyze the other notes in relation to those chord harmonies.

Exs. 32 and 33

221

Continued next page

Example 34 returns to the tune "Worried Man's Blues," but now utilizes all of the concepts covered in this article. The harmony tones have been circled for the first several measures. Go through the rest of the song and circle the other harmony tones. You will be able to see where the non-harmonic tones come into play.

Ex. 34

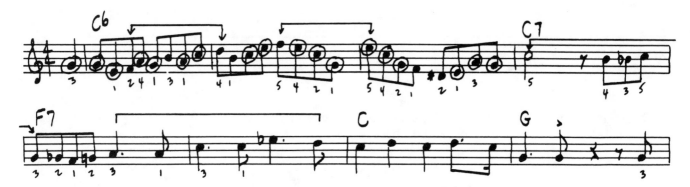

Here are some of the features of this improvisation: the phrase which begins the opening measure is repeated at the beginning of the second measure, starting on a different pitch. At the end of the second measure there is a phrase which finds a near relative at the beginning of the third measure. The pattern in the fourth measure with the C^7 chord is repeated at the beginning of the next measure, although the rhythm is different.

The ninth measure also contains a rhythmic pattern repeated in the eleventh measure. There are many other relationships in this improvisation like the ones just mentioned.

This is only one possibility, of course. From the standpoint of musicality, I would consider example 35 to be much too busy, although it does help to illustrate the principles involved in improvisation. As you practice the art of improvisation, you will tend to move further away from the strictness and rigidity of these examples, both in the notes chosen, and in the increasing flexibility of rhythm. We could vastly improve example 35 simply by editing out some of the notes, as in following example 36. Try this editing-out technique often, after you feel comfortable enough with the chord progression you are playing on.

Ex. 35

In order to find your own jazz style listen as much as possible to artists you like and appreciate, and continue to refer to this article on the basics of jazz improvisation.

SI

Harmony at the Keyboard

JAZZ IMPROVISATION

We asked jazz master Lou Stein, who has played piano with such musical luminaries as Benny Goodman, Percy Faith, and Bobby Hackett, to name just a few, to give us a sample of his style of improvisation on the children's favorite, "Mary Had A Little Lamb." (This little lamb is very hip, indeed.)

Notice how Lou keeps his improvisation in a limited area of keyboard by constantly changing direction of the jazz line. He never has more than four successive notes in one direction, ascending

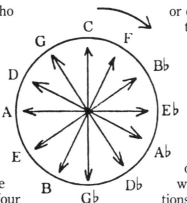

or descending. Most often he uses just two or three notes before changing direction of the line. This technique yields the nice "tight" solo for which he is famous.

Also notice that Lou ignores the tonic chord "C" as the opening chord, substituting instead the F# diminished. This substitution principle was explored in an article on the circle of fifths (January 1981), which explained how many substitutions are created by using a chord directly opposite the original chord in the circle.

Have fun playing this improvisation!

Mary Had a Little Lamb

Arranged by
Lou Stein

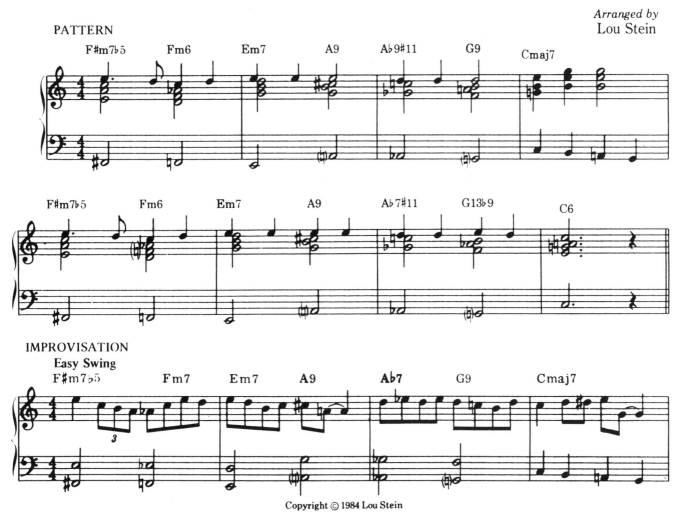

223

Continued next page

Introducing LOU STEIN

Lou Stein began his piano study at the Settlement School in Philadelphia and acquired a thorough classical training under Gregory Ashman, accompanist to Ephraim Zimbalist. Early in his career he performed with the Glen Miller Band, Charlie "Bird" Parker, and went on to become an integral member of the Charlie Ventura group. That was just the beginning. Throughout the years his broad performance career has included playing with such notables as Percy Faith, Kostelanetz, Jackie Gleason, Bobby Hackett, Benny Goodman and Clark Terry. His recordings — too numerous to list here — appear on such labels as Epic, Decca and Capitol. Mr. Steir currently devotes his time to teaching, studying, touring and composing.

LS ♪

photo by Paul J. Hoeffler

Andy LaVerne

Modes of the major scale
by Andy LaVerne

Andy LaVerne studied with Bill Evans, worked with Stan Getz and Woody Herman (and many others), and recently released See How It Feels (Black-Hawk BKH 51401) with Chris and Dan Brubeck, and Liquid Silver (Digital Music CD-449). The latter is a tribute to Bill Evans using piano, guitar, bass, drums and string quartet. We welcome Andy LaVerne as a new writer.

Modal playing in jazz first came to prominence in the late 1950's. Miles Davis's Kind of Blue (Columbia PC 8163) album is generally acknowledged as one of the first recordings to employ modes as a basis for composition and improvisation. Along with Davis, Bill Evans and John Coltrane contributed to this album. Both went on to develop modal playing in different directions.

The question arises, "How do I get into modal playing?" If you follow the procedure given here, it will unlock the door for you. The first step is to examine the seven modes of the major scale (**JKW** vol. 1, no. 2). Each of the modes has its own characteristic sound.

Two common pitfalls we may encounter when learning the modes are 1) learning the seven modes using only **C** major as the relative major scale and 2) limiting knowledge of modes to the Dorian and Mixolydian modes.

In order to avoid these pitfalls, I have devised an exercise that overcomes both problems simultaneously. The exercise uses a common tonal center (at first, **C**) as opposed to using a single major scale for demonstration and practice purposes. By using a single tonal center, we are able to have a different relative major for each mode. (See table 1 below.)

We can also readily see the difference between each mode and the major scale starting on the same note. This demonstrates the characteristic sound and intervallic structure. (See table 2 below.)

The third common problem we encounter regarding modes is that of left hand voicings. A simple solution to this is to superimpose a major triad over a bass note — the bass note being the root of the mode. Each of these triads spells out the characteristic tones of the modes, thus giving the listener and player alike the overall sound and quality of the prevailing mode. (See the exercise below.)

After you feel confident playing this exercise using **C** as the tonal center, start transposing it up in half steps. (**Db, D, Eb**, etc.). Don't go on until you have a facility and understanding of each tonal center. By playing this exercise in all tonal centers, you will have added 7 × 12 = 84 scales to your vocabulary!●

1

Mode		Relative major
C	Ionian	C maj.
C	Dorian	Bb maj.
C	Phrygian	Ab maj.
C	Lydian	G maj.
C	Mixolydian	F maj.
C	Aeolian	Eb maj.
C	Locrian	Db maj.

2

Mode		Altered tones of major scale with same root
C	Ionian	none
C	Dorian	b3, b7
C	Phrygian	b2, b3, b6, b7
C	Lydian	#4
C	Mixolydian	b7
C	Aeolian	b3, b6
C	Locrian	b2, b3, b5, b6, b7

Exercise

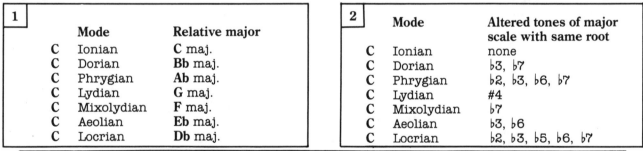

Next time, Andy will get you started improvising modally. In the meantime, two excellent records in this vein are McCoy Tyner's The Real McCoy (Blue Note BST 84264) and Chick Corea's Now He Sings, Now He Sobs (Pacific Jazz LN-10057).

Continued next page

Andy LaVerne

Modes of the major scale – part 2

by Andy LaVerne

Last month, in part 1, we examined the seven modes of the major scale. Now that the sound and feel of these modes are more familiar, we can delve into modal improvisation.

With your right hand, play the mode up and down two octaves, while still using the triad/bass note voicing in the left hand. At this point I suggest introducing the assistance of a metronome. At a slow tempo, have each click of the metronome represent the second and fourth beats of $\frac{4}{4}$ time. Now, play the modes in eighth notes, with the note values closer to $\sqrt[3]{}$. Keep the accent on the offbeats. This procedure will help in achieving a nice, swinging rhythmic feel.

The next step is to take each mode and play on it for four measures. You might want to ease into this step as follows. Try improvising a right hand melody line using just the notes of the mode. (In other words, don't use any non-modal tones.) For four bars each, play a modal melody using whole notes (o). The next time through the cycle, use half notes ($\downarrow$), then quarter ($\downarrow$), eighth ($\boxed{}$), triplets ($\boxed{}$) and finally, sixteenth notes ($\boxed{}$).

Remember to think melodically, making use of

scale passages, arpeggios, various intervallic relationships and sequential passages. Use rhythms to provide even more color and variety.

Listening will help give you ideas on how to use modes. Below, I've listed the names of some musicians to correspond to each mode. While all of these players are conversant in all modes, their characteristic personal sounds seem to gravitate toward some more than others.

Ionian – Bill Evans

Dorian – Bill Evans, Herbie Hancock, McCoy Tyner, John Coltrane (saxophone)

Phrygian – Chick Corea

Lydian – McCoy Tyner, Joe Henderson (saxophone)

Mixolydian – Bill Evans, Herbie Hancock, McCoy Tyner, John Coltrane

Aeolian – Richie Beirach, Chick Corea, Keith Jarrett, Ralph Towner (guitar), John Abercrombie (guitar)

Locrian – Richie Beirach, Chick Corea, Herbie Hancock, Joe Henderson

Lately, I find myself gravitating to the Locrian and Mixolydian modes in my own writing and playing. It will be interesting to see what your favorites are.●

Andy LaVerne's **MONTUNO OF THE MONTH** is on page 16.

LaVerne will perform a solo concert featuring modern piano compositions from the early sixties to the present day on December 4, 8:30 pm, at Cami Hall in New York. It will be recorded by DMP, the label for his *Liquid Silver* (DMP CD-449).

Harold Danko's
Sound approach to modal improvisation

In the study of contemporary music we often hear the term "modal" describing a work or sections of larger works. It has also been used to define a style in which many jazz artists perform. For practical purposes we use the term mode interchangeably with scale*, particularly when referring to scale formations generated from various degrees* of the familiar major scale. In earlier times, the major scale was called the Ionian mode.

FIGURE 1.
C Major Scale or C Ionian Mode

The use of modes dates back at least to ancient Greek music. In fact the names of the seven modes (Ionian, Dorian, Phrygian, Lydian, Mixolydian, Aeolian, and Locrian) are Greek. You can also find them in use as the "church modes" in music during the Middle Ages, particularly in the Gregorian Chant. In the early part of the twentieth century, modes surfaced once again in the music of Ravel, Debussy, and others.

Miles Davis has been largely responsible for the popularization of the modal style of jazz improvisation. His albums Milestones (Columbia PC 9428) and Kind of Blue (Columbia PC 8163), dating from the late 1950's, had a tremendous impact on other musicians. They feature modal compositions and the innovative playing of John Coltrane, Bill Evans, and others.

Dorian mode in particular has become a prevailing sound in contemporary jazz, pop, and "new music," through compositions like Davis's "Milestones" and "So What," Herbie Hancock's "Maiden Voyage," and Michael Jackson's "Billie Jean." The same Dorian sound occurs frequently in compositions of the Minimalist school, such as in the work of Steve Reich.

It is recommended that pianists acquaint their ears and fingers with the sounds of the modes as follows.

Figure 2 shows the seven diatonic modes possible from the note C. The key signature designates the major scale from which the mode is derived.

For my own students, I have developed a visual method presenting scales as paths on the keyboard.** I like the word "path" because, just as your feet negotiate a path when you're walking, your fingers create a path of whole steps and half steps when you play a mode on the piano. Figure 3 illustrates three modal paths (the major scale, Mixolydian, and Dorian) from the note C.

FIGURE 3.

MAJOR SCALE - PATH ON C

MIXOLYDIAN SCALE - PATH ON C (flatted 7th)

DORIAN SCALE - PATH ON C (flatted 3rd and 7th)

Besides acquainting yourself with modes as a variety of scales or paths on the keyboard, you can play them as sets of triads* over a pedal point*. Figure 4 gives characteristic triads of the Ionian mode over the pedal point C, the "root" of the mode.

FIGURE 2.

Continued next page

FIGURE 4.

C Ionian

If the triads of the Ionian mode are played with their individual roots C, F, G, and C, then you hear a familiar cadence*.

FIGURE 5.

But if the triads are played over one pedal tone, the root of the mode, they take on the modal flavor.

As you play the triads of each mode in Figure 6, let your inner ear hear familiar melodies that fit with them. The melody of "Tonight" (from West Side Story) has a Lydian sound. "On Broadway" (the Drifters' and George Benson's hit) is Mixolydian. The Russian folk melody "Song of the Volga Boatman" is Aeolian.

Here are some ways to prepare for improvisation with these sounds.

1) Transpose the examples in Figure 2 to begin on all twelve notes. For example, starting on G, play G Ionian, G Lydian, G Mixolydian, G Dorian, etc. You can find 84 modes on the keyboard in this manner alone! Each has characteristic triads.

2) Play the triads as broken chords. Figure 7 shows a broken chord exercise on the triads of the C Ionian mode. Run broken triads on all seven modes on C. Try them on a different root every day.

FIGURE 7.

C Ionian

3) Play the triads in the Charleston rhythm:

FIGURE 8.

Now you're ready to improvise using notes of the mode in a melody as the chords are sounded. This is an ideal exercise for students and teachers. First the student can play the chords while the teacher improvises in eighth notes, using only the notes of the mode. Then, when the student hears some of these patterns of notes, the roles can be reversed.

Figure 9 is a melodic example in C Ionian. By changing key signatures, play the same melodic example in all modes on C with the appropriate triads in your left hand.

FIGURE 9.

Working with the sounds of the modes in the above manner will enable you to appreciate their importance. If more emphasis were to be placed on them, both in terms of ear training and keyboard facility, pianists would be better equipped to enjoy and participate in the music of today. ●

FIGURE 6.

C Lydian   C Mixolydian   C Dorian
C Aeolian   C Phrygian

Harold Danko teaches in the Master's program at Manhattan School of Music and is a clinician for the National Association of Jazz Educators. His two recent records on Sunnyside are Ink and Water (SSC 1008), a solo album, and Shorter by Two (SSC 1004), compositions of Wayne Shorter played on two pianos by Danko and Kirk Lightsey. Danko has recorded with numerous others including Lee Konitz, Woody Herman, Chet Baker, and the Thad Jones/Mel Lewis Band (1976-78).

*See Glossary, p. 16.

**For the method — with scale paths and exercises presented for all modes of the major scale as well as minor, pentatonic, whole tone, diminished, and other scales — see Harold Danko's book, The Illustrated Keyboard Series — Complete, Columbia Pictures Publications/Studio P/R, 15800 N.W. 48th Avenue, Miami, FL 33014. SB 130, $11.95.

GLOSSARY

CADENCE — A progression of chords that effectively concludes a passage of music, as if by formula. A simple example is the musical "Amen" at the end of a hymn.

CHROMATIC — Melody or harmony that can use any of the twelve tones of the octave.

CONTRARY MOTION — Hands simultaneously playing in opposite directions on the keyboard.

DEGREE — Classification of a note with respect to its position in a scale. C is the first degree of the C scale, D is the second degree, etc., up to B, which is the seventh degree of the C scale.

DIATONIC — Melody or harmony that uses only the tones of a particular major or minor scale, and therefore is not chromatic.

DUPLE METER — Time signature in which the number of beats per measure is evenly divisible by two. Any duple meter (for example, 2/2, 2/4, 4/4, 6/8) can be played with two equally spaced accents per measure, falling on the beat.

INVERTED MORDENT — An embellishment consisting of a pair of notes played rapidly before a principal note. The sign ∿ represents an inverted mordent.

 is played

MODULATE — To move out of one key into another in a continuous musical process.

PARALLEL MOTION — Hands simultaneously playing in the same direction on the keyboard.

PEDAL POINT — A single low note, sustained beneath a melody or a series of chords.

PHRASE — A group of notes which form a subdivision of a melody. PHRASING is the way in which a melody is divided, as a poem is divided into lines.

SCALE — The succession of tones defining a key or tonality. Major and minor scales use both whole and half steps to create their individual characteristics. A chromatic scale proceeds by half steps.

SYNCOPATION — An accent falling on a weak beat or weak part of a beat.

TRIAD — A chord consisting of three notes which can be arranged as two superimposed thirds.

TRITONE — The interval of a flatted fifth or augmented fourth, comprised of three whole steps. Examples are

WHOLE TONE (or WHOLE STEP) — The musical distance between two adjacent half steps; a major second. For example, the interval between C and D or between C# and D# is a whole tone. A whole tone scale is a succession of whole steps on the keyboard.

The Thumb Slide

Jazz and pop keyboard technique is not at all like classical technique. The classical style, which aims for a clean, elegant and often delicate sound, is quite different from the funky, down-and-dirty approach desired by many blues musicians, for example. Here is an exercise to help you practice one kind of jazz technique, the thumb slide.

The thumb slide is used in bluesy embellishments, in which a note is preceded by the note a half step below it. The lower ornamental note is usually played very quickly before the beat; it then slides onto the main note. The following pattern is given first for right hand practice, then for left hand practice.

229

Creating an improvised line

Stuart Isacoff

Improvisation has never been the sole province of the jazz artist. A tradition of spontaneous variation and embellishment played an important role in early classical music, and we can take some important cues from that tradition on how to think about improvising, and how to teach it as well.

How did the classical performer approach improvisation? Mozart claimed that he simply played whatever occurred to him at the moment. But earlier musicians left behind clear evidence of their methods, which were based for the most part on the use of ornamentation. Here is Bach's ornamented version of a theme by Vivaldi.

A comparable contemporary example is this excerpt from John Coltrane's performance of Thelonious Monk's "Round Midnight" (from the recording <u>Basic Miles</u>, Columbia PC 32025). We've transposed it from Eb minor to D minor.

Here's the original (transposed) melody.

Words by BERNIE HANIGHEN   Music by COOTIE WILLIAMS and THELONIOUS MONK
1944 (RENEWED WARNER BROS . INC)   All Rights Reserved   Used By Permission

In each of these cases a basic melody was embellished to form a new extended melodic shape. This method has its roots in the sixteenth century, when charts containing examples of ways to ornament an interval appeared in several manuals of Renaissance music instruction.

Ganassi's Tables*

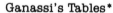

---

*Ganassi was a 16th-century Venetian church musician who wrote treatises about the instrumental techniques of the time.

Pianist and composer Stuart Isacoff is the editor of <u>Keyboard Classics</u>.

Increased chromaticism and rhythmic complexity make jazz improvisations seem quite different from Ganassi's Tables, but the basic principles bear many similarities. No matter what the century, the improviser still has to think about the same things:

1) melodic shape
2) rhythm
3) form
4) color

Let's take these considerations one at a time, beginning with the first on the list.

Shaping the melody

There are three basic choices for adding ornamental melodic notes: above, below or in between the notes of the interval.

One of the keys to interesting melodic lines is that they weave above and below the intervals being ornamented. In the Ganassi examples, this occurs, but in a limited way. In many successful improvised jazz lines, the weaving line ornaments an interval and connects it to another melodic interval.

We can think of each of the chords that harmonizes a tune as consisting of several intervals. For example, when playing on a Gm⁷ chord, we might keep in mind the intervals from G to B♭,

B♭ to D, D to G, and so on, including all inversions (B♭ to G, D to B♭, etc.). Creating an improvised line then becomes a simple matter of ornamenting these intervals according to our above, below, or in between concept.

Of course, most improvised lines will use combinations of embellishing tones. Playing on a Gm⁷ chord might involve playing a note between G and B♭, followed immediately by a note below the interval, etc.:

The trick is to reverse direction often enough so that a varied shape results. Below are some more typical examples of improvised lines.

Producing a solo with order and balance requires more than simply placing ornamental tones, of course. Two elements that help add cohesiveness and direction are rhythm and motivic design. We'll begin to look at these next time. ●

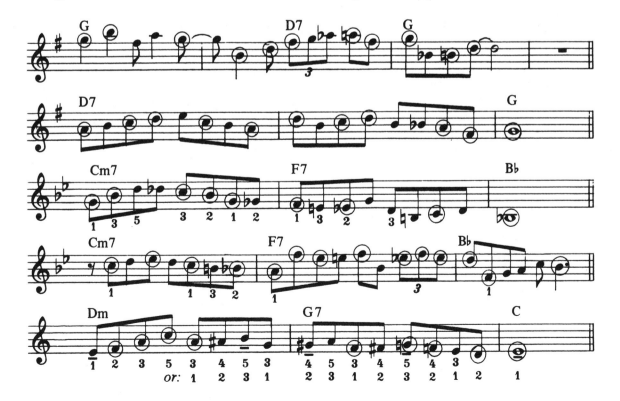

231

Continued next page

Creating an improvised line – part 2

Stuart Isacoff

Last issue's look at how to create "weaving" lines in your improvisations did not deal with some important aspects of jazz soloing, such as form and rhythm. This time, let's take a closer look at how your various weavings can knit together a full-length phrase.

The simplest device for establishing a structure within a phrase is repetition.

Fig. 1

If we take this idea and repeat it starting on different pitches, the result is a sequence.

Fig. 2

A sequence can be extended over changing harmonies, as in the examples below. This device will help bring a meaningful sense to an improvisation.

Fig. 3

Another device frequently used to bring a feeling of direction and cohesiveness to a solo is the alternation of question and answer phrases. The first phrase states the question; the second responds, often with a sense of finality.

Fig. 4

An endless sequence can become awfully boring, so it will always be most effective to vary the shapes of your solos (in the same way you vary melodic direction to create weaving lines). One way to achieve this is to construct building blocks, as in the question and answer format. In the examples below, a pattern (A) is alternated with another (B) before A reappears. A and B themselves are sequences.

Fig. 5

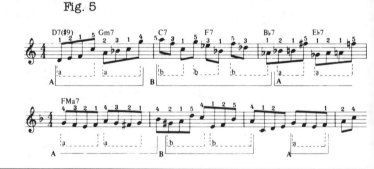

Scale patterns may be used the same way. The first example in Figure 6 is a five-note scale. It is the basis of a pattern A in the example ABA. B uses notes from a different scale.

Fig. 6

So far in this continuing series, we've played with the melodic shape and form of an improvised line.

IMPROVISATION

Creating an improvised line – part 3

Stuart Isacoff

With this article about harmonic color, we conclude our series.

Thus far we've looked at ways to create ornamental lines that weave and turn for melodic interest, and at rhythmic variety for those lines. Another ingredient you will want to consider when improvising is color. It's hard to define color, but it's easy to hear it. Just listen to something in major followed by something in minor. There will be a difference in atmosphere, in emotional connotation, in . . . color.

Transforming a major scale into a minor scale is relatively simple, yet the result can be earthshaking. By making a few more changes in our basic scale a whole rainbow of sounds can be created.

These less-common scales are known as "modes," which is a term that pretty much means the same as "scale." (The well-known major scale was called the Ionian Mode by medieval musicians.) By choosing particular modes when improvising, a player can obtain very specific qualities or colors in an improvisation.

Say, for example, we wanted to highlight the color created by the use of the flatted fifth. We might think, during an improvisation, of the following mode (played over a C7 chord):

How can we use modes in forming our weaving lines? You will recall that we placed tones above, between, and below melody or chord intervals in order to form our lines. To create specific colors, we may simply use particular modes when choosing these pitches. Using our b5 mode (above) to ornament a C7 chord, for instance, we might produce this line:

There are an endless number of modes — oriental, medieval, contemporary — and many jazz musicians make up their own. Three very interesting modes appear in a book by French composer Olivier Messiaen about the technique of his musical language. Messiaen writes music based on both rhythmic and melodic modes, and he singles out a group he refers to as "modes of limited transposition."

These are modes which can be transposed to various pitches only a limited number of times

before they repeat themselves. The whole tone scale, for example, can be transposed only once before it repeats: you may begin it on C, then on C#, but when you play it on D you are actually back to the scale you played on C.

The diminished scale can be transposed twice: begin it on C, then on C#, then on D . . . but if you begin again on D# you are back to the same pitches you used for the scale on C.

Here is a mode which may be transposed only three times:

Inventing modal patterns

Many contemporary musicians like to create patterns out of the pitches of these modes. Here are a few examples.

By trying these modes, learning the "flavors" each may add to your solo lines, and by varying which ones you use (even in a single line you may choose to switch modes several times), you will gain control over a sizable palette of musical colors. They can add drama and expression to your playing in ways you never expected! ●

More practice for a continuous melodic line

by Dick Hyman

Last time, I suggested a method of practicing for developing the ability to improvise a continuous melodic line. The first step was to set up an eight-bar chord sequence and corresponding bass line. Then, playing with a metronome, we constructed nonstop right-hand melodies, first in whole notes, then half notes, then quarter notes, and so forth. We began by limiting ourselves to the diatonic mode in C major (strictly white keys).

See how inventive you can be over the course of several minutes.

This time, we'll move on to chromatics and see how the process develops. We'll use the following bass and harmonic pattern as our game plan.

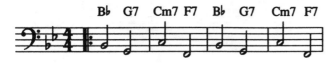

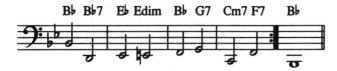

Setting the metronome to ♩ = 100, improvise a right-hand melody of your own. Start with a melody in whole notes, as shown last time. When you're comfortable with whole notes at this tempo, move on to half notes. It can be tricky to select melodic tones that make musical sense when you only have only one or two notes per bar to choose.

When you can play a half-note melody with no hesitation, move on to quarter notes. Now the line begins to show a more distinct jazz flavor.

Notice how the seventh chords become flatted ninths, and how neighboring tones make it easier to get around the harmonic changes.

Keeping the same tempo and continuing to use the original bass line and chords, let's improvise a melody in quarter-note triplets. Again, you should play through the progression a number of times while improvising your own melody. The eight bars shown here are just to get you started. Repeat the bass line as you invent new melodies with the metronome running. See how inventive you can be over the course of several minutes. (See example with quarter note triplets below.)

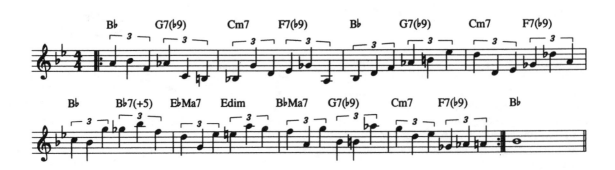

Now take a look at a sixteen-bar run-through of the same chord sequence with a melody in eighth-notes (example 4). This is the most common manner of jazz blowing. Note how it is possible and, at times, desirable to go outside the exact harmonies, either with a sequential series of figures or with something modal. For now, use these devices sparingly. It's easy to fall into them, but the point of this sort of practice is to invent melodies which reflect the chord changes rather than run counter to them. Play this example with jazz accents and with a swing (triplet) feeling.

When you're comfortable doing nonstop improvisation at this speed, you can go one step further, with a melody constructed in triplets (example 5). Remember, keep it moving! The value of this type of exercise is in teaching you not to stop, no matter what.

Subsequent topics are the virtue of taking breaths to create phrasing, and being less regular in rhythm than these exercises illustrate.●

Example 4 - Improvisation in swinging eighth notes

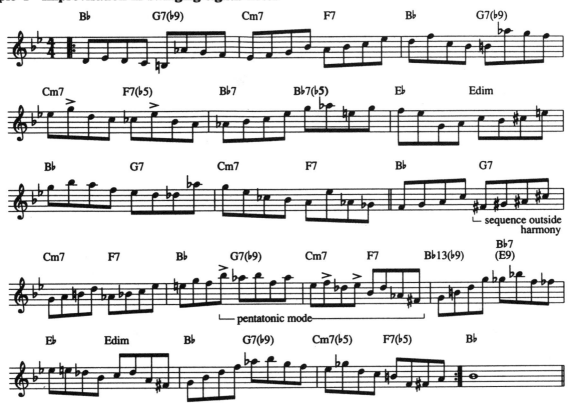

Example 5 - Nonstop improvisation in triplets

235

Using Jazz Runs

by Stuart Isacoff

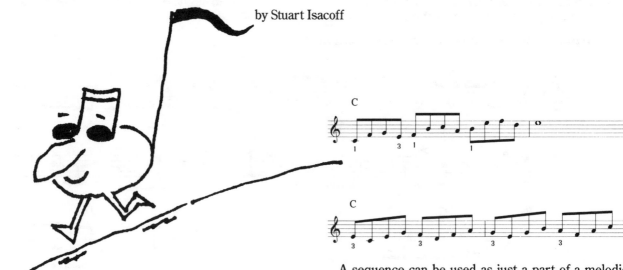

When people hear the term "jazz runs" they often think of complicated, technically difficult phrases that will make a pop arrangement really splashy — and beyond the level of most hobbyists. But jazz runs don't have to be too difficult, and professional musicians often put them to use as introductions, endings, fillers, or for modulating from one key to another. For example, to lead into a song beginning on a C chord, the run might fit over a G7 harmony (creating a V-I feeling).

One way to create a run is to use the idea of the musical sequence: take a brief phrase and repeat it on different pitches. Here are some examples that use only the notes of a major scale:

A sequence can be used as just a part of a melodic phrase. (Continuing the same pattern for too long can create monotony.) Here's a sequence in the key of E♭; first it appears intact, then broken up a bit:

To make your sequences a bit more colorful, try adding accidentals. This is most often accomplished by inserting a note either a half-step below or a half-step above any member of the sequence. Such "chromatic" notes mix smoothly into the sequence and create more variety in the shapes and sounds being played:

Illustration by Art Glazer

Birdlike

With the current popularity of Clint Eastwood's movie on jazz great Charlie Parker ("Bird"), many musicians are taking another look at the work of this founding member of the bebop school. In many ways, Parker's music was the foundation of all modern jazz playing. Even keyboard players can benefit from studying his rapid, improvised lines.

One of the keys to Parker's style is the art of constructing continuous, weaving patterns that move around and through the tones of a song's chords. And one of the ways to gain that ability ourselves is to play through some of his patterns . . . to get them "under the fingers" so that they become less and less foreign to what we are used to playing.

The following "Jazzercise" is designed to get your finger joints "well oiled" for rapid movement around the keyboard, while helping to familiarize you with the sound of Charlie Parker's jazz. As a homework assignment, continue to transpose this little exercise through all the keys. You'll find it more useful for pop playing than Hanon . . . and more fun, too!

Continue down cycle of fifths.

Section 8
TECHNIQUE SESSION (Part 1)
Classical Skills & Studies for the Keyboard

TECHNIQUE
A Sight-Reading
Workshop
Part I
BY ROBERT DUMM

"The three guardian monkeys–see no evil, hear no evil, and speak no evil–remind us of the three elements of good sight-reading."

Almost everyone is familiar with the three guardian monkeys—see no evil, hear no evil, and speak no evil. They remind me of the three elements of good sight-reading, which combine sight, hearing, and touch. If you don't want to just monkey around at the keyboard, keep in mind that a good sight-reader is guided by what he or she *sees* (on the printed page), *hears* (either before, or after a note is struck), and *feels* (on the keyboard).

Hearing is important; ideally, your inner hearing guides your hand and fingers, keeping them on track. However, the average pianist will perform a little trial and error before finding the right notes; this is often true even for a familiar piece. Take, for example, the melody of *Beautiful Dreamer:*

When you arrive at the * and play a C or an E instead of the correct note, something tells you it's not right. You may try again, and play a B natural or E flat. You flush a little, try them all until the right note is sounded, and by this time you've lost your place on the page!

How can this be avoided? Music reading requires the harmonious cooperation of all three elements: you see, you touch, and you hear together. This cooperation can be strengthened through practice, so that you will see and hear recurrent patterns, and your touch will become in turn more accurate.

Touch

Chances are, your sense of touch is weaker than your sense of sight. "Reading" the keyboard is similar to reading Braille, the sequence of tiny bumps that spells letters and words for blind people. A good sight-reader feels his way through a piece, not note-for-note, but handful-by-handful.

241

"You flush a little, try again, and by this time you've lost your place on the page!"

Many adults have a quick comprehension of the printed page—of what it "signals"—but are helpless with the keys. They endure considerable frustration in trying to find a key to press for *each* individual signal. The eyes do a jiggle from page to hand, and rhythm, musical shape, and continuity disappear in the hunting and hesitation. They are spelling their musical "words" letter by letter!

So we must begin improvement with *keyboard feel.* The answer is scales! Behind every melody or chord there lives a scale, and the *feel* of that scale is your tactile "slide-rule" for measuring the correct movements of your fingers.

First, feel the major scales in five-finger "slices" up and down the keyboard:

Then, derive the major chords (triads) by first playing the five-note scale, and leaving out the passing notes between chord tones:

Work through the same patterns in all keys, in this order: C, G, F, D, A, E, B, D-Flat, A-Flat, E-Flat, B-Flat and finally G-Flat. Try to find the notes of each scale by "ear" first; if that doesn't work, you can then fall back on this formula:

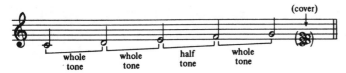

Be patient with yourself. In most everyday activities, whether you are handing someone a pencil or turning a page, your four fingers work *against* your thumb. Scales, on the other hand, ask you to open the hand partly, then keep it half-open while each finger in turn lightly squeezes down its key, then lets go. You may feel a little "thick" at first, simply because you are getting brain signals through to unexplored places!

The next step in familiarizing yourself with the feel of keyboard patterns is to play other types of scales and intervals.

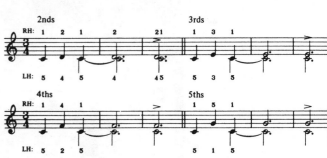

Next time, we'll continue our survey of scale-type figures, and discover how they can lead us into an awareness of chord inversions. Then, we'll move on to reading the map of "musical constellations" found on the pages of our printed materials.

Robert Dumm was named Dean of the Boston Conservatory when he was only twenty-five, and became a critic for The Christian Science Monitor *a year later. He served fifteen years as head of graduate Piano Pedagogy at The Catholic University before retiring in 1979. In 1983, Mr. Dumm was awarded the highest certification—Master Teacher—by The Music Teachers National Association.*

Continued next pa

TECHNIQUE

A Sight-Reading
Workshop

Part II

BY ROBERT DUMM

RACHEL GORDON

"One important aspect of good sight-reading is an infallible sense of 'touch.' Here are helpful exercises to develop that sense. No peeking!"

Let's continue to develop the sense of "touch" necessary for good sight-reading, with some of Hanon's five-finger exercises. Hanon, whom one of my old teachers, Maurice Dumesnil, remembered at the Paris Conservatoire as the bent and wizened gnome of *La Mecanique*, invented the "escalator clause" in music. His five-finger scales "leave out a note, but *not* a finger," which allows the action of the fingers, moving in sequence, to slowly spiral the hand forward on the keys.

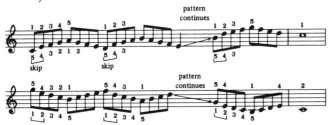

One octave is enough, then turn back, working that octave toward the starting point. As soon as you can, play this with eyes shut — no peeking — which, especially in scales with black keys, will improve your touch to the point that you will have "eyes in your fingers."

Next, try what I call "Hanon On Wheels," in triplets. They keep your wrist flexing ("breathing"), as you play.

Hanon's exercises can be helpful in getting the feel of triad inversions, which account for more keyboard chords than the root position triads we built last time. When you structure Hanon No. 1 by accenting fingers 1, 2, and 5 in the right hand, you have the first inversion of an A minor chord.

Notice how often first-inversion chords appear in pieces and arrangements you play:

You can tell them by their "gap" — the wider spacing (of a fourth) between the upper two tones:

The upper note of that "gap" is the root, or *name* of the chord. "Meet me at the top of the gap," I say to my students, recalling to them the *spelling* of the chord they are seeking.

Second inversion chords have their "gap" between the *lower* two notes:

Here is a way to work all triads, in all three positions, into your hands. This will "program" a large part of piano music into your "memory bank":

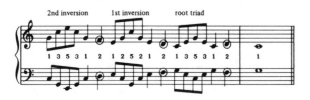

Be patient with yourself. Work slowly, making good tones, and try each of these studies with just one hand first, then with both, moving in *parallel* and *contrary* patterns.

Seeing

Now that we have worked through several exercises to teach your fingertips to feel, and your hand to cover standard shapes and anticipate changing forms, let's begin to examine how printed notes signal your movement on the keyboard.

"This is a way to 'program' a large part of piano music into your memory bank!"

Each C on the keyboard begins and *names* an octave. Here are those names:

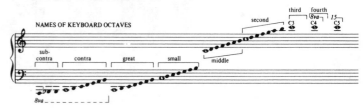

Since the "Grand Staff" roughly corresponds to the full piano keyboard, you should become familiar with *any* location it charts. Look out for those *Ottava* and *Ottava bassa* signs ("Play one octave up," or "Play one octave down"), with their light dotted lines, which are hard to see. You should also be aware of the little word *"loco"* which appears after one of these signs; it means return "in place" to play the notes *as shown*.

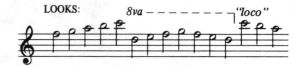

Next time, we'll explore "star maps" of the musical galaxy; lines and spaces in musical phrases; and "anchor tones," which cue your fingers to the position of the next note! ∎

Robert Dumm was named Dean of the Boston Conservatory when he was only twenty-five, and became a critic for The Christian Science Monitor *a year later. He served fifteen years as head of graduate Piano Pedagogy at The Catholic University before retiring in 1979. In 1983, Mr. Dumm was awarded the highest certification—Master Teacher—by The Music Teachers National Association.*

Continued next page

TECHNIQUE
A Sight-Reading
Workshop
Part III

BY ROBERT DUMM

"Here's a way to combine the *sight* aspect of reading with the *feel* of the notes beneath your fingers."

In our last installment we looked at a chart of the full keyboard and named each of the octaves it covers. The "Grand Staff" corresponds roughly to the range of most piano music, so it is important to become at ease with any location on it. I give my students this "Star Map" of the musical galaxy, and ask them to practice reading and playing notes in its various regions.

Practice writing down and playing in random order little "star treks" out and back from the landmark notes in the example above.

Such experiments help you to read steps and skips of a single, horizontal melody line accurately. Pianists,

however, are two-handed players, and we'll want to practice reading and feeling all intervals which lie under the five-finger position. We can group intervals on the staff as "likes" (line-to-line) or "unlikes (line-to-space).

The feeling aspect of this exercise is most important. It is a good idea to play through little progressions such as the following one, without ever breaking touch with the keys. Hold the common-tones, which I call "anchors," even if you must substitute another finger to hold a note as you move your hand into position for the next interval.

245

Mistakes are due either to mis-readings (something not seen or forgotten — such as a key signature), or to *mis-feelings*. In order to cultivate the ability to feel your way around the keyboard, it is necessary to "program" each key securely into your fingers. The note groupings and hand shapes in a piece will likely reflect the scales and chords of the key it is in.

In F Major, for instance, there is a B Flat in the signature. B Natural does not exist in that scale. So you'll want to "program" the B Flat into your playing mechanism before approaching a piece in F. Work the scale through by slices, in five-finger positions.

KEEP YOUR EYES CLOSED if you can. Now you have experienced most of the "handfuls" a composer will present to you in a piece in F Major. The piece will be yet another "program" of patterns placed on top of these basic scale-chord patterns.

The next step is to work on chord inversions. (You will meet them more often than chords in root-position!) Again, develop a sense of touch, using the following "feelies."

Now you are ready for a practical application of the points we've been discussing. Work through the G Major chords of Purcell's little *Prelude* before you "sight-read" it like a pro.

Last time we worked on spotting the "gap" in each chord. Here, you have begun to combine this *sight* aspect of reading with the *feel* of the notes beneath your fingers!

Next time, we'll look at *accidentals,* and alert you to some troublesome obstructions to good sight-reading. ■

TECHNIQUE
A Sight-Reading
Workshop
Part IV

BY ROBERT DUMM

In this conclusion to our sight-reading series, we will look at various pitfalls that should be kept in mind when reading a piece.

"**Accidentals**" are the sharps (#), flats (♭), and natural signs (♮) which alter any regular scale tone, however briefly. Sharps "push" a note to the right; finding a flat beside a note signals a move to the left. In a way, these signs function as turning lights on the

musical roadway. Everybody knows they remain in force for only the bar in which they appear and are then cancelled by the barline, but hardly anyone remembers this in sight-reading.

For example, in Bach's "Little Prelude" No.1 in C Major first sharps appear in the left hand, then flats in the right hand of the next measure. (See example 1.)

Example 1

"Pulls" toward F major

"Leans" toward A minor

Continued next page

These alterations — I call them "Promissory Notes" — forecast a new scale or key to come, and may or may not be "paid." They inject variety and expectation. (If you notice the *same* sharp or flat inserted again and again, a new key is being asserted by the composer.)

In order to play these correctly, try to analyze and keep in mind what is taking place in terms of possible key changes. In the Bach example above, the sharped notes direct the music toward A minor; the flatted notes create a pull toward F Major. Making sense of those accidentals make then easier to read.

Here are some other obstructions to good sight reading.

Repeated Notes: Busy eyes are likely to see them as moving up or down instead of staying in one place. You can mark them with a straight arrow as a reminder.

Tied Notes: That second black note-head is very likely to signal your muscle to twitch and play the same note again. A good cure is to *lightly* press the held key at the new beat.

Breaks: At the end of lines, look ahead to "cue" the next notes in the continuation of the music.

Skips: "Choreograph" your hand movements in relation to each other (with black-key groups as sensors).

"Road Closed" Signs: Watch for these nearly always tiny warnings of immediate key changes, signaled by miniature key signatures often hidden at the ends of lines.

Register Changes: *Ottava, Ottava bassa, 8va, col 8,* indicate changes of register; the word *loco* restores play to the notes as printed.

You will go a long way toward removing these pitfalls to accurate reading by:

1) Surveying The Scene (before you play), especially the key signature — the most overlooked of all signals!

2) "Pawing Out" The Music, that is, laying it out and experiencing it by handfuls. This has a lot to do with finding the fingering natural to your hands. Try to feel the "handfuls" in the music — the way your hands naturally fall over the keys — so that you will come to form automatically the physical posture needed for smooth playing. (See example 2.)

3) Playing Freely, with the confidence allowed by "feeling ahead."

4) Listening To Yourself. Taste each note-group as a "tune," and savor the continuing sound of each chord.

5) Above all, Taking Your Time. Probe with your fingers, approving each probe with your ear.

Keep these elements in mind, and you won't ever again be afraid to face the notes on a new page of music. Sight-reading can be fun, and these few steps should help to smooth the way to many rewarding moments at your piano. Happy sight-reading! ■

Robert Dumm was named Dean of the Boston Conservatory when he was only twenty-five, and became a critic for The Christian Science Monitor *a year later. He served fifteen years as head of graduate Piano Pedagogy at The Catholic University before retiring in 1979. In 1983, Mr. Dumm was awarded the highest certification—Master Teacher—by The Music Teachers National Association.*

Example 2

TECHNIQUE
Playing Scales

"If you pay attention to these points, you will acquire a great technique in just a few weeks."

Walter Gieseking was one of the most brilliant pianists of his generation (1895-1956), known particularly for his interpretations of Debussy. Together with his teacher, Karl Leimer, he wrote a number of essays on technique and pedagogy; the following first appeared in 1932, in a publication called The Shortest Way To Pianistic Perfection.

I am not absolutely opposed to finger exercises, scales, and arpeggios, nor do I reject the study of etudes; but I am of the opinion that these means for developing technique are, as a rule, used too much. To sit at the piano and practice scales and exercises for hours and hours, generally without concentration, is a very roundabout way of obtaining results.

If this intensive work is done by the help of strong concentration, it is possible for technique to improve so rapidly that marvelous results will be sometimes obtained. Almost always, however, brain work is left out, and the pupil is obliged to spend many years of practicing daily, and for hours at a time, in order to acquire a somewhat serviceable technique.

To a certain extent, of course, the practicing of finger exercises and scales cannot be avoided, and it is well therefore to make a few further remarks, which I think will be advantageous when studying.

Scales are played with a view to training the fingers, so that they do their work evenly and smoothly. Every tone of a scale must be struck with a certain vigor, and the ear must be carefully trained to hear the exact volume of sound required. We must have an accurate knowledge of the notes appearing in the scale, in order to be able to play it from memory; and we must further acquaint ourselves with the fingering, that is, the use of the thumbs and the third and fourth fingers. Not before the notes and the fingering are familiar to the pupil should he begin playing.

As the ear must pass judgment on the correct volume of sound, it is the first condition, when playing scales, for each hand to practice alone. If this is not done, the left hand is drowned by the right hand, or *vice versa,* for it becomes almost impossible to find out the grade of strength of the different tones with the two hands playing together.

In the scale of C major, for instance, **C** in the left hand is played with the fifth finger, in the right hand with the thumb; **D** in the left hand with the fourth finger, in the right hand with the second finger; and so forth. As the fingers are unequal in strength, they cannot at first be expected to touch the keys evenly. It is almost impossible for the beginner to hear these dissimilarities if both hands are played together.

The most important thing when training the fingers (the control of which we call technique) is to be able to judge correctly the dynamic value of the tones, by means of the ear. One must, therefore, bear in mind that the tones of a scale must be played with equality of strength. For the thumb there must be an extra pressure; for the second and third fingers there will be a certain amount of restraint; and then again for the fourth and fifth fingers there will be an added strength of stroke.

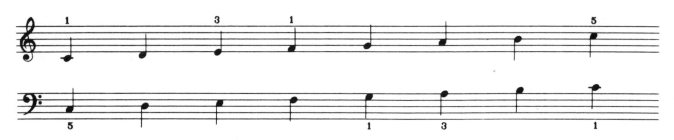

Continued next page

Strange to say, it is little known that in many cases the thumb touches the keys too feebly, a sure sign of how imperfectly the ear is generally trained. The movement which comes naturally to the thumb is to bend it under the other fingers, whereas the striking of a key from above downward necessitates practice. Its position, by reason of its being somewhat closer to the keys than the other fingers, encourages a weaker playing. For the same reason the thumb very often strikes too feebly when bent under the fingers, or else too vigorously, either through want of relaxation or through clumsiness.

After the thumb has been bent under, attention must be given to the secnd finger and, in descending, to the third and fourth fingers. Only by playing very slowly can we assure ourselves of the dynamic value of each tone, which is necessary in order to discover and to correct inaccuracies of equality in power. The best and quickest way to do this is to play short passages of the scale, and to practice five tones ascending and descending. The most careful attention must be given to the rhythm and touch of every tone.

Having taken note of the volume and the rhythmical value of tone, attention must be given to movement of the muscles. The feeling for absolute relaxation must become second nature to the pupil, and it must be continuously felt when playing scales. If the player gives constant attention to these points, keeping watch over both hands, and practicing a short time every day, in a few weeks he will have acquired so great a technique that he will be able to play scales in a much better manner than many pupils who have been studying for years and have practiced scales one hour or more a day. If the pupil follows these rules, his playing will become smooth and rippling. Then the hands may be occasionally practiced together, in order to accustom the ear to the precise striking together of the tones of the two hands.

A great difficulty when playing scales is the passing over and under of the fingers. We must think ceaselessly of relaxation. I advise the passing under of the fingers to be practiced principally by rolling of the lower arm; this is usually done by a side movement of the hand over the keyboard. It is quite easy to relax the muscles when using a rolling of the lower arm, and this is difficult when the hand is bent sideways.

Without relaxation it is quite impossible to play a pearly scale. After having touched a black key, it is comparatively easy to pass the finger under; but this is not so after having touched a white key. For this reason, the scale in C major is the most difficult to play smoothly. It is therefore advisable not to commence with the C major scale.

I do not consider it necessary to play scales in all their variations of sixths, thirds, contrary motions, and so on, as too much valuable time is wasted thereby. Scales, or parts of scales, however, as they constantly appear in compositions, should be carefully studied, so that in time their rendering will, with the help of relaxation, become more and more perfect.

WG & KL

E T U D E S

This study by the great Hungarian composer Bela Bartok focuses on shifting hand positions. Practice it slowly, and make use of the phrasing and accents to create a smooth, musical line.

from 43 Little Pieces And Studies for Piano

STUDY No. 36

BELA BARTOK
(1881-1945)

Sparking Your Scales

BY ROBERT DUMM

"This procedure will have you skimming your scales like greased lightning!"

Many pianists with a good knowledge of scale fingerings can manage smooth scales at ♩ = 76 (♫ 's to-the-beat), or even at ♩ = 96, but at a Classical *Allegro* of ♫ = 112-116 the ♫ 's (and surely ♬ 's) will begin to bunch in groups with little gaps here and there. How can you increase the speed of your scales and still keep their smoothness? That is the question!

Experience shows the trouble to lie, not with the finger-groups, but with a single finger — the thumb. Many a well-meaning book or article on scale playing gives a detailed explanation of how the thumb is supposed to move, its tip gliding behind fingers 2 and 3 (as they play their scale tones), to be ready when it is needed.

Like all exterior descriptions of movement, this puts the cart before the horse. For, like all the fingers, the thumb moves *as part of* the hand, and the hand, of course, moves from the wrist. Both thumb and hand *depend* (*Latin*, "to hang down from") on the wrist, and their freedom of motion is a result of freedom in the movement of the wrist.

Tightness in the wrist, which can happen unconsciously when you are making the effort to play faster, can, literally, *lock* the thumb at its root, and render it, along with the whole hand, heavy and sluggish. That's because arm weight, without a "shock absorber" in the wrist, bears down into the keys. As for achieving speed in this condition . . . well, everyone knows you cannot run carrying baggage!

The surest way to lighten both hand *and* thumb, and to balance their weight for swift sideways skimming over the keys, is to pause and test for looseness in the wrist, thus maintaining its resilience. The following procedure is helpful. Begin by bouncing the hand on a repeated thumb-tone:

The dwindling dynamic lets your hand lighten while marking time, just as a boxer hopes to lighten his whole body by jumping rope. Now use those hand-bouncing upbeats to spurt you up a segment of the scale, thumb-to-thumb like this:

Notice, we didn't stop dead on the next thumb-tone of the scale, but let it continue bouncing to a natural rest point.

Now recommence your upbeat hand-bounces on *that* thumb-tone to trigger (at *) the next quick spurt of four-scale tones, ending on the *next* thumb tone (with its afterbeats).

Continue this work, one hand at a time, mm = 76 (the right hand goes *up* the keyboard, while the left goes *down*).

You might work back in *two* different ways. At first, move from thumb-tone to thumb-tone:

The *next* time you return to keyboard center, bounce your hand on the other fingers as well: 3's, then later, 4's, like this:

This plants the weight on fingers other than the thumb, a sure way to lighten the thumb. By repeatedly "shaking out" the thumb from its root in the wrist, you can free it to swing as a whole. This is a freedom many pianists never know.

Don't worry about accenting the thumb — something your first teacher rated worse than sin. By minimalizing its action through a *decrescendo* during the upbeats, you can control the thumb to accent only the *first* of each note-spurt.

Be patient, and practice *rhythmically*. The quickness you already achieve for short spurts of three and four notes will soon add up to an octave streak. You can fill out your octave by adding a note-at-a-time to your "streak":

An octave is already far to go on a single thumb "spark." Stick to it. This procedure will have you skimming the scale like greased lightning! ■

Robert Dumm was named Dean of the Boston Conservatory when he was only twenty-five, and became a critic for The Christian Science Monitor *a year later. He served fifteen years as head of graduate Piano Pedagogy at The Catholic University before retiring in 1979. In 1983, Mr. Dumm was awarded the highest certification—Master Teacher—by The Music Teachers National Association.*

The Secret Life Of Dots And Slurs

Part I

By Seymour Bernstein

Seymour Bernstein

Distinguished pianist, teacher, composer and author Seymour Bernstein is an ASCAP award winner. His book, "With Your Own Two Hands," and his video lesson, "You And The Piano," are both available from Hal Leonard Publications, Milwaukee, WI.

All of us know the rewards of feeding good information into our "automatic pilot." And we know, too, that misinformation of a musical or technical nature results in wasteful practicing that may take years to re-program. As an example, I was taught from early childhood on that this (•), and this (▼) always indicate shortness of sound. By the time I was sufficiently advanced to play the following example, I responded to all of the staccatos seemingly without thought: I pulled away from the notes so marked as though they were "hot":

BEETHOVEN: Sonata, Op. 13 (Pathétique), first movement (the pedal indications are mine)

That they were difficult to execute at a fast tempo was, I reasoned, my own problem; Beethoven's markings were sacrosanct, and obeying them was a matter of conscience.

I practiced, and practiced, and, if anything, I merely became more and more tense.

Subsequently, however, I learned that dots and wedges from early classical music through to the romantic period may also indicate *accents*. Whether or not they do depends primarily upon the context in which they appear. Two things in particular influence our decision: the testimony of the musical ear, and technical comfort. While it is true that most composers place musical content above technical ease, still, from the performer's viewpoint, physical awkwardness adversely affects musical intentions.

Accordingly, there is a musical and technical basis for interpreting the dots in the Beethoven example as accents.

> *"Dots and wedges from early classical music may indicate accents; two things influence that decision."*

Musically speaking, the dots outline structural melodies in both the treble and the bass. Moving in contrary motion, these melodies stand apart from the turbulent eighth notes which surround them.

Used frequently in all periods of music, this compositional technique in which an independent melodic line is extracted from a single voice is known as a *polyphonic melody*. Occasionally, composers indicate them with double stems:

BACH: Prelude, from Prelude and Fugue in *D* Major, Bk. 1, measure 32.

But when polyphonic melodies are not indicated, we are free to create them ourselves. Thus, from a series of sixteenth notes,

BACH: Prelude, from Prelude and Fugue in *C* Minor, Bk. 1, measures 1-3

we may create quarter-note polyphonic melodies in the treble and bass.

In accompanying figures, such as the following bass line in eighth notes,

MOZART: Sonata in *G* Major, K. 283, first movement

we may create dotted quarters on each downbeat. By so doing, we need no longer cope with complicated pedalings; and, in fact, we can dispense with the pedal entirely for measures 1-4. Holding bass notes in Mozart, and other composers as well, is perfectly acceptable. Do not feel guilty about it; as the following example proves, I don't!

As a young student, my constant desire to hold bass notes in alberti and broken chord figures stemmed from musical instinct alone. Later, however, I noticed that composers, more especially in their chamber music works, actually double the bass notes of the piano part by assigning prolonged bass notes of the same pitch to the cello. See below measures 231-234 from the first movement of the Quartet in G Minor, K. 478 by Mozart:

I have already mentioned the technical basis for deciding to play accents instead of staccatos in the first example — namely, the fast tempo militates against playing staccato. Besides, if one pedals at the half bar, playing staccato is superfluous.*

In spite of all the reasons I have given for playing the staccatos as accents, still, many pianists take the staccatos literally. In the next example, however, pianists generally agree that the staccatos appearing every four notes indeed indicate slight accents:

BEETHOVEN: Sonata in *A* Flat, Op. 110, first movement, measures 12-13

The effect is of a shimmering cascade of sounds which the late pianist Sir Clifford Curzon, so fond of metaphors, used to refer to as "stardust." As though influenced by Beethoven, other composers such as Schumann, also used staccatos to indicate accents and polyphonic melodies:

SCHUMANN: Sonata in *G* Minor, Op. 22, first movement, 2nd ending of exposition

(In all such passages where there is a moving voice against a stationary one, there is a tendency to neglect the repeated note. In the above example, be sure to rotate fully toward the right (pronation) for each B♮, and then, of course, back toward the left (supination) for each note of the polyphonic melody. This rotational twisting of the forearm, always initiated by the fingers themselves, inhibits involuntary contractions of forearm muscles — those nasty cramps which may lead to tendonitis.) ∎

to be continued . . .

---

*A word about the *crescendo* in this example: crescendo usually induces a heightened emotional response, and with it, an increased flow of adrenaline. Hence, we tend to play too loud too soon (the opposite obtains when we see the word *diminuendo*). This, coupled with the fact that our left hand tends to overpower the right, requires the following strategy — one that is helpful in controlling all *crescendos:* 1) Assume that a crescendo begins half way through a passage. 2) Always initiate crescendos with the right hand alone. 3) Finally, add the left hand crescendo near the end of the passage. In almost all passages marked crescendo, the pitches, registers and rhythms have an intrinsic excitement all of their own. As Ex. 1 proves, the rising polyphonic melody, the descending bass in contrary motion to the treble and the turbulent eighth notes — all create the illusion of a crescendo, even without our playing each note successively louder. Thus, the word *crescendo* means to begin a passage *piano;* while the word *diminuendo* means to begin *forte.*

Continued next page

The Secret Life Of Dots And Slurs

Part II

By Seymour Bernstein

The Riddle of the Wedge

Perhaps no musical symbol causes more confusion than the wedge, or dash. That they mean staccato and piano in the following passage seems clear enough:

MOZART: Sonata in *G* Major, K. 283, first movement, measures 31-33

And, in the next example, that Mozart uses dots and wedges to distinguish a light, finger staccato in measure 77, from a slightly heavier arm staccato (poco marcato) in measure 78, seems probable indeed:

MOZART: Sonata in *C* Major, K. 309, third movement

If dots and wedges imply finger versus arm touches, how then are we to interpret the right hand thirds in the next example?

MOZART: Sonata in *G* Major, K. 283, first movement

No light finger touch here. The thirds in measure 63 seem far more comfortable when they are played with a combination of 1) fingers sliding along the surface of the keys toward the palm, and 2) a gentle upper-arm-roll for each third (the wrist will undulate up-down for each third). Perhaps Mozart, by placing wedges on the upbeat D's in measure 62 and dots in measure 63 is graphically demonstrating a musical truth — that music is often far more expressive when upbeats are louder than downbeats.

But wait: one look at the next example and we realize that we are far from solving the riddle of wedges in Mozart:

MOZART: Sonata in *G* Major, K. 283, second movement

Previously, we assumed that wedges indicated a slightly louder sound; but now our assumption is proved false by the *subito piano* on E. At this point, all is confusion, and we wonder what,

---

"Perhaps no musical symbol causes more confusion than the wedge."

---

in fact, a wedge really means. Moreover, we have not even considered the duration of notes marked with wedges.

Interestingly, Beethoven himself sheds some light on the duration of dots and wedges. While scrupulously correcting the orchestral parts of his *A* Major Symphony, he made it clear to his copyist that the dots:

are to be replaced with wedges:

(Considering Beethoven's stormy relationships with his copyists, we can only imagine the abrasive language which must have accompanied these corrections!) Moreover, in August, 1825, Beethoven wrote to his friend Karl Holtz about another editorial matter concerning his *A Minor Quartet*. Here, he insisted that, "(♪ ♪ ♪), and (♪ ♪ ♪) are not a matter of indifference!" (Gustave Nottebohm, *Beethoveniana*, Leip-

---

"As far as I know, no publication has reproduced Beethoven's articulation signs faithfully."

---

zig and Winterthur, 1982, p. 109); the implication being that wedges are shorter than dots — a fact that his own pupil, Carl Czerny, pointed out in his writings on keyboard practices of the time. This being the case, what ever could Mozart have meant by placing wedges over tied whole notes in his Jupiter Symphony?

Making a Physical Connection to Notation

Quite obviously, Beethoven and Mozart, even with his wedges on tied whole notes, were on very safe ground. The confusion we experience today derives from the fact that the interpretation of articulation signs varied even within Mozart's short lifetime (1756-1791). As far as Beethoven was concerned, his articulation signs varied according to his musical responses: thus he notated more variations of staccatos than did any other composer of his time — simple dots, elongated dots and dashes of varying lengths. As far as I know, no edition has reproduced them faithfully. But then, how could they? For to this day, musicians still try to decipher what amounts to "ink spots" throughout Beethoven's manuscripts: are they dots, wedges or merely smudges? In fact, so confusing are wedges that C.P.E. Bach avoided them entirely and relied on dots alone, his chief reason being that his pupils confused them with the fingering numeral "1." Besides, Bach reasoned that it was up to the performer himself to vary the interpretation of dots according to note lengths, tempo and dynamics. (Carl Philipp Emanuel Bach: *Essay on the True Art of Playing Keyboard Instruments,* translated and edited by William J. Mitchell, N.Y., W. W. Norton, 1949, p. 154).

Beyond all of this, I like to think that there is a musical truth that transcends all notational devices. Discovering this truth requires a lifetime of thinking, experimenting and, above all,

having the courage to follow one's own instinctual responses to music. Feelings are one thing, of course, but expressing them on an instrument is quite another. To do this, we must learn to make a *physical connection to musical feeling*. In the language of movements and "muscles," the wedges in the second example from Mozart's Sonata in G above ought, in my opinion, to be depressed with an abundance of pressure derived both from the finger pads lying on the surface of each key, and the entire arm from the shoulder joint down to the fingertips — so much pressure, in fact, that a *noise element* is heard. Simultaneously, the right pedal goes *down* when the *E* is depressed, and *up* with its release. The noise element is the consequence of three distinct events related to the mechanism of the piano itself: 1) each key being "squeezed" into the key bed, 2) each key being released again, and 3) the dampers falling back onto the strings when the pedal is released. The result — a faint knocking sound; a "putt-putt." It is one of the few instances in piano playing when a percussive sound can be used to good advantage; when we can proudly join with singers and other instrumentalists in the art of inflecting sounds. Apart from this inflection, and a few others, pianists, alas, can only simulate those special musical effects which singers, and other instrumentalists, articulate quite naturally. As an example, delaying a high note and also playing it softer creates the illusion of a slide. But the inflection I have described — the "putt-putt" — is actual, and not just imagined.

Returning briefly to Ex. 8, the following dynamic scheme may suffice for expressing those enigmatic wedges in the Jupiter Symphony: *sfp*, or *fp*. Note: Speaking about *fp* — Schubert, whose piano works are, in essence, orchestral reductions (one might say the same of Beethoven) requires an inflection which, at first glance, seems quite impossible to achieve on the piano:

SCHUBERT: Sonata in *B* Flat, Opus Posthumous, fourth movement

Yet, the results of the step-by-step procedure which follows, would, I believe, make Schubert himself proud of us:

1) Play the *G* octave *mf*. Depress the notes down to the *key bed*. Keep the middle fingers of the left hand firm, pointing straight ahead and slightly toward the left. Try to hold them together — or, if separated, at least in a mold.

2) Simultaneously, depress the right pedal.

3) As soon as you hear the sound of the *G* octave, rebound the keys again — but only to the surface. Instantly, depress the octave *G* a second time, silently, but this time only slightly below the surface — to the *escapement level* of the keys.

4) Having done this, change the right pedal, *up-down*.

Changing the right pedal instantly reduces the *mf* to *piano*. Holding the octave *G* to the escapement level releases the dampers from the strings, thus assuring a continuance of the sound. ∎

Continued next page

The Secret Life Of Dots And Slurs

Part III

By Seymour Bernstein

Slurs

Like staccatos, slurs in music have an ambiguity all their own. Music and the notational means of expressing it are, as we know, subject to many interpretations. It is heartening, therefore (and somewhat of a relief) when all musicians agree to at least certain facts. Two of them concern slurs: one is that slurs, up to, and including, Mozart, always indicate *legato;* the other is that from Beethoven to the present day, slurs, besides meaning *legato,* may also indicate *phrases.* In other words, a slur came to mean one of the following: legato, a phrase, a phrase played legato, or a phrase with varied ar-

> *No rules exist requiring us always to take a "gulp of air" between slurs.*

ticulation, that is, notes that are marked either legato or staccato — all under one slur.

All slurred notes in Mozart are to be played legato — in one bow, so to speak. As a matter of fact, the slurs in Mozart and his contemporaries derive from bow indications for stringed instruments. And this brings up another question: Should the last note of one slur be connected to, or disconnected from, the first note of the next slur? On these points, opinions vary considerably. In other words, whether a singer should take a breath, a string player lift his bow, or a pianist his hand is more or less a question of taste. But one thing is certain: no rules exist requiring us *always* to take a "gulp of air" between slurs, or *always* to play the final note of slurs softer.

Returning once again to Mozart's sonata in G, K. 283, a separation between the upbeat *B,* and the downbeat *D* (and later between *F#* and *A*) would result in nothing more than a musical "hiccup":

Later, in measures 33-34, a separation between the two-note slurs seems far more appropriate:

Often, when playing a slow, cantabile melody, one choreographs two-note slurs by lifting the hand and "seaming" the juncture with the pedal:

MOZART: Sonata in *G* Major, K. 283, second movement (the pedal indications and dynamics are mine)

All of us wonder how to fill in that enigmatic space between slurs. Princely Mozart, as though anticipating our dilemma, occasionally makes the decision for us. Considering how

255

relatively few expression marks he wrote into his scores, we are amazed at, and also grateful for, the exquisite care he làvished upon silences:

MOZART: Sonata in *G* Major, K. 283, second movement

In fact, all of the notation in this Andante alone may be viewed as a sort of musicophilosophical treatise on the interpretation of articulation signs in early classical music. Seeing what Mozart himself has, or has not, written "between the notes," literally speaking, I infer the following (see the example below): 1) The two-note slurs in measure 9 are separated by rests; therefore, the two-note slurs in measure 11, to cite one example, are to be played legato. 2) Rests in Mozart are, with very few exceptions, sacrosanct. The 32nd note rests in measure 9 make the notes before them very short indeed (be careful not to accent them, however!); therefore, the wedges in measure 10 are *not* to be played with the same shortness. I personally use quick pedal insertions after these wedges so as to bind the fragments together (see below my pedal sug-

gestions for measure 10, and later, for measure 11):

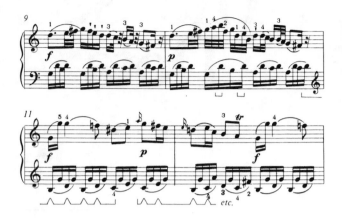

MOZART: Sonata in *G* Major, K. 283, second movement.

The Secret Life Of Dots And Slurs will conclude in the next issue of Keyboard Classics. *Readers with questions on this and related topics are invited to write to Mr. Bernstein c/o this magazine.*

■■■
■■■

The Secret Life of Dots And Slurs

Part IV

BY SEYMOUR BERNSTEIN

Diminuendos or Crescendos?

More often than not, we must draw upon our own musical instincts in determining whether or not to connect the final note of a slur or phrase. And just as often, we ourselves must determine the dynamics with which slurs and phrases end. While it is true that most slurs or phrases end softly, others want to swell in intensity. Clear notational indications are like gifts from the composers themselves. See, for instance, the first measures of the following examples:

BEETHOVEN: Bagatelle, Op. 119 No. 11

Frankly, I am puzzled at the vast number of musicians who are convinced that entrance to musical heaven requires two things in particular: *always* lift your hand at the end of a slur, and *always* play the final notes of slurs and phrases softer. Other conscience-stricken musicians consider it a musical sin to pedal through rests. With *Für Elise* fresh in our ear, let Beethoven himself settle this matter once and for all — not only for *Für Elise,* of course, but for all piano music up to the present day. To get right down to basics, pure musical feeling is often served best when a pianist lifts his hands and connects the sounds with the pedal:

Continued next page

SCHUMANN: Waldszenen (Forest Scenes), No. 2 — *Jager auf der Lauer* (Hunter in Ambush)

At other times, however, our musicality may dictate a crescendo which the composer did not notate. In the following example, I have taken the liberty of inserting one, my feeling being that a crescendo on the two-note slur in measure 25 lends greater direction and unity to this passage:

BEETHOVEN: Klavierstücke (Für Elise), WoO 59

These pedal indications are by Beethoven. The rests are exactly what they imply — the hands are lifted, and the sounds are connected by means of the pedal. The custom of placing (*) between all *Ped.* indications during the classical and romantic periods has created a great deal of confusion. The more contemporary practice of using brackets for pedaling is far more accurate. I am sure you will agree that the following pedal indications clarify Beethoven's intentions:

Turning to the romantic period, here is my favorite example of urtext pedal marks under rests — favorite, because I have often roused audiences to gales of laughter during my lectures on pedaling by demonstrating how the following passage would sound when one literally adheres to the rests in measure 5. Quite obviously, Chopin placed the pedal indication under the B Flats to give us time to

---

Our musicality may dictate a crescendo which the composer did not notate.

---

prepare the ii⁷ chord in a register far removed from the B Flats:

CHOPIN: Scherzo in B Flat Minor, Op. 31

While I have never heard any pianist play measure 5 without the pedal (for nothing would be funnier than an abrupt silence after the fortissimo B Flats), still, many pianists give far too little consideration to pedal indications under rests, and, for that matter, to pedaling in general.

In my opinion, the wedge in measure 9 above requires a special emphasis of sound by means of stretched fingers, an upper arm roll and a quick down-up insertion of the pedal. Play this chord slightly softer than the climactic one three measures earlier.

That slur marks began to signify phrases, and not only legato (bowing indications) is, I believe; very evident in the following examples:

SCHUMANN: Carnival, Op. 9

In the example above, lift the hands — rather "laboriously" — and connect the sounds with the pedal.

SCHUMANN: Phantasiestücke, *Grillen* (Whims), measures 16-20

In the above example, notice all of the subsidiary articulation symbols; a two-note slur in the left hand, measure 17, staccatos in both hands, measure 18, and finally, a separate slur with dots in the left hand, measure 19 — an indication for portato — half staccato. (The word portamento is often erroneously used. This indicates a manner of singing in which the voice glides, or slides from one pitch to the next.) Unquestionably, then, Schumann's long slur over all of this indicates a phrase.

We know, of course, that most of the great composers of the past were virtuosi of the keyboard. We can only imagine with what transcendental beauty they must have played. To achieve such a standard of performance, they must have choreographed everything, using more especially upper arm, forearm and wrist movements of all sorts. In the final analysis, then, no fact concerning slurs can be divorced from knowing how to implement them physically. To cite two examples — when playing a two-note slur, the wrist goes down-up; for a three-note slur, the wrist goes down on the first note and glides up for the second and third notes, and so on. (Wrist motions are far more controlled and also economical when they are initiated by the forward-backward movements of the upper arm.) To state the full truth — the entire body is engaged in the performance of even a single note.

Music has often been compared to language, especially in the case of phrases. Large and small musical phrases have their counterpart in whole sentences and adjectival or prepositional phrases, for example. Expressive communication in both music and language requires the exact dynamic, duration and inflection on each and every note or word, as the case may be. Notes and words thus group themselves together into larger ideas, with each idea having a directional point — a tone or a word that is louder or even softer than all the other notes or words in that idea. Occasionally, this directional point may occur during a silence — one that may be even more intense in feeling than sound itself.

Finally, when looking at a composition as a whole, an entire piece will move inexorably toward a directional note, harmony or silence, and then recede from it. How does one find that one decisive moment in a phrase and in a piece? Sometimes through instinct, but more often by pondering for years on end what that F Sharp ought to be doing in that phrase. Finally, when a decision seems as clear as the difference between a dot and a wedge, a musician may then change his mind.

If we are to assess what music really means, we must fortify our instinctual responses with a clear knowledge of musical notation — fact and fiction. As to misinformation, I have tried to say enough here to free everyone's conscience concerning the interpretation of dots and slurs, the premise being that a free conscience assures greater freedom of expression. And this, in turn, brings us closer to the music we are interpreting. ∎

Shake On It!

Repeated Notes
Part I

BY ROBERT DUMM

There are two ways to repeat a note using the same key: you may (1) vibrate the key with the *same* finger:

Verdi: The Anvil Chorus

or, you may repeat the key using a sequence of *changing* fingers:

Chopin: Valse Brilliante in Bb Major, Op. 18

and later on:

In either case, your hand weight must be counterbalanced somewhere farther up the arm, so that it does not jam the finger(s) acting on the key. First, sit tall and let your arms hang free from your shoulders. With your fingertips resting lightly ON the keys, open out your elbows a couple of times, like wings. Then let them drop sinkingly loose till they find a passive place to hang beside your body. Now, while your right arm is thus hanging, raise and lower your right wrist slightly (fingertips still touching the keys), till the hand finds its own balance-point, neither arched nor sunken, just a little lower than the line of your hand knuckles.

Now, let's try repeating a note with just *one* finger. Close your eyes. Keep that sense of readiness that accompanies the balance of hands and arms. It helps me to raise my wrist a little (without leaving the keys) as an upbeat "breath," before I drop it with the first note of each group (a little kick-off energy will carry through the note-group). After that (implied) drop, the wrist will rise naturally with the repeated notes:

Pause a moment. What actually happens as you keep the beat, yet increase the number of repetitions with each drop-wrist impulse? I sense a quivering action at two points: (1) in my finger tip, contacting the escapement point deep in the key action which nudges the hammer to quickly return to the string with no wasted motion of recovery or reset, and (2) in the vibration of my (rising) wrist. Experiment a little here, eyes closed, to feel these fine stirrings.

Trouble is more likely to come with long stretches of uninterrupted repeated notes, as here where a heaviness can come from the hand or fatigue of the small muscles.

Ravel: Alborada del Gracioso

The piano action may itself become sludgey with humidity, worn parts, or poor regulation at times.

I have found it better to acquire endurance not by repeated single notes, but by octaves. If you play a stretch of light octaves in both hands by accented groups, you will sense both the shaking in the wrist and the bobbling at the fingertips that produces the rapid repetitions of the piano hammers:

Step 1: Octaves, "Overland":

To be continued…

This column is dedicated to our reader, Robert Goodman, who asked the question that inspired this discussion (see Letters).

259

Shake On It!

Part II

By Robert Dumm

Here is a continuation of our series on repeated notes, begun last issue.

Step 2: Finger sequencing and finger repetition

For slowly repeated, *crescendo* repetitions use a heavy, "lazy" hand-drop, "rubbing" the keys with your finger tips as you play (as if to dissolve a stickiness):

The left hand plays alone, starting from C2, working up three octaves till it arrives at an accent on the C above Middle C:

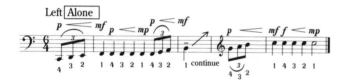

Step 3: Matching triplets

Now you are ready to play your repeated notes just as fast as the triplet pick-up which precedes them. "Shake" your hand into those pick-up notes, and drop it into the accented thumb (*). This drop causes the hand to rise for the softer repeated notes which follow. Continue each hand alone for three octaves to an accented C, with four beats of triplet repetitions—not a bad beginning, if you can do those without jamming!

Step 4: Hand "flipovers"

Now try these 4,3,2,1 sequences fairly fast. You'll flip the hand over onto finger 4, and thus prepare it for the next "act." When you get to the accented terminal C, round off with four beats of a brisk *crescendo* tattoo. (If that gets at all gummy, return to Step 3 pronto!)

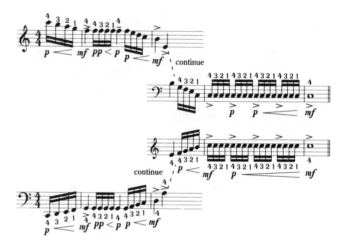

Even if you can perform Step 4 right off, I would stay with it for some time (weeks?), to harmonize your smooth drop-lift wrist action with the rhythmic recurrence of accents (Mf) followed by repetitions (p).

Step 5: Reprise Steps 3 & 4

Now proceed to play both steps 3 & 4 with BOTH hands, parallel motion down (then up) the keyboard. Watch the symmetrical fingerings, and follow the dynamics and accents closely: they synchronize your wrist action with the rhythm you hope to project—the rhythm, incidentally, that knits your hands in a single skill:

While you may play through Ravel's "Alborado" tomorrow, you are now certainly more light-handed, tip-conscious, and sensitive to the key action. You have sharpened your repetitions by grouping them between spaced stresses, and your hands play together at those stresses, which lightens them instantly for the "trick" of repetition. Nice going! ■

TECHNIQUE

A Fair Shake*
Some Steps to Better Trills

By Robert Dumm

Trilling is often considered to be purely finger action. When a trill sticks, lumps, or spasms to a stop, it seems logical to drill the offending fingers in a willful goose step until they *work*. At least, that seems to be the evidence of etude books past and present, which often dismisses the subject with some variant of this figure:

But so much is left unanswered. How many accents? Where? How fast? How do I speed up without tightening? It hints of gradual steps to be taken, but simply pictures an end result.

Such prescriptions ignore the rotary nature of trilling, and the *co*operation of fingers, hand, and arm. Musically, the trill should be a *thrill* in the melody. Its *vibrato* lies in the shift of energies, from one finger to another and back. We may begin trilling by oscillating each pair of fingers toward an accent. Try moving these shifts through the hand, out from the thumb and back again:

Once you have worked this figure through all the keys (at a moderate tempo), you can activate the trill-germ by a quick mordent after upbeats:

*Shake is the English word for trill.

261

"Musically, the trill should be a thrill in the melody."

And while you work, the cheerful tick of the metronome, set for the ♪, times your finger "spark." Do you recall paintings of Elizabethan girls at the virginals, their hands drooping from raised wrists, their fingers tapering whitely onto black keys? That is a picture of the arm balance and natural finger action a trill requires.

The arm hangs passively from the shoulder in an elbow "sling," while the hand dangles freely from a slightly raised wrist. The arm "slings" the hand over the note to be trilled, and the fingers, then, seem to "drop" the trilled notes, like dewdrops, from their tips. I spoke of "slinging" the arm into place to suggest its balanced weight; a passive, not a *dead* weight.

The trick is to minimize your finger "spark" so that the key is so lightly tapped that its instant rebound "springs" that finger free, ready for the next finger. To sense a near-weightless finger flick by contrast to a (hand)weighted touch, try this procedure:

While the "Trill" section of Hanon's *Virtuoso Pianist* is of the uninterrupted "drive-them-to-spasm" school, he does append two training routines by Mozart and Thalberg respectively. Both virtuosi instinctively sensed the need to deflect hand weight away from trilling fingers by changing fingers with strong beats:

Mozart's trill

Thalberg's trill

Continued next page

Hanon's real genius lies in an innocent skip between fingers one and two, which converts the static five-finger figure to a spiraling sequence through the changing shapes and sounds of the scales, freshening the ear while keeping the hand pliant and responsive to the continual changes of "real" music.

After Hanon, I would apply trilling figures to scales, such as:

First, work one of these jingles *through* a five-finger pattern. Then, apply it to one octave of a scale, *using the scale fingering:*

Now I hear you asking: "But, how do I get my trills *fast?*"
I might refer you to Gyorgy Sandor's stimulating new book *On Piano Playing* (Schirmer Books, 1981):

> It is best to start a trill at a moderate tempo with slightly articulated finger and forearm motions. The speed of the trill should be gradually accelerated while the player carefully guards against tension in the arm, hand, and fingers. (That's the rub!)

He even offers a reprieve:

> Trills need not be executed at a frantic pace; those that are played effortlessly at a moderate tempo are often completely satisfying.

Actually, the effect of "speed" in piano playing derives from *both* tempo *and* shape. As you work, then, gradually escalate the metronome for all the aforementioned exercises. But keep your accents! As your quick notes become lighter, your accents will become less forceful, but nonetheless piquant, like casting darts among hummingbirds. Step by step, increase the ratio of quick notes to accented "arrival" tones, but do not dispense with those "arrivals" too soon, in haste to work by "speed." You need them to discharge tension, spark the next spatter of trilled notes, and make "sense" by grouping sounds.

Robert Dumm was named Dean of the Boston Conservatory when he was only twenty-five, and became a critic for The Christian Science Monitor *a year later. He served fifteen years as head of graduate Piano Pedagogy at The Catholic University before retiring in 1979. Mr. Dumm is active as a teacher, contest judge, and writer on musical subjects.*

ETUDES

Etudes is a department which features technical exercises composed by masters throughout history.

Brahms used to take difficult passages in musical works, and practice them with accents on different notes. He gave much attention to the thumb, and to keeping a loose wrist. When he gave his students trilling exercises, he had them play in triplets and in groups of four, and demanded that they try a variety of accents in each phrase.

BRAHMS'S TRILLING EXERCISES

Continued next page

Taking Turns

By Robert Dumm

The TURN is one of the most melodic and flowing of all musical ornaments. Its sign is ∽ (sometimes ᘔ) but you will just as often meet it written into the melody as small notes. It "ornaments" its note by draping it with two neighbor-tones, either starting from the note *above*: or from the note *below*: . A well-played turn flashes its *first* note as the strong one: (when the turn falls on a strong beat, or strong part of the beat); or draws your attention to the note on the next beat (when the turn falls between beats) as Schubert clearly shows by his accent here:

Schubert: *Scherzo*, **B-Flat (D. 593) Allegretto**

Played:

Turns seem fundamental to Beethoven's improvisations:

Beethoven: *Rondo*, C, Op. 51, No. 1, opening

At (1) you have a turn around B, strictly speaking, though it rolls right into an unstressed C on beat 3. At (2) Beethoven's dotted C, triad outline, and separate slur suggest a five-note turn (which begins ON the main note) ending at the dot that lends panache to the triad:

At (3) an "inverted turn" (from below) plays in the passage work.

While earlier composers mostly thought of the turn as beginning on the upper note (the scale tone above the

printed note), accenting its grain of dissonance, you can see old J.S. Bach having regular flipflops with turns up *and* down in the Invention he devised to teach his son, Wilhelm Friedmann, how to play them best:

J.S. Bach: *Invention 14, B-flat*

Later composers liked to get their main note sounding before they did a flip around it. See Johann Strauss at work:

Fledermaus Waltz:

He announces the dance with two short twitter trills (at (1)), then begins the "turning" with a five-note turn-from-below: it's no wonder that the waltz derives from an old German word meaning "to churn" (turn) around. Thus magnified, the "turn" figure has a lilting swing-and-sway purely for the fun of it.

Chopin glories in turns, just as did his favorite operatic larks—Grisi, Rubio, Malibran—when they thrilled the Paris Opera with their highest solo flights. He begins his A-Flat *Valse* (Op. 69, No. 1) with a five-note turn (Bar 1) whose interval ghost can just be made out (notes with *'s) in bars 3 and 4:

Lento ♩ = 138

Some opuses later, Chopin spins his Fantasy Impromptu (Op. 66) from a light upbeat turn:

Continued next page

But later, Chopin uses turns to pivot the direction of the passionate midway melody: (*)

Reverse

Turns light up your piano songs as a lightning bug lights its tail while it keeps flying.

The following workout will lighten your turns to sparkling effect. The secret is to work briskly, and stress NOT the quicker notes, but the long note that follows them. TURNOVERS: Accent the *long* notes.

Now for versatile two-ways turns, vary that exercise like this:

The Missing Link
or How To Feel Triad Inversions

BY ROBERT DUMM

Apart from scales and their segments, chords make up a great deal of piano writing. We have all seen somewhere a chart showing how root-position triad chords are turned upside-down — "inverted" — so that what had been their bottom note is now the top note:

> "I have found the following workout very helpful in giving your fingers 'eyes in the dark.'"

Even if the bass remains absolutely static, as it does during the climactic middle of the same piece, you're not going to have any time at all to feel these triads beforehand; they've simply got to be *there, in* your right hand:

Same, Bars 72-75:

Root   "Root position"   1st inversion   2nd inversion   "Root position" again

It is one thing to understand that process in your mind, and quite another to work the feel of those three shapes into your hands and fingers. Consider how often you meet an accompaniment like this:

That was a fairly standard spill of inversions compared with this little chord sign-off, (*) marked *Presto*, that Beethoven wants dashed off with a flare. It has been the toe-stumper for many a fine pianist.

Czardas by V. Monti (arranged by Gustav Saenger)

Con pedale

Beethoven, *Bagatelle*, Op. 126, No. 6

Even though the *largo* tempo gives you time enough to cover those left hand inversions, you may be "all thumbs" when it comes to finding the correct finger(s) for the second note of the second chord (at *).

Schubert: *Impromptu*, A Flat Major, Op. 142, No. 2:

The placement of the hands becomes difficult as chords change voices, moving *away from* a moving bass (*).

You must have all the inversions of all the common chords *in your hands,* as muscle memory, as well as in your minds. I have found the following workout, where the hands play symmetrically (using the *same* fingers at once, working out-then-back to a central rest position) to be very helpful in giving your fingers "eyes in the dark."

1. Prep-step

(*) *It is your second or "pointer" finger that helps you feel your way from one position to the next.*

Continued next page

First, the "Prep Step" of 1,2, 1,2 ONLY with 1 crossing smoothly under 2 and back. Let your thumb tip touch the back of 2 as it slides to the third note and back to the first again. That smooth cooperation of only two fingers at their tips will not only raise and lighten your hands, sensitizing your sense of touch at that point, but will act as a smooth "conveyor belt" that will carry your hand TO (and not beyond) the next position of the triad.

Work through all the white keys first. When you come to keys where the thumb must ride up and over a black key, say, D Major, simply lift the wrist at that point (thumb on F# in D Major), which lets the thumb simply fall vertically into place.

Try it. Experiment with the smooth-running of this quiet "conveyor" action of 1 with 2 a long and loving time before you attempt step two, playing a broken triad inversion each time you reach thumbs on that two-handed "conveyor belt."

Keep this a *two-handed* work-out, for one hand will learn from the other. And note how naturally *both* hands choose 1,2,5,2 in the *second* position, that necessary fingering that is so confusing to learn when you play triad hands parallel motion. Just tell yourself: "Second position has 2 (in the middle). All the rest have 3 (in the middle)." You will be surprised how this little triad tune will jingle you into fluency in rippling chords up and down the keyboard. ■

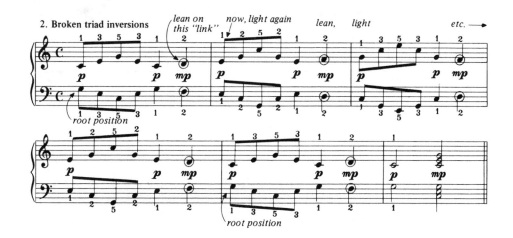

TECHNIQUE

"Palm Springs"

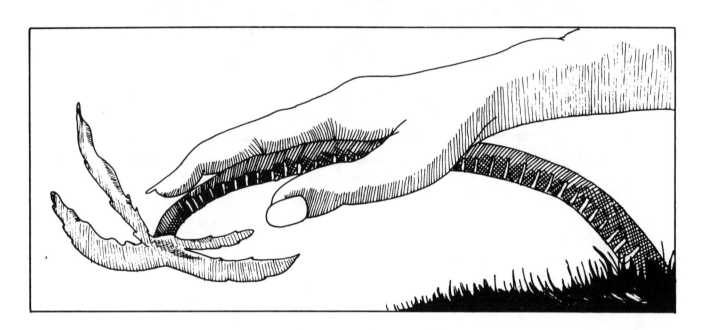

"A ringing tone quality depends upon the invisible spring action of the palm."

 ichelangelo, who was as much a sculptor as a painter, often spoke of "the hand that obeys the intellect." For a pianist, too, it is the vital animated hand that portrays his musical ideas. We have all heard chords crashed or thumped from the keys with what, I am sure, the pianist *thought* to be an impressive sound. Chances are, however, the player was aiming a fixed hand at those chords—what I call a "cookie-cutter" hand.

It is the touch of an *active* pliant hand—with "springs" deep inside its palm—that rings the strings clear as a bell, and produces the grand sound we expect of a piano.

To assure this quick flex inside the hand at the instant it touches the keys, we must (1) remain supple at the wrist, and (2) sense everything we play, from chords to single tones, as "springing" from deep inside our palms. This spring of the hand's action lies in its "hinges," the small muscles underneath the hand knuckles. The need for minute, almost instantaneous action of the hinge is what kept your patient childhood teacher telling you to "raise your arch" and "curve your fingers" (they jiggle more easily when hanging freely from the hand knuckle).

To locate and feel the action of your hand hinge, place both hands flat down on a tabletop. Then flex your palms without moving your flattened fingers, mentally saying "open," then "close," as if an overturned turtle was lying there, gasping for air. But *your* "turtle" is right side up, ready to crawl. Slowly *draw* your fingertips toward the centers of your palms, letting your flattened fingers skid across the surface. Keep skidding until your hand-knuckle rises high enough to show "snow on the mountains"—the

270

Continued next page

"We have all heard chords crashed or thumped from the keys with what the pianist *thought* to be an impressive sound."

cartilage of those knuckles showing white under the skin.

This daily exercise will give your hands a more lasting flexibility:

And the next exercise serves the same purpose for smaller hands:

For more advanced players, you can preserve flexibility during wider expansions of the hand with:

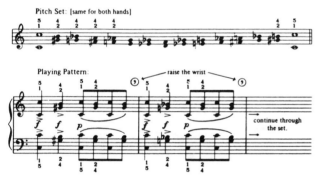

The alternation between the repeated, unchanging octave, with slowly shifting inner notes (the "windshield wiper") effectively massages the hand free of its tension. BUT! Be SURE to lift the wrist high at the end of each measure, just before you drop into each stressed octave, so that the falling arm weight will naturally "dip" your wrist down-and-up, like a young girl's quick curtsy before the queen. The lift-off lets the wrist "breathe" before again "diving" into the keys.

Next, this exercise has your arms reaching from center to both ends of the keyboard. Let their weight, dropping into each octave, cause the wrist to dip-rise more noticeably, like two rubber shock absorbers.

Never think of hand- and finger-action apart from the arms and body. When the body is poised and ready, the shoulders, elbows, wrists, should *all* jiggle like a line of "shock absorbers" at the impact of fingers on the keybeds, or there will be no spring-rebound from that point. In fact, the whole body, sitting tall and poised, often comes into piano play. The impulse for the following FF chords comes from thighs and abdomen: it is similar to the feeling a good jockey gets as he urges his horse over a fence:

Chopin: *Prelude*, C minor, Opus 28, no. 20:

Bodily poise includes letting the arms hang loosely down from the shoulder. "Elbows like lead, wrist like feather," said the late Ludwig Deppe to his students. Tall, lanky pianists (apart from sitting far enough back to make their arms a gently slanting "bridge" to the keys) may just want to "open their wings"—a slight, outward elbow flexion at the thought of the sound.

While the power of these chords comes from weight and energy, their ringing tone quality depends upon the invisible spring action of the palm hinges *at the instant of contact with the keys.* Those "hand springs" are the last, the final tuning of multiple energies rolling down the arm.

Carl Philipp Emmanuel Bach reports that his father, Johann Sebastian, would place his hands ready on the keys, fingertips in a line:

"The impulse thus given the keys, or the quantity of pressure, must be maintained in equal strength, and that in such a manner that the finger be not raised perpendicularly from the key, but that it glide off the forepart of the key, by gradually drawing back the tip of the finger towards the palm of the hand."

Was Bach—nearly three hundred years ago—not inviting us to "palm springs"? ■

RD

Robert Dumm was named Dean of the Boston Conservatory when he was only twenty-five, and became a critic for The Christian Science Monitor *a year later. He served fifteen years as head of graduate Piano Pedagogy at The Catholic University before retiring in 1979. In 1983, Mr. Dumm was awarded the highest certification—Master Teacher—by The Music Teachers National Association.*

Finger Fitness
with Robert Dumm
"Skids" And "Brakes"

When we run, we usually run *to* something: to the finish line, the goal post, or the store before it closes. So in piano music, "runs" mean action, and they usually take you to a special spot, a note that is important, such as this C:

You run best when you are lightly dressed, and not carrying any weight which loads you down. The same is true in music; your "running" notes are often lighter, played by fingers alone, and your "goal" tones are heavier, played with some hand weight added to the fingers, as if to say: "Home at last!"

Try this little tune, which "runs" toward its goal, but doesn't want to stop, so it carries through to further, smaller goals (*).

If you have just a little farther to run, or, say, up a small hill, you sometimes make a "running start." Let's add to our run, in order to carry around-the-bend one extra note, like this:

After that becomes easy, how about *another* extra note?

Now run all the way around to your starting point, like a boomerang. Keep your hand and wrist loose for those "get-set" upbeats!

Good for you! You made it in one "home run" because you knew your goal, lightened your hand, then really "arrived" with an *accent* on the goal.

It is by similar patient, repeated practicing of notes *by groups* that you will be able to increase your speed while keeping your playing crystal clear.

Chopin's Tricky Filigree

By Robert Dumm

For every song there is a dance. Think of it: Prelude and Fugue, Introduction and Allegro, etc. Emotion pent up explodes into activity.

It often seems the "song" must soar in wild abandon, to burn away its accumulated feeling before it settles down to "dance." Two such examples concern one of our readers, Henry J. Altmeppen, of Bakersfield, CA; the first occurs in a Chopin Nocturne, the second in a piece by Liszt.

"I would like to be able to include Chopin's *Nocturne* in E-Flat, Op. 9, No. 2 in my repertoire," he writes, "but I keep tripping up on that run at the end. Everything is fine when I play it slowly, but as soon as I bring it up to speed my fingers become stymied and the whole passage falls apart." (See the example at right.)

Chopin: *Nocturne,* E-Flat, Op. 9, No. 2, end

At this point in the piece, Chopin's "song" drives in impassioned fervor into B-Flat (at the ⌒ , marked *a,*), the dominant of the key, which then quivers or vibrates a dozen groups of fours before "falling" to E-Flat, the tonic or keynote tone, in the next-to-last bar *(b)*. This passage is not an interpolated *cadenza* — something added — but a *part* of the melodic line. It derives its expressive power not by how loudly or brightly you can play it, but by how it arrests that important B-Flat — insists upon it — till B-Flat "yields" in a melting *cadence* (Latin for "falling") towards E-Flat. In practice, always approach the tremolos from before, to establish the big "soundwave" out of which the tremolo emerges *(c)*.

A computer can tell you how many different ways four notes may be practiced, but it's not a computer that's playing. Human hands like to rest on their thumbs, so it is with the thumb (not the initial C-Flats) that I would begin practicing the groups:

Now work Chopin's pattern in two complementary ways:

Then simplify each figure by small rotary "flicks" of the hand from 1 to 4, then 4 back to 1. The important thing is to leave the thumb hanging *free* after each flick, or to shake it free by a slight lift of the wrist (still touching the key) just before beginning each group, then letting it drop into the starting note. These wrist-breathers are each marked with a ✍:

Consciously "let go" between each group. Then think "Ready!" (hand lightly poised in place) before you let yourself play the next group. That "let" is important; most people automatically go on and on, to the point of pure spasm. It is by establishing this habit of taking "cat-naps" between each group that will keep your fingers from getting "stymied." Above all, drop the idea: "I *will* conquer this place!" (a sure way to adrenalin wipeout), and replace it with the thought: "This is the part that just 'plays itself.'"

Taking care to thus space each note-group, you might now try some time-honored "add-a-note" practice, still starting

273

each group *from the thumb:*

Till you can play through *two* groups on a single impulse:

Next, try for *three* groups at a time, not hesitating to return to *two* if you can't remain loose. Be patient. What if playing three-at-a-time takes you a few days, a week, or more? One day you will find your vibrations spilling into the *thirteenth*

group. But don't let it continue aimlessly. Take it only this far:

Next time: Solving the Liszt dilemma! ■

Robert Dumm was named Dean of the Boston Conservatory when he was only twenty-five, and became a critic for The Christian Science Monitor *a year later. He served fifteen years as head of graduate Piano Pedagogy at The Catholic University before retiring in 1979. In 1983, Mr. Dumm was awarded the highest certification — Master Teacher — by The Music Teachers National Association. He teaches privately in the Rockville, Maryland area, outside of Washington, D.C.*

Liszt's High Flights

"These are famous trouble spots . . ."

BY ROBERT DUMM

Reader Henry J. Altmeppen of Bakersfield, California, asked for help in mastering two passages in Liszt's *Liebestraum*. These are famous trouble spots, but we'll do our best to help.

The first high flight of Liszt's *Liebestraum* functions like a cadenza in a concerto. It erupts after a sighing break in the melody, and punctuates the stanza just ended, preparing the listener for a fresh start at the *più animato*. It should affect us as a gust of wind from the open window that nearly blows the candle out.

Structural tension spanning from the E♭ bass at (a) to the B at (b) (not the expected tonic A-Flat) not only supports the shower of small notes, but plants us with unexpected freshness in the key of B, arrived at by ascending the whole-tone scale, Liszt's favorite "stairway to the stars":

Liszt: *Liebestraum,* the first 'cadenza'

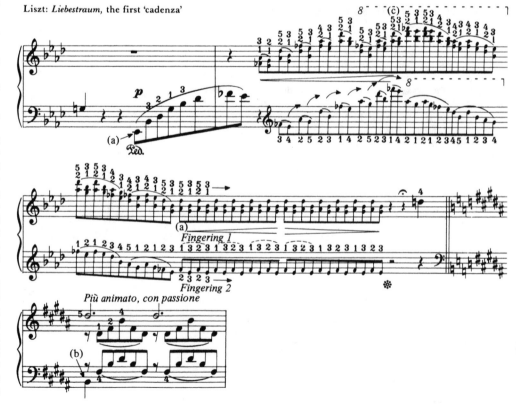

274

Continued next page

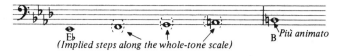

(Implied steps along the whole-tone scale)

So first establish that E-Flat sound by warmly rolling the bass at (a), not too quickly, before you tackle the smaller notes.

When you do practice the smaller notes, take the left hand *first,* to confirm the continuity of its long line — sweeping as an ocean breeze. I have indicated a new fingering that will keep your hand moving in *one* direction, though I know how hard it is to reprogram the synapses to a new finger-route! Feel a little lift, or upward "boost" with each note pair marked:

Now take the right hand in two-note groups that pause like this:

At the dotted white notes, place your hands silently over the next notes, loosely poised to play, then play the actual written notes.

Let the left hand join into this practice, pair by pair. When you arrive at the top, turn-around tone of this ascent (and Liszt's first slur marking) (c), think in terms of this little grouping for a smooth "skater's turn":

For the descent, lean into the left hand line with the given fingering.

There are many ways to perform the final triple tremolo that begins at (d), all the way to a shimmering virtuosity. I suggest you choose either fingering (1), for a pulsing undercurrent of the tremolo, or fingering (2), for the smoothly vibrant effect of a single "hovering" harmony. I prefer the former, since it hints at passion continuing beneath the smooth sound surface.

The second cadenza of *Liebestraum* deserves a lesson in itself, since it is a rapid scale in chromatic broken thirds (see the example to the right).

I recommend the fingering given here, by Rafael Joseffy, a student of Liszt's. Take the thirds together at first, like this:

The second 'cadenza'

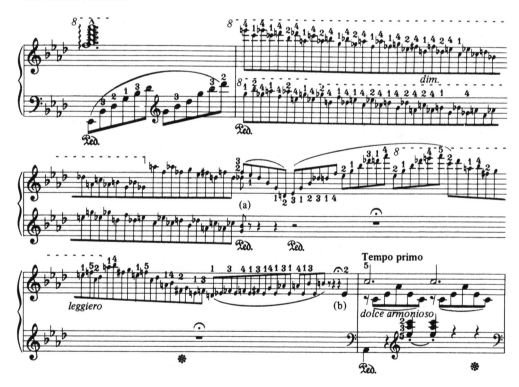

favoring the *upper* voice in the right hand, all the way to the chords at (a), where the left hand ceases. But continue the right in unbroken solo past that point, to the pause at (b).

Try for a light spinning-out of a single line, dazzled into silence. Then refine your chromatic thirds by taking them broken as written, with a slight stress on the after-notes:

Robert Dumm was named Dean of the Boston Conservatory when he was only twenty-five, and became a critic for The Christian Science Monitor *a year later. He served fifteen years as head of graduate Piano Pedagogy at The Catholic University before retiring in 1979. In 1983, Mr. Dumm was awarded the highest certification — Master Teacher — by The Music Teachers National Association. He teaches privately in the Rockville, Maryland area, outside of Washington, D.C.*

Technique

The "Howl," The "Cloud" And Other Super Pedals

BY ROBERT DUMM

Let's look at an impressionistic effect I call the "howl" or "wind" pedal, which is often (lightly) applied *during* a rapid run (not at its beginning or end):

Beethoven: "Fuer Elise"

Debussy's piano music is perhaps where you most often need a light ("surface") pedal color, held throughout each musical shape. Debussy also asks for a "cloud pedal" when he writes long bass tones impossible to hold by hands busy elsewhere, as here:

Debussy: "Clair de Lune"

It is the *damper* pedal, lightly held (the "surface pedal") that Debussy intends everywhere, for he neither had nor wanted the *sostenuto pedal* (the middle one); its selective spotlight of a single bass tone (or tones) was unsympathetic to his intention of having columns of overtones seemingly rise — directly *from* the bass.

Debussy's pianistic "grandfather," Chopin, is often well served by a light spray of pedal "mist":

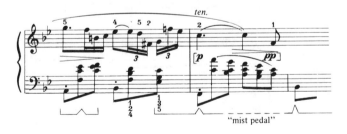

Chopin: "Cantabile" (1834)

All these are ways to group sound into shapes, as is the bold result of the "overlap pedal" *(legatissimo pedal)*. In this case, you apply a deep pedal and hold it *through* both the first and part of the second sound, clearing it while you still hold on to that second sound:

Mendelssohn: "Wedding March"

276

Continued next page

By far the most common use of the foot working WITH the hand is the straightforward *"Rhythm Pedal."* What would you just naturally do here if no one had told you a thing about pedaling? Sure enough — you'd "keep time":

Scott Joplin: "The Entertainer"

That regular injection of pedal sound lends buoyant energy to the bass downbeat, while releasing the pedal with the second beat gives it an added "life":

Beethoven-Busoni: "Ecossaises"

And if in a dance, the harmony allows you to prolong your "rhythm pedal" a little longer, the natural dip-rise of dancing becomes that much more joyous and free:

Johann Strauss, Jr.: "The Beautiful Blue Danube"

Nor does the pedal-energized rhythmic stress have to fall always on the downbeat:

Schubert: "Impromptu in A-Flat," Opus 142, No. 2

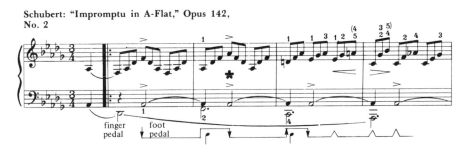

But notice how Schubert never fails to support his dancers. He gives his bass downbeat a "finger pedal" holding three beats, which suggests you should stress it *somewhat,* to carry it through the bar (and give the offbeat accent something to react to).

One word of caution! Never let your "rhythm pedal" degenerate to a mechanical pump that stresses every downbeat to the same degree. Music — and especially, dance music — groups itself several bars to the phrase: musically "strong" bars alternate with one or more "weak" bars, which, so to speak, get a "free ride" from the impulse of the "strong" bar. For example, Chopin's "Minute" *Valse* goes a long way before making even a slight "touchdown" to earth (*). It would never do to "ground" it with too much bass baggage! ∎

Chopin: "Valse in D-Flat Major," Opus 64, No. 1

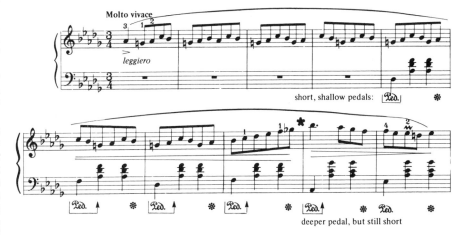

Robert Dumm was named Dean of the Boston Conservatory when he was only twenty-five, and became a critic for The Christian Science Monitor *a year later. He served fifteen years as head of graduate Piano Pedagogy at* The Catholic University *before retiring in 1979. In 1983, Mr. Dumm was awarded the highest certification — Master Teacher — by* The Music Teachers National Association.

Section 9
TECHNIQUE SESSION (Part 2)
Pop/Jazz Skills & Studies for the Keyboard

FINGERING

Good fingering is simply one that "works" for you, letting you play with as much ease and comfort as possible.

The "right" fingering can help you sound like a pro, but the "wrong" fingering may cause you to miss notes and sound less than your best. Finding the "right" fingering requires a little thought and some experimentation but, in the end, it will pay off.

Good fingering is simply one that "works" for you, letting you play with as much ease and comfort as possible. Most importantly, it is one that lets the music come through.

Look at your hands. They are different from anyone else's. Most people, however, have three longer fingers (2, 3 and 4) and two shorter ones (1, always the thumb, and 5). The short fingers fit most comfortably on the longest keys (the white keys) while the longest fingers fit easily on the shortest keys (the black keys). You can see this by placing the thumb of your right hand on an E anywhere on the keyboard, and placing your fifth finger on B. The three longest fingers (2, 3, and 4) fit over F#, G#, and A#.

This is the most natural position of the hand on the keyboard and probably the one that is most comfortable for you. From this demonstration we can form a rule of fingering. *RULE: If you can, avoid placing the 1st or 5th finger on a black key.*

The next thing to realize about fingering is that all fingering consists of groups — usually five finger positions. Here are several examples from last issue's music.

Groups like the following, which most often have more than five notes, can be connected by "turning under" your thumb, as in this example from *Nagasaki:*

Nagasaki – M. Dixon & H. Warren

When you are choosing a fingering you need to decide where the best spots are for "turning under" the thumb. This is usually done after a black key, as in the preceding example, and in this one from *Skylark:*

Skylark – J. Mercer & H. Carmicheal

RULE: You can usually turn the thumb under after one of your other fingers has struck a black key.

Scales are one of the best ways to study fingering because they combine so many different problems and techniques. Scale fingering is a combination of two finger-groups (1, 2, 3, and 1, 2, 3, 4) connected by turning the thumb under:

Even a scale which begins on a black key has the same two finger-groups. However, the scale begins on an incomplete group:

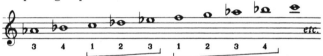

The four-note group is F G A B and the three-note group is C D E. This incomplete group at the beginning of the scale points up the fact that finger groups are often quite different from rhythmic groups. Look at this example from *Autumn Nocturne.* The finger group begins on the second sixteenth note while the rhythmic group begins on the beat:

Autumn Nocturne – K. Gannon & J. Myrow

Be careful not to let the rhythm force you into using an uncomfortable fingering, such as beginning with the thumb on a black key.

A useful trick to know is the "slide." You may sometimes need to move from a black key to a white key with the thumb or fifth finger. Simply slide that finger from one note to the next, as in this example:

These techniques are all for single note passages and runs. A future article will deal with chords, octaves, and repeated notes. By keeping these principles in mind you can find a fingering that is "right" for you.

Portions of music from Nagasaki, Skylark and Autumn Nocturne used by permission of Warner Bros. Publications, Inc. **-DR**

Continued next page

FINGERING
PART II

Last month we discussed ways to find the "right" fingering for single-note passages, such as scales, runs, etc. If you experimented and are now familiar with those techniques you are probably ready to move on to the techniques required for fingering chords, arpeggios, octaves and repeated notes. Keep in mind that your hands are unique in shape and size. Because of this, a fingering which is perfect for you may not be right for someone else.

Fingering chords can be somewhat less confusing if you keep in mind that a chord is really a finger passage; the notes are simply sounded together, rather than separately. For example, you would use the same fingering for both:

and

When playing either a blocked or broken chord, many people wonder whether they should use the 3rd or 4th finger. A simple rule solves the problem:

If the chord has an interval of a 4th below the 5th finger (or in the left hand above the 5th finger) use the 3rd finger.

Example:

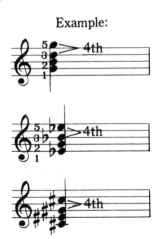

But: Use the 4th finger if the interval is a minor 3rd or smaller.

When the interval below the 5th finger is a major 3rd you can use either finger.

If you have a large hand with a wide palm and long fingers you may prefer the 4th finger but pianists with smaller hands may prefer the 3rd instead. Consider this example from *Winter Wonderland:*

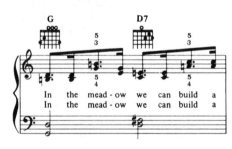

Play this passage once using the 3rd finger, and then play it again using the 4th finger. You should be able to decide easily which feels best for you.

The best fingering to use in the left hand of *Winter Wonderland* is easy to find if you play the notes first as a chord:

1st measure

3rd measure

Since many pieces have similar bass patterns you will find lots of places where this "trick" can be applied.

It seems obvious that octaves can best be played with fingers 1 and 5.

But, if you have a black-key octave followed by one with a white key you may find it easy to take the black-key octave with the 4th finger. Look at this passage in *Nagasaki:*

This fingering makes it possible, too, to make the top notes *legato.* People with large hands may even want to play some octave passages with the 3rd finger:

This fingering gives a perfect *legato* but is only for those lucky people with large hands.

Groups of repeated notes played at a quick tempo are usually easier to play if you change fingers with each note:

This fingering makes it easier to control the rhythm and tone quality of the notes. However, at a slow tempo — or when a passage has fewer repeating notes, it might be easier to use the same finger for each note:

Adding these principles to your arsenal of piano techniques will improve your playing and take you closer to your goal of becoming the best pianist you can be.

-DR

FINGERING

PART III

When deciding on a fingering, a good "rule-of-thumb," so to speak, is to let the size of the intervals between two notes determine which fingers you use. If the music has a 2nd, use two consecutive fingers, such as 1 and 2 or 4 and 5.

When the interval is a 3rd you might use 2 and 4 or 3 and 5.

If you have a 4th, 1 and 4, etc.

Look at this example from *Solace:*

Most pianists, whether they are near beginners or experienced professionals, have some difficulty with fingering when they are sight-reading a piece. Usually, you use whatever finger seems right at the moment so that you can keep going and form an idea about the music. However, the fingering you used to "get through" the piece the first time around may not be the best one. When you repeat the song, analyze the music and try to locate the finger groups — the spots where you can turn your thumb under, etc. Don't try to finger one note or chord at a time, but instead, look ahead to see what follows. Consider this example from *Forty-Five Minutes from Broadway*. On first glance, you might be tempted to begin with 1 and 3, but considering what follows you will see that 1 and 2 would be a better choice.

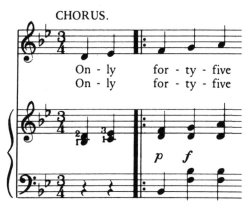

In this example from *The Wabash Cannonball* you would probably play the G₇ chord with 1-4-5 on the first glance. But if you look ahead even one beat you will see that 1-3-4 would have been a better choice. In short: PLAN AHEAD!

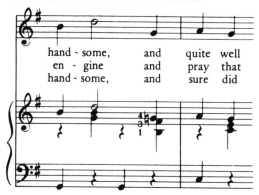

Many times the music suddenly changes direction leaving you on the thumb or second finger without a black key to use in order to turn under. The solution to this problem is to switch fingers. That is to play the note with one finger, and, while still holding it down, change to a different finger. Look at this example from *Just a Closer Walk With Thee*:

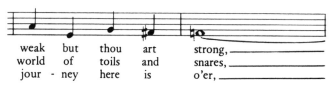

Teachers have been known to say in cases like this one—"Use the 25th finger, please."

When deciding on a fingering be sure to pick one that is right for the music. It might be easy to play:

But you can't achieve the *legato* that the song demands unless you use this fingering:

WILL THE CIRCLE BE UNBROKEN?

Many players say that they have difficulty remembering the fingering. You can work to overcome this problem if you remember that it isn't this or that finger that you have to remember but that you must think of groups of fingers. These groups should be associated in your mind with the "shape" of the notes on the keyboard and with their sound.

When you have formulated what seems like a good fingering, try it out at several different tempos to make certain that it "works." A good fingering for a slow tempo may not be as successful at a faster speed. Write the fingering that you have chosen in your music. Use a pencil, so that if you want to change it later on, the numbers can be easily erased. Above all, don't be afraid to change a fingering once you have written it down. After you have practiced a piece for a few days you may find a different fingering that "works" better. Don't forget: No fingering is ever wrong if it is comfortable for you to play and lets the music come through.

-DR

FINGER JAZZ
The Fun Way To Exercise Your Fingers!

Finger Jazz is a new *Sheet Music Magazine* feature which takes the boredom out of finger exercise, and teaches you jazz lines for improvisation too! This exercise, Study No. 1 in F, is based on what are commonly called "rhythm changes." The chord progression, or chord changes, are those found in the Gershwin song "I Got Rhythm." (And many other songs as well.) *Practice hint*: separate hands practice is strongly suggested, and when the right hand feels fairly comfortable, try playing the second half of the exercise, measures 9 through 16, looking at the bass clef line only. And remember, *speed isn't everything.* ■

Study No.1 In F

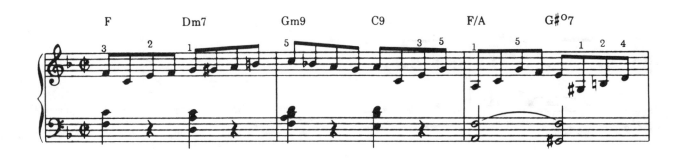

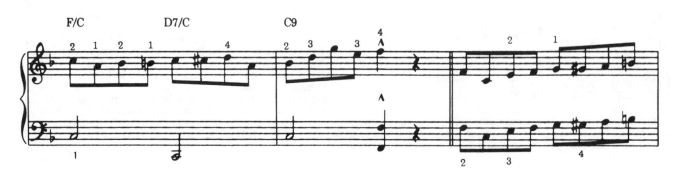

-ES

FINGER JAZZ
The Fun Way To Exercise Your Fingers!

Finger Jazz is a new *Sheet Music Magazine* feature which takes the boredom out of finger exercise, and teaches you jazz lines for improvisation too! This exercise is based on the chord progression, or chord changes, used by some jazz musicians in the Duke Ellington song "Satin Doll" (1st sixteen bars). *Practice hint*: separate hands practice is strongly suggested, and when the right hand feels fairly comfortable, try playing the second half of the exercise, the two hand-drill, looking at the bass clef line only. And remember, *speed isn't everything*.

Study No. 2 In C

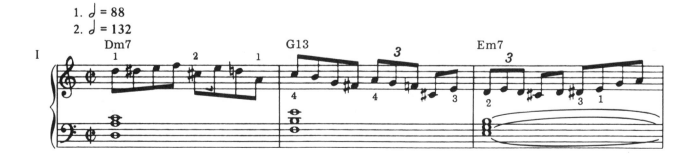

Continued next page

-ES

FINGER JAZZ
The Fun Way To Exercise Your Fingers!

Here's another installment in our continuing series of "Finger Jazz" exercises—a way to take the boredom out of finger studies, and learn jazz lines for improvisation at the same time! The first study below, in Bb, can be practiced hands separately. When both hands are up to performance speed, you can tack on the following final chord as a kind of coda:

The second finger study is a bit less contemporary in flavor—it fits in with a 1950's be-bop approach, as exemplified by the playing of Charlie "Bird" Parker. This time the hands don't play in strict unison; the second line finds them in harmonic counterpoint. Take your time with these. . .playing them slowly is the best way to get those finger joints well-oiled! 𝄐

-SI

ꝕoꝕ-ꝕiano

Jazzercises

Exercises are important for finger dexterity. While many find the practice of scales and Hanon to be drudgery, exercises taken directly from music we like to play can be fun.

I call these exercises *jazzercises,* as they are based on the many chord progressions regularly used in jazz tunes. This column contains the first of a series of jazzercises which will appear in SHEET MUSIC MAGAZINE. Jazzercises are designed not only to develop finger dexterity, but, when mastered, to be used in actual pieces as well.

Study and play the harmonic pattern which follows. This is the bare bones harmonic structure upon which this set of jazzercises is based. This particular chord pattern fits the *I Got Rhythm* chord changes and many other bop tunes, too. When you have played the harmonic pattern several times and have the sound firmly in your ear, proceed to Exercise I.

Play Exercise I through carefully, hands separately, then put both hands together. Play it four times.

Follow the same procedure for Exercises II and III. In Exercise IV, add the bass line. Practice all jazzercises at a slow tempo, and play the eighth notes evenly.

HARMONIC PATTERN

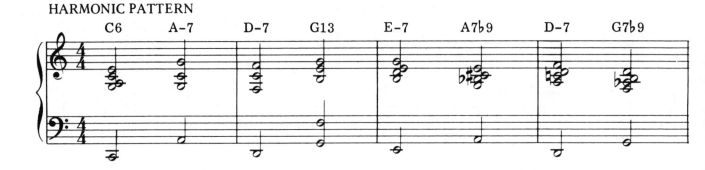

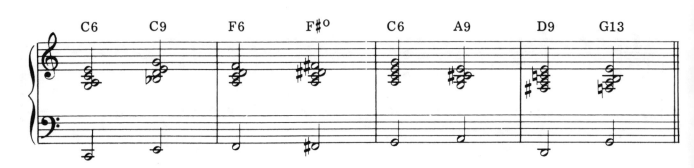

Ex. I *Play 4 times*

Ex. II *Play 4 times*

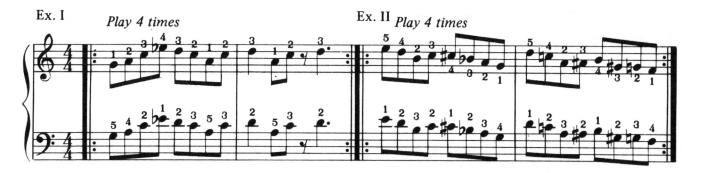

Diminished Scale

Ex. III *Play 4 times*

Ex. IV EXERCISES WITH BASS NOTES = JAZZ SOLO

Play 4 times

C6 A−7 D−7 G13 E−7 A7♭9 D−7 G7♭9

C6 C9 F6 F#° C6 A9 D9 G13

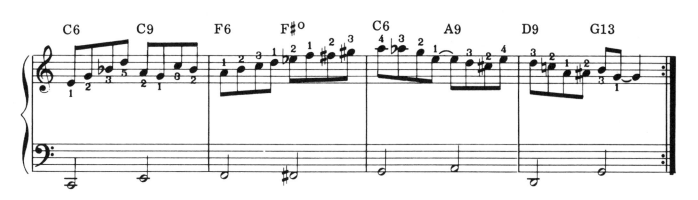

-LS

Lou Stein's Jazzercises

Exercises relating to jazz playing are good for finger dexterity and for learning how to "run the chord changes." That means to improvise a melodic phrase that fits with the given chord progression. One of the most common progressions we run into in jazz is the ii-V-I pattern.

In the first three examples, I have written exercises based on the ii-V-I pattern with each chord lasting two beats, except for the I chord. It lasts for an entire bar. Then in the fourth and fifth examples, I've written exercises on ii-V-I with each chord lasting one bar.

Each pattern should be practiced in every key. Some of the fingerings might be a little awkward in the different keys, and you will need to make adjustments. Begin practicing slowly, starting with three keys (C, Db, D); then add one new key at a time.

When you feel secure with each exercise, set your tempo, count off two bars and swing the Jazzercise!

"one .. (snap) .. two .. (snap) ..

one .. two .. three .. four ..
(snap) .. (snap) .."

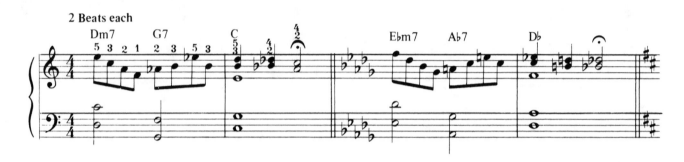

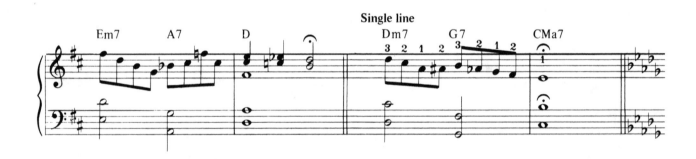

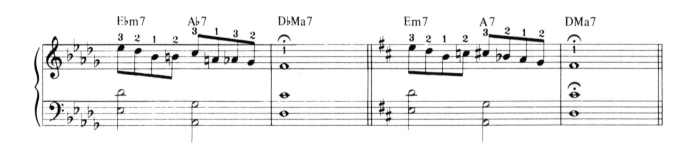

Lou Stein's album <u>In It for Life</u> features a trio of piano, drums and tenor sax live at John Word's in Mobile, Alabama. It's on the Nomad Records label. One of the standards on the album is "Just Friends."

290

Using triplet

Continue in all keys

4 Beats each

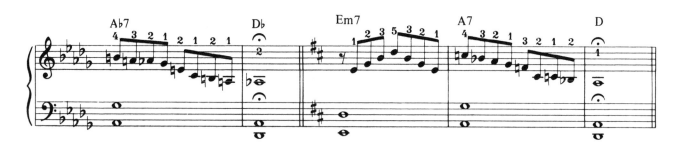

With syncopation

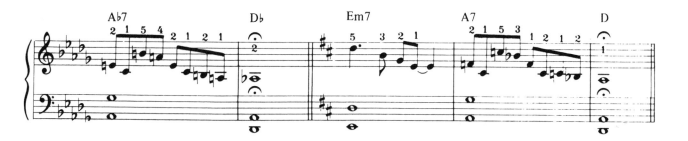

A 5 Minute Workout

Here's a drill that will get your fingers "warmed up" and moving in just 5 minutes. Although it's made up entirely of five-finger patterns, some are on white keys while some are on black keys. When you play on the white keys, with the thumb on a white key, play toward the outer edge of the key. When playing on the black keys, with the thumb on a black key, play toward the cover of the keyboard.

Try playing with the right hand alone, then the left hand alone before putting them together. Begin with a tempo of ♩ = 120-144.

"Helping Hanon"

BY ROBERT DUMM

After you work a while with stationary five-finger exercises, you should proceed to Hanon's *Virtuoso Pianist,* which begins with a set of what I call "six-finger exercises," since they cover the keys of *six* scale steps, leaving your thumb or little finger one place to move. This means that each repetition, instead of using the same pitches, moves up or down one pitch, relieving the ear and asking the hand to adapt to changing keyboard shapes.

That was Hanon's great invention: he found a way to move *while* repeating a given figure or set of notes, providing enough repetitions to develop a skill without dulling the ear by grinding away at the same thing. Hanon himself seems to have been a man-of-all-work at the Paris Conservatoire during much of the last century. Whenever any enrolled piano student proved lacking in any aspect of technique — what the French called La méchanisme — he was promptly sent down the hall to Hanon, who used his five-finger invention to oil their mechanism — with spectacular results, if old recordings of grads playing into their nineties can be trusted.

Success must have spurred Hanon on and on. Like Czerny, he turned drudgery into challenge, and spun his webs for years. I recall one of my high school teachers, Maurice Dumesnil (himself in his seventies) rear to his full Norman height, saying, with a Gallic glint-of-the-world in his eyes: "Old Hanon — I can see him still, bent over and shuffling down the hall in his eighties!"

You can spot the point of each Hanon exercise by how it varies from the others. The first one simply gets you used to going up and down in sequence. Once that sequence is smooth, try repeating fingers 4 and 5 in a slow but insistent "trill," three times with a building *crescendo,* like this:

Hanon In A Tizzy

ETUDES

Etudes is a department which features technical exercises composed by masters throughout history.

Scott Joplin wrote his "School Of Ragtime," he said, to help pianists play "that weird and intoxicating effect" he intended in his music. Joplin was referring, of course, to ragtime's jolting syncopations. These exercises can benefit classical pianists, too, since almost all music contains syncopated passages of some kind.

The dotted lines indicate where the held tones (syncopes) would normally be struck. Try playing these examples slowly at first until—as Joplin put it—"you catch the swing."

SWINGING SYNCOPES

SCOTT JOPLIN
(1868-1917)

Boogie Your Way To Dexterity

By Bonita Luciotti

Boogie Woogie patterns are not only fun, but a great way to develop finger (and, in the case of organists, foot) dexterity. Here are some patterns to practice, based on the 12 bar blues form.

The first patterns are for the right hand alone. Next, there is a variety of left hand Boogie bass lines. Finally, there are two examples of organ pedal patterns. For the last pattern, get your right foot off the volume pedal and play the upper notes in each eighth-note grouping!

All patterns can be played together, so get your musician friends to join in . . . or create a duet with yourself by taping one set and playing along with the recording using a new set of patterns the second time around!

Right hand pattern #1

Right hand pattern #2

Left hand pattern #1

Left hand pattern #2 (done in "jazz eighths")

Left hand pattern #3 (done in "jazz eighths")

Spinet pedals

Console pedals (done in "jazz eighths")

Section 10
THE ORGAN STUDIO

organ studio

Instrumental Sounds at the Organ

One of the wonderful aspects of today's electronic organs and synthesizers is the ability to produce authentic-sounding instrumental sounds. However, many players often overlook the limitations of range of the instruments they are registering, with the result that they sound anything but authentic!

So, here are some charts designed for quick and easy reference, to use when you are looking for the true sounds of the orchestral instruments at your command. If you play within the ranges shown, the tones of the violin, clarinet, trumpet - any orchestral instrument - will fall within the tonal range in which the actual instrument would be played.

(If you have a spinet, do the best you can. This is one of those times when a full console is a desirable asset).

I hope you find this helpful in creating as many authentic sounds as possible on your instrument. Be sure to experiment with each individual instrument, and learn the full capability of the registrations on your particular keyboard.

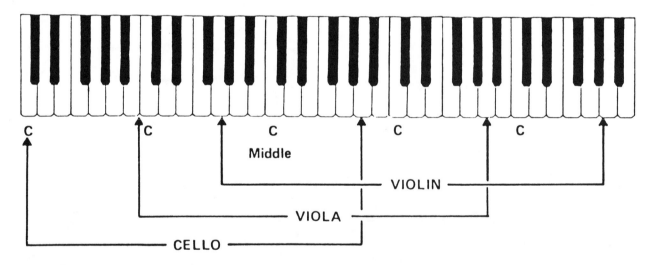

String Instrument Ranges

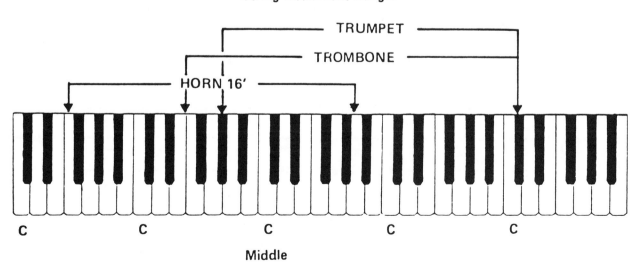

Brass Instrument Ranges

299

Continued next page

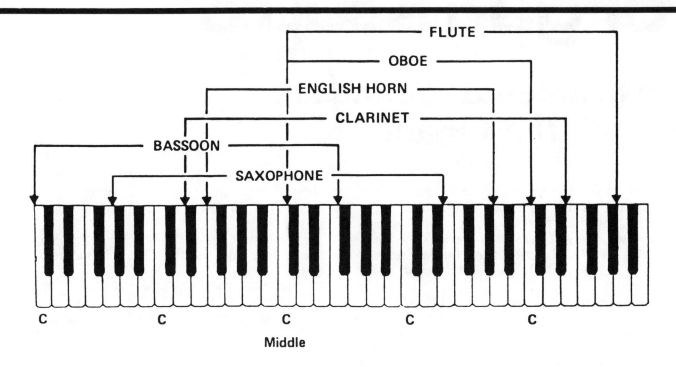

Woodwind Instrument Ranges

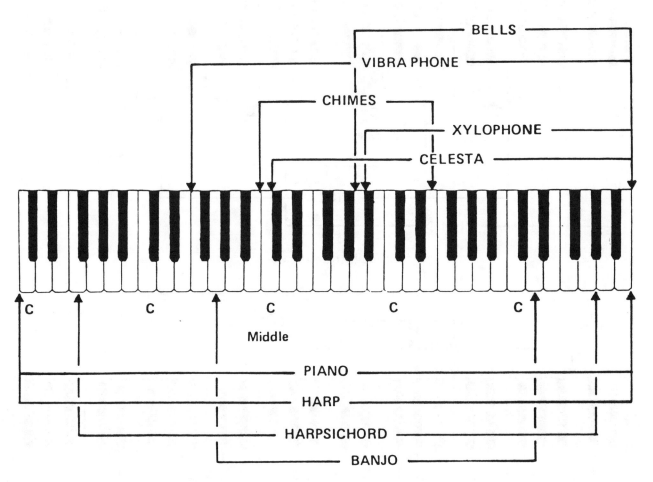

Keyboard and Percussion Instrument Ranges

MAKING YOUR ORGAN AN ORCHESTRA

The sound of the organ has changed drastically over the years. Although we can still sound "like an organ" we can also authentically recreate almost every orchestral voice.

Many of us have listened to a salesman demonstrate "that beautiful violin," buy the instrument, and never find "that beautiful violin" again. That's because the salesman knew the tricks of not only pushing the correct button, but treating that voice as if it were a real violin.

We have to consider each instrument individually. It helps to know how the sound is produced, the instrument's range, type of vibrato used (if any) and any other special treatment necessary to make each voice sound as authentic as possible.

With the wide variety of organs on the market, it is impossible to be extremely specific in some cases. We will try to use general terms that will clue you as to the feature name on your instrument.

Keep in mind the idea of phrasing. Many instruments we will discuss are wind instruments—meaning that air produces the sound we hear. A trombone player who is not allowed to take a break every few measures will probably pass out!

The goal of this lesson is to help you to understand the instruments better, and, ultimately, to make the time you spend on the bench even more enjoyable.

VIOLIN

Range:

Best Organ Range:

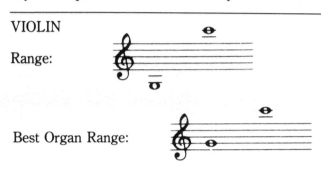

The violin dates back to the early 16th century and can be used for a broad variety of musical styles. It can be played either legato or staccato, and you can play single notes or two, three, or more notes to create an entire string section. The vibrato is created when the player moves his hand against the strings.

If you listen to a violinist, notice that the sound intensifies as he draws the bow. On the organ, this effect can be imitated by backing off of the volume pedal and gradually adding volume as the note is played. (This only works for notes held for several beats.)

The vibrato is delayed—it comes in a short time after the note has been introduced. If your instrument has a "delay vibrato" feature, use it. On some organs, the vibrato's depth and speed can also be controlled. I would suggest a medium setting for both. The most realistic vibrato comes from the "touch vibrato" feature, where the vibrato is produced by physically moving the key.

Whichever vibrato you use, it will give the violin a much warmer tone and make it useful for many types of music.

The accompaniment should provide a contrast (unless you are duplicating a string ensemble), so use a flute 8' by itself or add a horn 8' to the flute.

SUGGESTED TUNES:

Fiddler On The Roof
The Godfather (Theme from)
Lara's Theme (Somewhere My Love)

These are by no means the only tunes to use with the violin. The sky's the limit!

CLARINET

Range:

Best Organ Range:

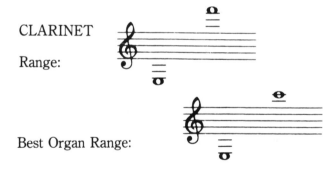

The clarinet is a cylindrical tube with a single vibrating reed. It dates back to the very end of the 17th century. It can play only one note at a time and can be played either legato or staccato. The clarinet can jump easily from high to low notes and smooth runs are no problem for the experienced player.

The clarinet can be played with or without vibrato. If vibrato is used, use the delay vibrato if possible. If you have control of the depth and speed, they should be at a minimum setting.

A bass clarinet is created by using the clarinet voice in the lowest range of the organ keyboard. It can be effective, so experiment with it.

The clarinet player can "glide" from one note to another. Most organs have a glide feature, usually located on the expression pedal. Be sure to activate the glide first, then hit the note and finally release the glide when appropriate.

Continued next page

The accompaniment will vary depending on the kind of music you are playing. For the faster tempos, use a flute 8' so that the clarinet is emphasized. A flute 8' with the addition of a cello 8' would be effective for a ballad, where the accompaniment might include some nice harmony or moving lines.

SUGGESTED TUNES:

Begin The Beguine
Clarinet Polka

TROMBONE

Range:

Best Organ Range:

The trombone is one of the larger brass instruments, using a slide with seven positions to create the different pitches. It is not always capable of playing very legato, since the slide might be moved quite a distance at times, from the closest position to the farthest.

The vibrato is created when the player moves the slide slightly, and it is noticeably delayed. Use the delay vibrato if possible, with a medium to full depth and a medium speed. The amount of delay used will depend on the melody played. The longer delay should be used for melodies with many notes held for several beats. A short delay is best for those melodies with few or no sustained notes.

The trombone is known for the "glide" effect. As with the clarinet, be sure to engage the glide first, strike the note, and then allow the pitch to rise. Don't overuse the glide. Two or three times per chorus is usually enough. If the melody includes half steps upward, the glide can be incorporated into the melody, as demonstrated on the tape. When you reach the point in the melody with the two effected half steps, first engage the glide and play the *higher* note (it will sound like the half step below). When the melody's rhythm calls for the higher note to be played, simply release the glide control. This effect can be a challenging one to coordinate, but it is very useful in creating an authentic trombone.

Grace notes and fast runs are difficult for the trombone, again due to the seven position slide.

The accompaniment will vary depending on where you want the emphasis. A flute 8' by itself would be best if all the emphasis is to be on the trombone. If the accompaniment includes countermelodies or interesting harmonies, try adding a cello 8' or string to the flute 8'.

SUGGESTED TUNES:

I'm Getting Sentimental Over You
Moonglow
Seventy-Six Trombones (no vibrato)

PIANO

Range: Entire Organ Keyboard

Best Organ Range: Avoid Highest Octave

The piano has been enjoyed by both players and listeners since the 18th century. The sound is created when the pushed key activates a hammer which strikes strings that vibrate.

No vibrato is used and any type of turning speaker should be avoided if possible. All of the orchestra voices will sound most realistic through a stationary speaker.

Since the piano tone dies away, don't attempt to play notes with long time values. Sustain can be used to add length to the tone. Strike the note and quickly let go, allowing the note to "ring." Use a medium amount of sustain for slow ballads and less for faster tempos or songs with a good deal of movement. Some instruments provide a damper feature, so that sustain can be added at any point and taken away when necessary. This feature allows the organist to play a very authentic piano, especially if he is also a pianist.

If you have no piano experience, begin by using the piano only for the melody, with your accompaniment sounding like a "normal" organ. The melody will be accented very nicely if you are able to play octaves (add the note one octave above the melody note).

The piano can also be used for the accompaniment registration. It can be played simply with a pedal-chord rhythm, or used with arpeggios. The accompaniment could be a variety of things; since the flute 8' is very similar to the piano tone, it might be best to accent it with a contrasting voice, such as a horn or string.

SUGGESTED TUNES:

The Entertainer
Send In The Clowns (Use piano for arpeggio accompaniment)
Maple Leaf Rag

TRUMPET

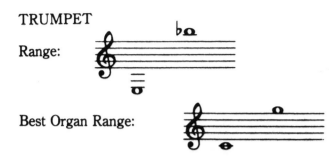

Range:

Best Organ Range:

An early version of the trumpet was used in the 17th century, and today's most popular version has three valves used alone or in combination to create the well known sound.

The trumpet player creates vibrato by moving his fingers on the valves. His lips also have a great deal to do with the tone he produces. Again, the vibrato is delayed. For those of you with a delay vibrato feature, a medium delay is best. The depth of the vibrato is medium and the speed slow to medium.

You can use the trumpet for both legato and staccato passages, as well as long jumps and runs. It is a very flexible instrument and is used for all types of music. Ballads, marches, country, big band and classics all sound authentic when played on the trumpet.

Although the trumpet plays only one note at a time, you can duplicate the entire trumpet section by playing full chords in the right hand.

A simple musical accompaniment should have a simple registration—possibly a flute 8' with a touch of flute 4'. An interesting musical accompaniment calls for the addition of an 8' string or cello.

SUGGESTED TUNES:

Bugler's Holiday
Tenderly
Theme From "Ice Castles"

OBOE

Range:

Best Organ Range:

The oboe dates back to the beginning of the Christian era and is a conical tube with a double reed. These reeds are positioned back to back and the player must "pinch" the reeds between his lips.

As the player blows into the oboe, the reeds vibrate and create the haunting, easily recognizable sound.

The oboe player uses a subtle, delayed vibrato. If your instrument has delay vibrato, use it. The depth and speed of the vibrato is usually at a minimum.

The best use for the oboe is as a single note melody, since only one note can be produced at a time. An "oboe choir" is extremely rare, so it is best to stay away from full chords with the oboe.

The accompaniment must be fairly soft, as the oboe is a soft instrument. I would suggest using a flute 8' by itself, or a flute 8' and horn 8'. The accompaniment should provide a rich background but be careful not to overpower it.

SUGGESTED TUNES:

Stranger On The Shore
The Way We Were
Caravan

FLUTE

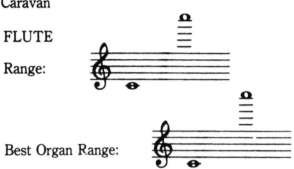

Range:

Best Organ Range:

The flute is a cylindrical tube that is stopped at one end and has been a part of the orchestra family since the mid 18th century. It is not a particularly loud instrument, but it has a very pleasing tone.

The flute voice is probably the most used voice on any organ, since most organs include several flute pitch levels and some organs base all of their sounds on a flute foundation. The 8' flute is the pitch that should be used for the solo flute.

The vibrato is actually more of a tremolo or "wah" (a change in volume or tone, rather than the change in pitch that is vibrato). Vibrato (delayed if possible) will work just fine if your instrument does not include a "wah" control. The type of tremolo used for any turning speaker, such as Leslie, is not the tremolo necessary for an authentic flute.

The flute 4', used with a slight vibrato and played in the upper range of the keyboard will sound like a whistle. The flute 4' can also be used to create a piccolo (it plays one octave higher than the flute).

The accompaniment should provide a contrast, so try using a horn 8' or string 8' with the flute 8'.

SUGGESTED TUNES:

Girl From Ipanema
Meditation
(Any Bossa Nova)
Sweet Georgia Brown (Use the flute 4' as a whistle)

DC

303

organ studio

Playing Like The "Real Thing"

Using solo stops more effectively

Without exception, everyone who owns a home organ has at one time or another experienced what I like to call the "demonstration — WOW!" This usually occurs when one ventures into an organ showroom and hears a demonstrator put the latest electronic organ through its paces. The successful "demonstration WOW!" (which inevitably leads to a successful sale) is made largely by the art of using solo stops effectively. By "using" we don't simply mean turning the stop on or off but rather playing the keys in a manner which best imitates the sound characteristic of the musical instrument named by the stop. In this workshop we are going to examine this playing technique more carefully.

First, what is a solo stop? A solo stop is a stop on the organ which duplicates the sound of an orchestral instrument. These stops include: trumpet, clarinet, oboe, orchestra bells, xylophone, violin, piano, accordion, harp, and chimes, to name a few. Selecting any one of these stops is simple; the difficult part is knowing how to imitate the way the actual instrument is played. The way an orchestral or actual instrument sounds is governed first by its timbre or tone color, and second by the characteristic way the performer plays that instrument. On the organ, the timbre of the solo stop is predetermined by the organ you are playing. The characteristic way that instrument is played, however, is governed by the manner in which the organist interprets the melody of a given song on the keyboard.

As our first example let's say we've decided to use a bell stop to play the following song. To make the solo stand out more clearly use a soft accompaniment at 8′ only, and a soft pedal stop at 8′. (I'm assuming your organ has some sort of bell effect; if not, register a flute at 8′ and 1′ with long sustain and no vibrato.)

(Original)

etc.

Upper: Bells (00 6000 006)

(Altered)

etc.

Notice how the rhythm of the melody was altered to make the organ's bell stop sound more like the real thing. This same rhythmic alteration would be made if we were using the chime or xylophone stop.

Now, here are some general rules for some of the other solo stops we mentioned:

Piano: Short, detached attack: alternate between single note and two note intervals in melody line (4ths, 5ths, and 6ths). Best effects obtained in octaves of middle C and treble C. No vibrato.

Upper: Piano 8'

Trumpet: Short, staccato attack; each note accentuated with slight volume pedal increase; usually single note solo, register with flute stop at octave pitch; give longer notes (whole, half, quarter) 1/2 their written rhythm value.

Upper: Trumpet 8' (00-8880-000)

Clarinet and **Saxophone:** Smooth, legato; usually single note solo, but can be effective in chords; register with flute stop at octave pitch, best single note effects obtained when played in octave of middle C; give notes their full written rhythm value. Full vibrato for saxophone, light vibrato for clarinet.

Upper: Clarinet 8' (00 8060 401) or Saxophone 8' (16 7662 310)

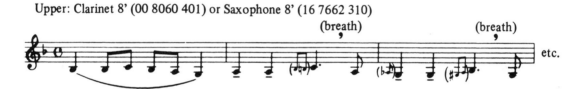

Oboe: same as clarinet except that the oboe, since it always plays alone in the orchestra, should never play more than one note. Oboes don't play melodies in chords! Once again, as with most reed stops, register the oboe along with a flute at octave pitch. Little or no vibrato.

Violin: Smooth, legato: single note solo; for more body try registering with a flute stop at sub-octave pitch (ex. 8' violin with 16' flute, or 4' violin with 8' flute); best effects obtained when played in upper three octaves on manual. Give notes full rhythm value or double value. Alternate between heavy and light vibrato.

Upper: Violin 8' (08 4663 000)

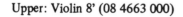

These examples should give you a good idea of what is meant by imitating the "way an instrument sounds" by playing the melody of a song in a special way for each solo stop. Remember, the designers of electronic organs have done their best to duplicate the timbre of orchestral instruments, but timbre is only half of the overall effect. To make the organ sound like that instrument you have to do your best as a keyboardist to play like the instrument you are imitating. This applies to all keyboard instruments which attempt to duplicate other instruments: drawbar organs, standard organs, electronic pianos, and synthesizers!

DK ♩

organ studio

How To Make — Registration Changes

Are you one of those conservative organists who luckily found a nice-sounding registration on the instrument a few years ago and has been using it, and only it, for a long time?

Do you yell at your spouse not to go near the organ because it is set up just right and any touching will destory the nice sound?

When you are playing a piece, are you like the politician who promises a lot of changes but never makes any?

Do you take the equivalent of a television commercial break when you daringly reach for some tab, lever, drawbar, pressure-sensitive switch, knob, et cetera, to make a registration change during a performance?

Have you noticed how unrelated your playing is to the automatic rhythm unit after you pause to make a registration change?

If you are one of those poor unfortunate organ hobbyists who suffers from that dread disease "neverchangingregistrationitis," don't just start to cry and leave the room keep on reading. There is still hope for you, and we are going to discuss that

aspect of registration right now.

To begin, registration is an inherent part of playing the organ. It should be—it MUST be — studied and the knowledge applied if you are to have pleasure at the organ. It is a basic part of organ study. In fact, the only thing more basic, and certainly much less complicated, is knowing what switch turns on the organ. Sometimes, even that on/off switch is hard to find.

When the organ is first turned on, it is necessary to set up the registration for the manuals (keyboards) and the pedalboard. This is not a study of registration, so I will not go into the complexities of all the components of registration—families of tones, foot lengths, animations, contrast, balance, et cetera.

Instead, I'm going to concentrate on the various techniques I use and teach my students to enable them, and you, to make quick, accurate, smooth, acceptable and *noticeable* registration changes.

Why did I emphasize "noticeable"? Because registration changes that are too subtle are a waste of the organist's time and effort. Of course, I will

306

not dictate or even suggest "taste" in the quality of your registrations. If you are reading traditional organ arrangements (I hope some of them are mine, published by Hal Leonard Publishing Corp.), then the registration is suggested. While it is, of necessity, a general suggestion (not all registration timbres [tone qualities] can be found on the various brands of organs), it is quite important that you make the effort to set up the organ as close to the suggestions as possible. Watch out particularly for the footages given for the different stops or settings. These are most important in relationship to the area of the keyboard where you will be playing. Then, if you are choosing your own registrations for chord work, where YOU are the arranger, your choices will depend on your knowledge of the various components of registration, your ability to hear the wide range of tones (known as your "ear"), and your "taste."

Now that you have set up the organ for whatever you're going to play, your first thought should be: Am I going to play the piece rhythmically or in a sustained (rubato, freely, ad-lib) manner?

If you are going to play without a steady beat, then registration changes are easy to make. They can almost be done leisurely. In nonrhythmic playing, pauses are acceptable and during them, either hand can usually be used to make the registration change. Prior to an actual pause, try ritarding the "tempo" (simply start to play even slower than you have been playing) so that the pause used to change the registration will seem natural, like a normal part of the performance. Even then, I would suggest that you practice making the planned change so that it can be made to look and feel as if it were done effortlessly. People do seem to enjoy performers "working" during a performance; that is, the more the performer perspires and appears to be working hard (not struggling) to please the audience, the more the audience responds to the show. However, there is always the audience who appreciates the music the artist is producing with no apparent effort. The words "You make it look so easy" are often heard at a concert, and the performer can take pride in knowing that all the effort put into the performance was concealed in the polished presentation witnessed by the audience.

The techniques used in making registration changes in the middle of a rhythmic performance run the gamut from simple to complicated and will depend quite often on your instrument.

First, there are some basic rules for changing registration while playing rhythmically.

If the tempo (speed) of the piece is slow, use your right hand to make registration changes. Generally, the accompaniment for slow ballads will have the left hand holding sustained chords while the pedals are played on all four beats of the measure. When the right hand is removed from the manual, the full background produced by the sustained chords in the left hand, plus the activity in the bass with the four pedal beats, will effectively maintain interest and continuity for the listener. However, when the left hand is used at a slow tempo, the bottom seems to fall out of the arrangement.

Conversely, if the tempo is moderate to fast, I suggest using the left hand to make the registration changes since the movement in the right hand will keep the listener's interest while the left hand is doing the work.

At all times, look for the opportunity to make a registration change during a pick-up, that is, melody notes in an incomplete measure. It is always effective in arranging to have pick-up notes played without accompaniment (N.C., Tacet, Soli). Of course, that is the ideal situation for the left hand to make the change while the right hand is busy.

When there is apparently no opportunity to try the above suggestions, moving the right hand down to the lower manual, usually playing the melody 8va (one octave higher than written to avoid running into the left hand) is a simple, quick, and generally satisfying way to make a registration change when there is no time to make mechanical changes.

It is also possible to move the left hand up to the upper manual to play the tune with both hands on the Swell manual. However, you must remain aware of the footages in the settings. With an 8' setting, you can use both hands in the middle register, but if there is a 16' setting, you will have to move both right- and left-hand parts one or two octaves higher to avoid a muddy sound in the left-hand accompaniment.

In my registration workshop, I show how several registration changes can be made without a lot of mechanical changes. For example: Always check to see what, if any, preset registrations are available, especially on the various brands you have not played before. Try them and notice what sound each preset produces. Quite often, the manufacturer sets up the presets so that the settings become bigger and fuller as you move from left to right. On several makes of organs, the manufacturer gives you the opportunity to set up your own special preset sounds. I suggest you follow the same order and have your adjustable presets expand from simple 8' settings to more complex 16' settings as you move from left to right.

BI

How To Make — Registration Changes
Part II

1. Look for solo pre-sets that can be set up with a single movement, such as a tablet/lever/switch for Piano, Vibraphone, Chime and any of the solo orchestral instruments. When more than one movement is necessary in order to set up a particular setting, it will take more time and greater dexterity of movement to accomplish the registration change. A case in point would be having first to cancel the present setting before the new setting can be used, or having to change the animation (tremulant or vibrato) to match the new setting. If you are having any difficulty in making changes, learn to handle the simplest changes quickly, cleanly, and in rhythm before attempting the more intricate changes.

2. Some instruments have knee levers that can be activated without removing your hands from the manuals. They are excellent for quick changes (they give you the equivalent of a third manual when they change the entire sound), but it takes a little practice to become accustomed to the coordination required. If you are playing another brand of organ that uses a knee lever, make sure that the movement to the right produces the same mechanical result with which you are familiar. Generally, the knee levers can be adjusted to the most comfortable position for you. There are several effects for which a knee lever is used including changing the present registration back to an original setting, creating a glide, turning the animation off and on, etc.

3. On larger electronic and pipe organs, foot pistons are used to enable the player to make rapid changes with either foot.

4. There is generally only one switch to turn the tremulant or vibrato on and off. This can be a very valuable aid in helping you to change sounds. For example, if you are playing a melody in chords with the right hand, using full tremulant, try changing to a single-note melody with the trem turned off. The left hand can make the cancellation easily at most any time, particularly during a tacet (N.C.) pickup. When playing pop music with no trem on, use a light, disconnected touch to avoid sounding liturgical. You'll find that the orchestral instruments used in jazz numbers sound authentic when played without trem or vibrato. If you do use the vibrato for the orchestral instruments, then be sure to use the vibrato *delay,* and if it's adjustable, don't have it come on too soon.

5. Swell pedal switches are very valuable in making changes. When there is just one switch (it may be placed on either the right or left side of the pedal), it is generally used to turn the automatic rhythm unit on and off. However, there are organs on the market that have two switches in the form of short metal posts standing up on both sides of the swell pedal in the general area of the toes. One switch will control the starting and stopping of the automatic rhythm unit and the other will control a number of changes that are pre-set on a control panel. Remember that even the act of turning an automatic rhythm on and off constitutes a change and will enhance your presentation.

All right, let's get to the pièce de résistance that I offer in my workshops. How to make several changes during a piece without touching—or hardly touching—any mechanical switches, tabs, drawbars, or levers.

In speaking of different areas of the keyboard, we use the term "register". The area around middle C would be considered the middle register. Then the octaves above would be the higher register and the octaves below referred to as the lower register.

Playing single notes and chords in the different registers doesn't actually change the sound, but with the change of octaves, the sound seems to have a different quality. Let's explore that thought.

On the upper manual, set up a rather full 16' setting, using 16', 8', 4', 2' flutes/tibias, with 8' and 4' strings and either an 8' or 4' reed. This will provide a variety of tonal textures that will enhance the effect of changing as we move the melody up and down the manual. Set up 8' and 4' flutes and strings on the lower manual with diapason 8' added for "body," if available. Use 16' and 8' in the bass pedals with sustain. Tremulant or vibrato on, full.

Remember that with a 16' setting, you must be very careful when playing even single-note melodies in the middle register, to avoid sounding muddy. With a 16' setting, you must never play melodies in chords in the middle register. Even when you use single-note melodies, you must be careful unless you are performing heavy classical or dramatic pieces that call for that kind of sound.

Choose any simple piece for the following experiment.

Use your right hand to play a few single melody notes on the upper manual in the middle register and listen to the sound. Then move your hand to the highest octave on the upper manual and play the same single-note melody. It *does* sound different.

Then have your right hand repeat the single-note melodies in the same registers on the lower manual. If you have a spinet, your upper register will not extend as high, but there will still be a slight difference in sound between the melody played in the middle and upper registers.

Next, return to the upper manual and have the right hand play the melody in chords, legato, in the area around C an octave above middle C—between the middle and upper registers. Then repeat in the same area on the lower manual.

Return to the upper manual and this time, play the melody in chords in the same place, but play the chords *staccato,* in a crisp manner. (Note: In the accompaniment for this melody style, I suggest using a sustained countermelody with after-beats.) Again, repeat the melody in staccato chords in the same area on the lower manual.

With the right hand on the upper manual, play a single-note melody with the animation turned off, cancel the trem and/or the vibrato, and use a disconnected touch. Try playing the staccato melody in chords with the trem/vibrato off.

If you have a solo pre-set that can be turned on with a single movement (piano, virbraphone, chime, etc.), use it for the melody.

Try playing the melody in various styles, such as three-part open harmony, block chords, pyramid chords, etc., on either the upper or lower manuals, between the middle and upper registers.

For a big-theater effect, easily and quickly available to you with this type of approach, use the block harmony style of playing both hands close together on the upper manual, with the left hand holding the chord conventionally and the right hand playing a single-note melody.

Instead of the left hand holding the accompanying chord on the lower manual with the right playing the single-note melody on the upper manual, move the left-hand chord to the upper manual and play it an octave higher. Add the right-hand single-melody notes immediately above the left-hand chords and *voila!* . . .the sound of Radio City Music Hall! (I relate to that, having grown up in New York City listening to the pipe organ in that magnificent hall.)

Now that you have a variety of sounds at your command with very few physical movements or mechanical adjustments, choose a tune and at least every eight measures, make some sort of "registration change." For example, start with a single melody note in the middle register on the upper manual, next play the melody in chords or the single-note melody high on the lower manual. Follow with staccato chords on upper, followed by single-note melody in the middle register of the lower manual. You can certainly figure out several ways to utilize the changes.

For a big sound, I end the demonstration in my workshops with the full theater sound (Radio City). It's usually well received.

There's always more to say on a subject, but that's all on making registration changes for this time.

If you have a particular playing problem, write to me in care of *Sheet Music* and perhaps I can provide some instruction through these pages.

'Bye now.   **BI**

Section 11
SPECIAL FEATURES

How to play by ear

by Rom Ferri

An Arizona reader wrote to us, "I've been playing the piano for 49 years, and still can't play by ear." He says he knows thousands of songs and asks, "Do you know who could tell me the secret to playing without a musical score?"

Rom Ferri taught ear training and other music courses as a member of the faculty at Fairleigh Dickinson University. He is now involved in a number of musical projects. He recently created background music for a play, "No Song of an Ingenue," a tribute to Dorothy Parker, performed at the 1989 Edinburgh Festival.

Playing by ear is a process different from improvising. For a person who has read music all of his or her life, playing by ear may seem impossible. It is *possible* through a process of *ear training*. Let's start with something we already know.

A common denominator that the vast majority of us have, even without formal musical training, is the ability to hear and sing a major scale. The first exercise we should dig into is the simultaneous playing and singing in our individual vocal ranges of all major scales. It is helpful to play the scales with both hands in octaves while we sing. Do it several ways.

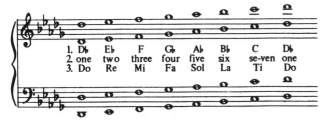

1. **Sing and spell with letter names, as shown in the example above.**
2. **Sing with numbers.**
3. **Sing with "movable Do" syllables. (In the "fixed Do" system, the syllable "Do" is always C.)**

Sing the scale in the usual manner — one octave ascending. Then, play each note of the scale in different registers, skipping all over the piano. Continue to sing the ascending scale in your vocal range. You may end up playing the scale this way.

This is valuable practice because it forces you to listen to a melodic design that you know, but played in a very different way. Ask yourself, "Do I hear better in my own vocal range? Am I able to sing a note that I hear in any other register?" The piano, of course, has a much wider range than your voice. Eventually, play any note in any keyboard register and sing it in your vocal range. Sing with *long tones*.

Melodic exercise

The word *diatonic* describes a melody or harmony made from a prevailing major or minor key. Diatonic is the opposite of *chromatic*.

Short diatonic major melodies are a good place to continue working because they use only the notes of the major scale. Nursery rhymes, folksongs, and popular songs are candidates. Sit at the piano, sing these melodies, and pick them out on the keys. You might try these:

Joy to the World (begins with the descending major scale)
Jingle Bells
Rudolph the Red-Nosed Reindeer
We Wish You a Merry Christmas
Hark! The Herald Angels Sing
Good King Wenceslas
God Rest You, Merry Gentlemen (minor)
Angels We Have Heard on High

After you can handle simple tunes, try some songs such as these half dozen wonderful diatonic melodies.

My Romance
The Very Thought of You (see December 1988 *PS*)
Young and Foolish (June '89 *PS*)
When I Fall in Love
That's All
Here I'll Stay (a less known favorite of mine, by Kurt Weill)

Go through your fake books, and locate the diatonic tunes that you know. Work on them. Remember, all keys! By the way, play the melodies in unison with both hands.

313

Continued next page

Harmonic training

Now, to go along with all of this, here are some diatonic harmonic exercises you should practice with both hands. (See boxed example below.)

There are many ways to practice these progressions. The main object is for you to hear the sound of the chord as a defined area of the key in which you are playing, and to name the chord.

. . . hear the sound of the chord as a defined area of the key in which you are playing, and to name the chord.

First, play just the root of the chord in octaves, and sing it. Then, follow the scheme below, using *very long tones*.

Notice that chords in *root position* alternate with chords in *inverted positions*. Root position chords have the root on the bottom, the third above it, the fifth above that, and the seventh on top. First inversion chords have the third on the bottom. Second inversions have the fifth on the bottom, and third inversions are sitting on the seventh. This exercise gives you practice hearing and singing chord arpeggios in the position that you are playing them.

Take a good long period of time to work on these melodies and harmonies. Ear training is a life-long, hard-work-but-fun process. You could work as slowly as one key per week, or structure your practice schedule this way:

Sunday	**A, A♭**
Monday	**B, B♭**
Tuesday	**C, C#**
Wednesday	**D, D♭**
Thursday	**E, E♭**
Friday	**F, F#**
Saturday	**G, G♭**

At times when the ear training process seems tedious, explore new territory — a diatonic melody that is new to you, or a familiar melody in a different key. Or go back to a step that you have already mastered, and appreciate your progress. Gains made in ear training are not lost.

After diatonic ear training, the next step is chromatic. Meanwhile, Merry Christmas and happy new ears!

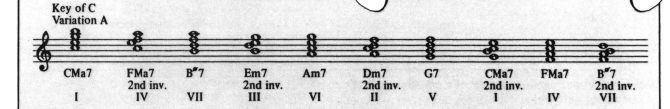

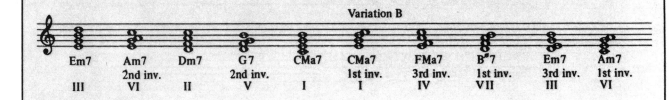

Who's Afraid Of An Audience?

Conquering Music's Greatest Phobia!

BY JO LOMBARD

The day of the recital, I awoke with a familiar feeling of chest tightness and stomach churning, a feeling of racing in neutral. Recalling the advice of several teachers, I resolved to "forget about feelings and concentrate on the music." Memories of previous nervous performances kept intruding, bringing visions of disaster ahead. But I hoped that will power would triumph.

The small hall was packed with other piano teachers and students. It was a festive occasion, the first in a new series of suburban musical evenings. My heart was beating so fast I scarcely noticed the first few numbers on the program. I couldn't concentrate on anything. Each performance just brought me closer to my own. "This must be how it feels on death row," I thought. While repeating my formula, "I know my music and I'm going to play beautifully," an even louder voice from my unconscious suddenly said, "What in the world are you doing here?" It was my turn.

As though I were dreaming, I walked to the stage. I couldn't feel the keys beneath my fingers. I was unbearably aware of the bodies in the first row, the bright lights, the shiny faces turned smiling toward me. I listened mentally to the first phrase but heard nothing. "This is it," I said, "I hope nothing goes wrong." And then everything went wrong.

Actually, practicing the Bach suite I planned to play had been a daily occasion of joy. As I memorized the ways in which the motifs fit together in these pieces, I marveled anew at Bach's genius. Weeks before the recital, I would play each piece silently on a table, or at the piano with one hand silent. Sometimes I would start after each cadence or at the beginning of each measure. I was leaving nothing to chance. I played for performance classes. Each day I played the entire work for an imaginary audience, rehearsing the performance scene in detail. I "visualized success" and gave myself positive messages. But I was merely rearranging the deck chairs on the Titanic, for I had not come to grips with the fact that I was a performance phobic.

Now, at the recital, I was able to play only the first few notes before there formed a complete blank in my mind — a total erasure. I was stunned. "Next landmark," I said to myself — but I couldn't think of it. I began at the third landmark, and time stood still. The blacks and whites seemed to be tilting slowly away, as if on shipboard. I was as sweat-drenched as a boxer after a fight. One by one, for each piece in the suite, I tried the carefully rehearsed landmarks. But my fingers belonged to someone else, and instead of hearing the interwoven motifs, I heard only my heart pounding in my ears. I saw the faces, no longer smiling, and felt the press of the darkened bodies against the brilliant stage light. I stood up, bowed, and retreated. "I'll wake up any minute now," I thought hopefully.

An hour into the recital, I decided to leave. I was coming down from a maximum panic attack, and something told me that when I realized what I had just done, I was going to cry.

As my car touched the driveway at home, the wave began to hit. I felt worthless, beyond help, degraded. I didn't sleep. The next morning I felt myself sliding into depression. I couldn't face my students and my friends who had been in the audience. I couldn't even make breakfast. I felt a moment of choice go by, like the place in a sonata where the development might go into the recapitulation. I could give up music, move away where nobody knew me, never teach again; I could admit failure. Or I could call the Phobia Program of Washington, which I had recently learned of on the radio. I had written down the phone number thinking it might be useful to someone else. I decided before sliding into the deep, to make just that one phone call.

At the Phobia Program I joined a class of ten for weekly meetings with Max, a professional group leader. Max told us he was a recovered public speaking phobic. He had dropped out of graduate school after a seminar in which his turn to speak had given him overwhelming panic. Yet here he was, speaking publicly in front of us, looking cool and re-

"Fear of your fear is the worst bogey of all."

Continued next page

laxed. "I still have anxiety before an audience," Max confided to us. "Right now on a scale of one to ten I'm about at a five."

We looked at each other. Could it be possible to function under that much tension? We squirmed in our chairs. I wanted nothing to do with any "level five" anxiety.

"But," said Max, "I don't run away from my panic any more, I go to meet it. That's the difference."

"Go to meet it!" I'd rather go to meet a tidal wave in a washtub. The woman to my left volunteered that she would never let her anxiety get started. "I'm afraid of groups too," she said, "and I always take valium. I just know that if panic even begins, it will shoot right up to the ceiling!" The rest of us nodded. We understood.

Max told her he hoped that the next week she would come with the valium in her purse instead of in her body. "You can always take it if you feel you have to," he said. "That will be your 'out.' Each of you will develop an 'out,' an emergency exit, from your phobic situation."

I had thought it would be difficult to talk about the devastating experience that brought me to the group. Surely these classmates would have nothing further to do with me once they discovered the depths of my incompetence. But as we went around the circle telling our stories, I realized how much we had in common. Gordon told of quitting his professional job rather than face a possible panic attack during the auto or bus ride to work. I thought how I considered giving up teaching rather than face another recital.

Emma spoke of feeling incompetent whenever she drove her car out of her neighborhood. "My heart starts to pound and I can't concentrate on anything, and the road looks so narrow that I'm sure I'll bump into the other cars and cause a big crash and maybe even kill somebody!" She was just as sure of this catastrophic outcome as I was of making major blunders whenever I played for an audience. In fact, I realized that when I rehearsed landmarks in a memorized piece I was actually rehearsing a scenario for the disaster that would require jumping forward to that landmark. It was a half-conscious rehearsal, but just as paralyzing as Emma's vision of bumping into oncoming cars.

I felt the most empathy for Donald, a public speaking phobic. His phobia didn't bother him as long as he didn't bother it, but a recent job promotion resulted in an upcoming lecture date that was terrifying. His whole reason for joining the group was to get through that speaking engagement. "I feel like a fraud when I get up to speak," Donald

---

confessed. "I always get flustered, my thoughts speed up and I forget what I'm going to say. It's torture!"

In that first group session, we all found something we couldn't have discovered by ourselves: other people facing the same problem. Nobody in the group laughed when I said I feared playing the piano because I might make a mistake or go blank. Not Brendan, who feared elevators because he might get stuck in one and never get out; not Nora, who feared eating in restaurants because she might shake and drop her fork; not Roger, who couldn't go over bridges because they might collapse.

We were ashamed of our phobias; we knew they were irrational but we were unsuccessful at putting them to rest by simple will power. Until now, each of us had been alone with a terror which others didn't understand. Friends and professionals had given us the futile advice: "Snap out of it." "Grow up." "Put your feelings aside." "Just relax." Our experiences were strikingly similar.

Here we found out that our anxiety attacks as learned responses must be unlearned. Later, as recovered phobics, we would have practiced ways of dealing with mild panic.

Each of us was assigned an individual partner, a recovered phobic with whom we were to practice assigned behavior modification tasks. Our goal was to bring on a low level anxiety attack and learn to handle

---

it. Brendan began by standing near elevators. Gordon took short rides on empty buses. My partner Jackie took me to piano stores where, posing as a customer, I played their pianos for the sales staff.

"Jackie, I can't just walk into a store and sit down at their pianos!" I said. "I'll feel like a fraud!" My old demon, fraudulence.

"Why?"

"The salesman will know I don't intend to buy."

"How will he know?"

"I'll have to tell him. Won't I?"

Jackie laughed. "Phobics always have a million great reasons why they can't confront their phobias. Do you want to think of some more reasons, or do you want to start dealing with the problem?"

Jackie went with me into the first showroom. She introduced herself as the customer and me as the helpful friend. I sat down at the $900 special and wondered if the word "fake" was written on my forehead. My hands were wet and clammy as I launched into Debussy's *Reverie*, the plain vanilla piece I had picked for my comeback. I began to think more about the salesman and less about Debussy, and sure enough, up came a memory blank. I jumped up from the bench.

"No, Jackie, you don't want this piano," I announced loudly, and moved down the line to better quality. As I stayed in the performing situation, two things happened. I began to enjoy the charade and I began to enjoy Debussy.

Five Ways to Foil a Phobia

1. Don't try to "will" your anxiety away. Instead, take a good look at it and then go out to meet it.

2. Take charge and start small. Consciously select a low level anxiety situation and, when you've succeeded in mastering it, congratulate yourself heartily and then move on to the next challenge.

3. Don't deny your negative feelings. Get in touch with them, express them, and let them go.

4. Whenever possible, develop an emergency exit for yourself. The stress level lowers when you know you have the safety of a "graceful way out."

5. Don't feel you have to conquer your fears alone. Look up the Phobia Programs in your area and find the support and help that can only be offered by those who "have been there."

316

The minute I felt uncertain about the music I simply switched pianos. What a relief to have an "out." Of course, there is no out in the real performance, but I was able to stay in the artificial situation long enough to find that my anxiety level actually came down while playing.

This was the first step in "befriending stagefright." We each monitored our feelings of tension, and rated ourselves on a scale from one to ten in each phobic encounter. The goal was not to be totally free of anxiety, but to study its rise and fall, thereby reducing its power to terrorize. Each week we went with our partners into a dose of low-level panic, then met as a group to share progress and setbacks. Only other phobics could give the moral support we gave each other. We cheered for Brendan when he reported riding an elevator to the second floor. We listened as Emma described the panic she felt waiting for traffic lights.

One Sunday I substituted on the organ at my church, playing two services at a tension level that went up to eight.

That was a big success story — not that I wouldn't rather have a level two, but that I found I could function at an eight.

We learned deep breathing and other relaxation techniques. We learned to go to meet our anxiety levels, to believe that a level which goes up must later come down, that panic attacks, however unpleasant aren't fatal. We were retraining our bodies not to go on emergency alert for the phobic situation, and retraining our minds not to fear a moderate anxiety level. Fear of the fear is the worst bogey of all. Most of us never found out the origin of our phobias.

As phobic personalities, we all tended to assume too much of the responsibility for any situation, setting ourselves up for stress if anything went wrong. The issue of control, we found, was a big one for each of us.

"If I were piloting the airplane, it wouldn't be so bad," said Earl, who feared plane travel. (He was a writer, and had refused some out of town assignments.) He might pilot the plane right into the ground, but it wouldn't scare him as long as he had control.

"If I could control the audience reaction," mused Donald, "if I knew for a fact that they'd like my speech, I could go ahead and give it without worrying." Exactly how I felt. We had to learn to tolerate uncertainty.

A big part of recovery was to come face-to-face with feelings. We shared our feelings, both positive and negative, in our class. Most of us had learned as children to hide negative feelings. We were walking time bombs. A musician, of all people, needs access to feelings. One cannot have a successful trip through a Chopin nocturne, or even a Bach fugue, without them. Keeping the lid on my own required a lot of emotional energy. After I told Jackie about these feelings, I felt enormous relief.

The thought and behavior reform begun in the Phobia Program has given me a far different attitude toward life. I now work at leaving stress behind, and go to meet the lesser anxiety levels with which I can cope. In teaching, I find these insights valuable. Most stage fright is not phobia, but nervous students can still benefit from relaxation, learning to control automatic thoughts, and discussion of negative feelings. For me, this is the key to coming out of it.

I eventually returned to the scene of the crime to play two Chopin etudes in a student recital. I thought I would topple from my chair before my turn came, but I played well in spite of feeling at a level nine. It was another solid brick in the ever stronger foundation of self esteem. ∎

Piano Partners

A Practical Guide To Playing Duets

BY DOUGLAS RIVA

For all of the rewards and pleasures piano playing brings us, it is a lonely activity. A typical pianist, whether beginner or professional, may devote long stretches of time to practice, interspersed with regular lessons, and hardly ever has the opportunity to play for anyone other than his teacher. For many pianists music remains an entirely individual pursuit.

Paradoxically, non-pianists find that making music with others is highly rewarding. Whether one plays in a large orchestra or a trio, the blending together of sound and the exchange of musical ideas gives an impetus for further musical growth. Even the beginning instrumentalist, a violinist for example, plays a "solo" with an accompanist. In reality the piece is not a solo but chamber music; neither part is independent since

both are necessary to perform the music.

Pianists, on the other hand, really do study and play solos — pieces written to be played by one person. Naturally, the piano has a great advantage over the violin and other monophonic instruments, since it is able to play melody and accompaniment at the same time. While this attribute of the instrument is a real advantage, for a developing pianist it might be viewed as a limitation. The violinist rehearsing a "solo" with an accompanist will have the opportunity to hear a different point of view, which may lead him to a more refined interpretation. However, a pianist studying a solo does not have the opportunity of exchange, except between student and teacher. In order to enjoy the special experience of making music with others, pianists must pursue chamber music.

Many works written for chamber ensembles, however, have a fairly complex piano part, requiring advanced pianism. A cellist or flutist has one musical line to concern himself with but a pianist must deal with all the difficulties found in solo works — chords, counterpoint, etc. — and take on the added responsibility of holding the piece together. Often it is necessary to act as a conductor, coordinating the other parts and indicating the tempo. Aside from these purely musical difficulties, finding like-minded partners for chamber music is not always easy. Many would-be pianists give up and return to solo pieces, denying themselves one of the most pleasurable of musical experiences.

Pianists have available to them a unique form of chamber music, though — the piano duet. Whether one is searching for an alternative to a chamber music ensemble or seeking an introduction to ensemble playing, duets may be ideal. Four-hand playing brings unusual challenges and rewards. Since duets may be played by a student and teacher or by two friends, it may be the perfect introduction to ensemble playing.

Duets have not always been common. During the seventeenth and early eighteenth centuries, multi-keyboard works were written for two or more harpsichords and also for harpsichord and organ. However, duets were almost unknown. Music for two players at one instrument began to be popular with the publication of the *Sonatas* by Johann Christian Bach in 1778. From that point, at the end of the Eighteenth Century, up to the beginning of the twentieth, duets enjoyed an enormous vogue. This popularity can be easily traced to the development of the piano. The harpsichord was not well suited to duet writing, being too small to accommodate two players easily. In addition, the musical style of the period, with its relatively delicate counterpoint, was not completely appropriate for four-hand writing. The piano, which had an increased range and power, was more appropriate to the

been a remarkable husband-wife team. Many pieces were written especially for certain family members to play together. Edward MacDowell probably wrote the *Lunar Pictures, Op. 20* for himself and his wife. More recently, Vincent Persichetti arranged his *Appalachian Christmas Carols* so that he and his wife Dorotea could play them for family celebrations.

For a developing pianist duet playing, with a teacher or partner, can aid in improving pianistic skills. As you study duets, rhythm and sight-reading will certainly improve. But, more importantly, duet playing can be a great help in learning how to listen — in molding the two parts together and in balancing the thick bass sounds, produced by the longest strings of the piano, with the treble, produced by the thinner and shorter strings.

Duet playing presents special difficulties and challenges which differ from solo playing. As a soloist the player is seated in the middle of the keyboard with the arms parallel to the keys. If a soloist needs to reach to the extremities of the keyboard it is easy enough for him to move his arms or body. Obviously four-hand playing sets certain limitations. Additionally, since the left hand of the *Primo* player is frequently close to the right

Pianist Douglas Riva, a frequent contributor to *Keyboard Classics,* has just released a new CD recording of "The Unknown Granados," on the Centaur Records label (CRC 2043).

difficult. If partners touch elbows it is easy to feel each other's motions of preparation, and thus accurately time a clean attack.

Duets are often written in an orchestral style. In fact, many composers have orchestrated their original duets. Both Ravel and Dvorak transcribed their duets *Mother Goose Suite* and *Slavonic Dances,* respectively, for orchestra. Granados' still-unpublished *En la aldea* (In the Village) contains notations in the score for possible instrumentation. John Corigliano's *Gazebo Dances* were performed in their orchestra and band versions long before the original four-hand score was performed and published. Because of this orchestral style of writing it is especially important for the two players to blend together as though a single player were playing both parts. When the melodic material passes from one player to another it is critical to match the tone carefully.

The range of repertoire for piano duet is vast. There are original compositions by major composers from Mozart to Stravinsky, ranging from concert works requiring virtuoso level technique in both parts to pieces written for teacher and student, with simple student parts for near beginners. And if one considers transcriptions or arrangements there are hundreds of other interesting pieces available. While discovering this music you can both improve your skills as a pianist and experience the great pleasure of chamber music. This issue's duet selection is a good place to start! ∎

"Duet playing has been called the 'ultimate parlour game.'"

---

more dramatic style and fuller harmonies of the Nineteenth Century. This new musical style benefited from the added volume of two players and from the melodic and harmonic doubling.

There were also compelling social reasons which led to the popularity of duets. In an earlier age piano duets provided a refined form of entertainment and an appropriate way for people to meet. Without recordings, radio or television, duet arrangements of symphonies and other orchestral works made this music accessible in the home. John Rockwell, music critic of *The New York Times,* has called duets the "ultimate parlour game."

Duets have long been a popular family activity. One of the most famous duet teams, and perhaps the first, was Wolfgang and Nannerl Mozart. Another brother and sister who certainly played duets was Felix and Fanny Mendelssohn. Robert and Clara Schumann must have

hand of the *Secundo* player, it is necessary to choose fingerings which do not conflict. A fingering which may be perfect when one is playing alone may prove difficult when the parts are played together. Sometimes it is necessary for one performer to play on the outer edge of the keys with the other playing closer to the fallboard (lid), in order to allow sufficient room for two pianists.

Traditionally the *Secundo* player takes charge of the pedal, not only because harmonies are built from the bass, but also because his right foot is closer to the pedal. Depending on the piece, it may occasionally be preferable for the *Primo* player to pedal, particularly in the case of a long solo section.

Precision between the two parts — good "ensemble" playing — requires careful listening and also watching the hand motions of your partner, so that you can "time" the descent of the keys carefully. Beginning exactly together is often quite

You Can Accompany Yourself! Part I

By Big Wilson

If you are a singer, either professional or amateur, I assume that you know the major scale . . . Do Re Mi Fa Sol, One Two Three Four Five, or No Nee Nay Nee Nah. I also assume that you can find middle C on the piano. Given these two assumptions, you *can* accompany yourself while you sing.

My daddy used to play piano for the silent movies. He started at the Binghamton Opera House. He taught me a few chords, and called them "changes." The first chord he taught me was a B Flat Major. The first "change" was an E Flat Major, and the second change was an F Seventh. Using these three chords, he ripped into a ragtime version of "Nearer My God To Thee." It was great, and I was hooked.

I spent lots of time at the piano learning and finding new changes, until I could play well enough to put myself through college. I then went into radio and television, often calling on the piano for background to commercials. In those days record artists would visit DJs, and I would get them to sing live. I've had the pleasure of accompanying Steve Lawrence and Eydie Gorme, Tony Bennett, Johnny Mathis, Ella Fitzgerald and others on my radio and TV shows. It was a thrill for me.

Many singers have said to me, "I wish I could play like that, and accompany myself." Therefore, I have devised the most simplistic method of learning to read guitar chord symbols, found on most sheet music. So, if you have the sheet music to the songs you want to sing, you can quickly learn to accompany yourself on the keyboard. You will not be a great piano player, but you will be a fine accompanist.

Let's start with a look at chords. All chords are based on triads. They are either Major, Minor, Diminished or Augmented.

All major triads contain the one, three and five.
All minor triads contain the one, flat three and five.
All diminished triads contain the one, flat three and flat five.
All augmented triads contain the one, three and sharp five.
Unless otherwise indicated, all chords are built on the major triad.
The symbol for a minor chord is a small m. Example: Cm.
The symbol for a diminished chord is a small °. Example: C°.
The symbol for an augmented chord is a + . Example: C + .

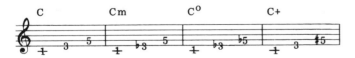

You Can Accompany Yourself!

You Can Accompany Yourself!

Part II

In the last issue, we saw how triads are built from scale tones. Let's extend the chart of chord types we began to write by adding sevenths and ninths. There are both Major seventh and ninth chords (Maj 7 or + 7 and Maj 9) and Minor seventh and ninth chords (m7 and m9):

When playing these chords from music with chord symbols, you can play the chord root with your left hand (try to hang around middle C with your left thumb), and chord tones 3 and 5 with your right hand. From this position, it is possible to play every chord (major, minor, seventh, diminished and augmented):

Try playing these voicings in many different keys. We'll place them in chord progressions next time! ⌒

320

You Can Accompany Yourself

Part III

By Big Wilson

Now that you've practiced all the basic chords, let's make things even simpler. When the music calls for a II-V7-I progression, try playing it this way:

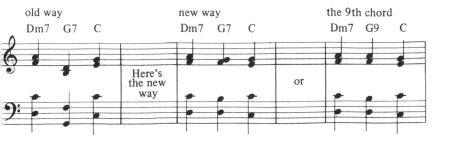

old way
Dm7   G7   C

Here's the new way

new way
Dm7   G7   C

or

the 9th chord
Dm7   G9   C

The left thumb moves down ½ step. The top note in the right hand moves down a whole step. And the C chord is played as always.

The same four notes are struck, but in a different order (inversion). The third way is even easier. Just move the thumb ½ step as shown in the 9th Chord version. The 7 chord is still a dominant 7th, but with a 9th added.

Practice this new way of playing II-V7-I progressions using the following drills.

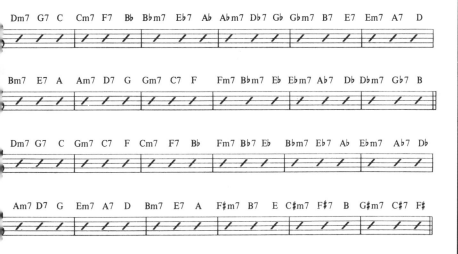

| Dm7 | G7 | C | Cm7 | F7 | Bb | Bbm7 | Eb7 | Ab | Abm7 | Db7 | Gb | Gbm7 | B7 | E7 | Em7 | A7 | D |

| Bm7 | E7 | A | Am7 | D7 | G | Gm7 | C7 | F | Fm7 | Bbm7 | Eb | Ebm7 | Ab7 | Db | Dbm7 | Gb7 | B |

| Dm7 | G7 | C | Gm7 | C7 | F | Cm7 | F7 | Bb | Fm7 | Bb7 | Eb | Bbm7 | Eb7 | Ab | Ebm7 | Ab7 | Db |

| Am7 | D7 | G | Em7 | A7 | D | Bm7 | E7 | A | F#m7 | B7 | E | C#m7 | F#7 | B | G#m7 | C#7 | F# |

You Can Accompany Yourself

Part IV: Transposing

By Big Wilson

Sheet Music is printed in "Standard Keys," which may be too high or too low for your voice range. If you sing a few bars in your range, then find the key the song is written in, you may discover that you are one, two, three or four notes higher or lower.

In order to transpose the music into "your" key, you will have to change the letter name in each chord symbol on the music. If the music is written in C and it suits you better in the key of F, you are a Fourth higher. Take your pencil and start changing the written chord symbols. In this case, C7 becomes F7. D becomes G. E becomes A.

I don't always transpose the music just to suit my voice, though. If a song is written in G and I like the key of B for singing, I'll write it down in Bb or C, because the chords in those keys fall more easily under my fingers!

Remember, in transposing only the *letter* of the chord symbol changes. A Cmaj.7 may change to an F, but it will remain a maj.7 chord.

The practice of transposing may seem tedious at first, but when you become more and more familiar with intervals you'll find you will be able to readily transpose any chord symbol. ⌒

David Leonhardt

How to "comp" for a singer

David Leonhardt

David Leonhardt has worked with some great jazz singers. He was musical director for Jon Hendricks (originally of Lambert, Hendricks, and Ross), and he's also played for Annie Ross, Michele Hendricks, Bobby McFerrin, Dianne Reeves, and Janis Siegel of the Manhattan Transfer.

Every professional jazz pianist will accompany a singer eventually. The interplay between vocalist and pianist can be the most intimate of experiences, as well as a source of great financial reward.

I've found that all great accompanists have a *good attitude.* Your role as accompanist is to help the vocalist realize a successful performance. Every note you play should be designed to make the singer sound better. If you cannot meet this criterion, then you are not accompanying — you are competing! This will not help you get or keep any gig, so leave your ego at home. Understanding this basic concept is the most important aspect of being an accompanist. Keep it in mind at all times.

The job of a vocal accompanist can be divided into three main areas: introductions, comping, and endings. An intro must accomplish three specific ends. It must establish the key of the song in an obvious way to enable the singer to find the proper starting note. It must set the tempo of the song, and the intro should establish the feel of the piece (swing, Latin, ballad, or whatever). It will help you to work out two or three different approaches, then use them as a basis for all your intros. Don't feel that each intro has to be spontaneous and never heard before. A thoroughly unusual intro will probably throw the singer off!

...you are the musical landscape over which the singer travels...

Intros are almost always four bars long on a ballad and four or eight bars long on an uptempo tune. A common intro is a simple **I-VI-II-V** turnaround (example 1) with the top note of your voicing being the starting note of the song. Another approach is to vamp from the **I** chord to the **V** chord (example 2), once again keeping in mind the singer's first note. If a singer comes in wrong, it is almost always due to a bad intro. Don't forget — singers are like customers. They are always right (even when they are wrong).

Do's and don't's for comping

You can approach *comping* (slang for accompanying or complementing) for a jazz singer in many ways, but there are some basic Do's and Don't's.

> Do listen to the singer and watch him or her for visual cues. A good singer will conduct the band.
>
> Don't play the melody. This will allow the vocalist more freedom and creativity of phrasing.
>
> Don't play cross relations that clash with the melody. For example, if the melody is the ninth, don't play the flat nine.
>
> Do listen for phrasing, and fill in when the singer breathes.
>
> Do know the melody and the correct chords of the song. Better no chord than the wrong chord!

Different singers will like different styles of comping. Some prefer the full sound of two-handed voicings with octaves in the right hand (example 3). Others want single note fills behind them (example 4) or simple sparse voicings (example 5). Most singers like a rhythmic comping style so they can feel the pulse. Remember that you are the musical landscape over which the singer travels in the song.

The last thing everyone remembers

Setting up a good ending behind the voice is a very important aspect of accompanying. After all, this is the last thing everyone will hear and remember. Once again, you can adapt a few endings to many different situations. The most common ending is a "tag." This is simply two or four bars added to the song by substituting some type of turnaround in place of the **I** chord (example 6). Some tags are extended into a "vamp" (example 7). Many times a vocalist will hold one note while you play a series of chords underneath to end the song. A useful ending of this type is the "tritone ending" (example 8). Another might be to start a whole step below the final chord (example 9). Endings must express conviction and a sense of finality. This is the pianist's job, and it can make a singer look good or ruin an otherwise successful performance.

With all these concepts in mind, listen to recordings of the great jazz singers and their pianists. Use their ideas as a catalyst for your own creativity in accompanying, and — most of all — keep your ears open! •

1. Turnaround intro

2. I-V vamp as intro

3. Full voicings

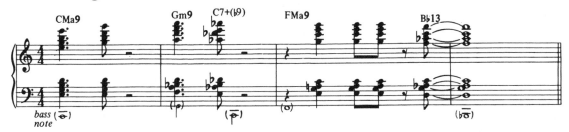

4. Single-note fill

5. Simple, sparse voicings

6. Turnaround as tag

7. An extendable vamp

8. Tritone ending (F# and C are a tritone apart)

9. Moving up to the last chord

Secrets of a Musical "COLLABORATOR"

Dan Routh

There's more to being an accompanist than meets the eye. Though pianist partners of leading soloists often remain far back from the gleam of stage lights, they exert a powerful influence on every musical performance; and they must call on special skills and talents to bring these collaborations off.

When music greats Itzhak Perlman, Pinchas Zukerman, Mstislav Rostropovich, or Beverly Sills perform at New York's Carnegie Hall or Washington's Kennedy Center, chances are they will ask pianist Samuel Sanders to join them. Sanders has been recognized for more than a decade as one of America's leading "collaborative" pianists. In addition to performing nearly one hundred concerts a year, he teaches accompanying at the Juilliard School, records extensively (two recent albums with Perlman and Zukerman have won Grammy awards), and acts as music director of both the Cape and Islands Chamber Music Festival, and the chamber ensemble Musica Camerit. Mr. Sanders has performed at the summer festivals of Marlboro, Ravinia, Wolf Trap, Saratoga, and at the Mostly Mozart Festival in New York, in addition to six performances at The White House.

Born with a serious heart defect, Samuel Sanders began piano lessons as a way to staying safely occupied through his childhood. He had several pioneering heart operations, and carried on a normal life until the spring of 1980, when he began having heart failure just before a concert. Since it was the inaugural season of the Cape and Island Chamber Music Festival, he continued on with the aid of drugs until twenty-four more concerts had passed! In the fall of that year he underwent open heart surgery twice, remaining in intensive care for a month and in the hospital for two

months more, during which time violinist Itzhak Perlman called him every day. One month after being out of bed, he made a recording with Perlman, and his career resumed at the same hectic pace.

Outwardly shy and modest, Sanders nevertheless takes musical command with ease. He likens his position to that of a catcher in baseball: "He's in on every single play," explains the pianist. "He has an overview and that's what you get at the piano because you are looking at all of the parts simultaneously, controlling many aspects, just as the catcher controls the flow of the game."

Keyboard Classics asked Samuel Sanders to write about the life and art of an accompanist, and he provided the following advice for our readers.

I have been an accompanist for over twenty years, and during most of that time I have taught music courses on the art of accompanying. People often ask me just what that means, and how one gets involved in my field.

I've never been able to answer those questions to my own satisfaction. I do know one thing: the use of the term "accompany" is unfortunate, but I really can't think of a better word. For example, if I were to say that I was a collaborator, it could be taken that I sided with an enemy government. "Partner" is nice, but no soloist would ever put up with that. "Assistant" is possible, but one doesn't really "assist" in any significant Beethoven, Brahms, or Strauss work that I know of. So we're stuck with "accompanist."

The real problem is the public's misunderstanding of the word "accompany." The dictionary defines it in some of the following ways: to go with; to add to; to support. Yet, any musician who plays one of the great song cycles or instrumental works knows that the piano and the voice (or instrument) are coexisting in that work on an equal basis; the pianist is not simply "going with" or "adding to."

In fact, anyone who wants to make his livelihood as a concert accompanist should be aware that he or she will need a first-rate piano technique, as just one of a number of essential skills. The physical requirements of a song like Schubert's "Erlkönig" or a piece like the Rachmaninoff Sonata for cello and piano demand the same total command of the keyboard that one must possess to play a large portion of the solo piano repertoire.

Let me give you a few examples. This fragment from the first movement of the Rachmaninoff *Cello Sonata* shows the difficulty one may find in an "accompanying" part. Note the leaps in the left hand while the right hand negotiates an unwieldy stretching passage. Rachmaninoff had a large hand and huge span; others of us are not so fortunate.

Here's another difficult accompanying situation. In the extremely brief song "Ich hab in Penna einen Liebsten wohnen," by Hugo Wolf, the pianist's concluding passage is a sort of high-wire act. This passage must be executed brilliantly, with seeming total abandon: the slightest mishap can cause the pianist (*and* the song) to fall flat on his or her face.

Beethoven's *Sonata No. 9* in A Major (Op. 47) for violin — Beethoven actually labeled it "for piano and violin"—has a passage which is noteworthy in another respect. The technical difficulty of this piano part is compounded by the need to synchronize with the violinist. *Both* players must listen carefully and phrase as one—not an easy matter!

The most renowned accompanists in the field today are indeed people who have fluent command of the piano from the purely digital standpoint. They include, among others, John Wustman, Geoffrey Parsons, Martin Katz, Sandra Rivers, Graham Johnson, Brook Smith, and Margot Garrett.

Now that we have established that one must be a very fine pianist to play both the instrumental and vocal repertoire, we can tackle the question of what accompanying is, and how one becomes an accompanist.

"Accompanists have to tackle problems that soloists never face. Here are some of them."

Accompanying is a profession that can be an end in itself, or it can lead to other aspects of music-making. Accompanists who play in recital can expect to play up to twenty-five or thirty programs a year. In general, concert accompanists, in spite of a busy travel schedule, also do a certain amount of teaching and/or coaching. For the concert accompanist, there is yet further specialization. Some pianists prefer to work only with singers; others feel they make their best music with instrumentalists.

In either case, there will be requirements that a solo performer does not have to deal with. Very often, for example, an accompanying pianist must play in concert a section of an opera or oratorio, or the ensemble part of a concerto. This brings up the problem of substituting for an entire orchestra.

These works were not intended for the piano, and piano reductions are often written by editors who do not play the piano. Naturally, the reductions are unplayable. For example, take a look at the second movement of the Prokofieff *Violin Concerto No. 2*. The passage printed here ideally requires three hands!

Continued next page

Faking is part of a musician's stock in trade; usually, pianists just go for the outer voices and fill in as much as possible. Certain notes must be left out to bring about maximum comfort, enabling the pianist to convey the *illusion* of an orchestra. My suggestion is to listen to the piece the way it was originally written so that you can extract an aural picture of the music. Once you know how it is supposed to sound, you can more convincingly create the right effect on the piano.

Pianists who specialize in accompanying singers will have more problems to contend with than one who just accompanies instrumentalists; for instance, he or she must have a command of French, German, and to some extent Italian. How can one expect to phrase and tonally inflect any song without understanding the text?

There is another difficulty in working with vocalists: one might master a tricky piece like Chausson's "Les Papillons" in the key of G Major (quite comfortable for that piece), and then have to perform it again in F Major (clumsy and awkward). Here it is in G:

Notice, in the new key, the discomfort in trying to fit your fingers between the black keys at a rapid pace!

In addition, many singers need a little more tender loving care—and justifiably; they are working with only their bodies and are more susceptible to the vagaries of weather,

Samuel Sanders performing with violinist Itzhak Perlman.

time, and place. An instrumentalist with a fever of 102 degrees might be able to gut his way through a recital, but a singer attempting such a feat risks an entire career.

Another skill that is helpful in accompanying situations is the ability to keep a straight face—or at least to maintain a sense of humor. Traveling with other artists can sometimes bring more than you bargained for.

I remember the time, for instance, when I was performing with cellist Mstislav Rostropovich in Cincinnati. He usually charges onto a stage and doesn't take time to tune; he just attacks the podium. At this performance, he was about to start when a very beautiful female latecomer sat down in the second row, center. Rostropovich turned to me, and in the most earnest but quiet manner said: "Not bad!" I was not able to recover in time for the opening of the piece.

That was mild, however, when compared to a concert we gave at the Kennedy Center in Washington, D.C. Backstage, Rostropovich cautioned me not to fumble around with the music; he wanted to rush out and begin immediately. When I arrived at the piano and opened the music, I discovered that he had pasted a centerfold from *Playboy* magazine across the first two pages. He sat on stage and pretended to be waiting impatiently for me to get ready. Frantically I tried to pry the centerfold loose without ripping the music, while the audience sat wondering what the trouble was.

On another occasion, I phoned violinist Itzhak Perlman on a beautiful Sunday afternoon in May to find out what time our concert was scheduled for. "We have to be there..." he began, then, with increasing panic, "We *had* to be there five minutes ago!" We arrived one and a half hours late, pulled the milling crowd back inside the theater, and apologized profusely.

Accompanists have to be prepared for *any* eventuality! Once I played for a soprano who started to go flat in the middle of a piece. She turned white as a sheet and asked me to help her offstage. I had to play a solo recital while a doctor attended her.

Musica Camerit, the chamber group in residence at Merkin Concert Hall in New York. Samuel Sanders is the ensemble's music director.

Some pianists who accompany do not enjoy that special feeling of panic that can greet one on the stage of Carnegie Hall. They prefer to do private coaching, playing for opera, choral, or dance rehearsals, and playing for students at their lessons. The vocal coach must know languages well enough to correct pronunciation and diction. A coach should guide a singer to repertoire which is particularly suitable to that individual's voice and help in program building—no small task. It is hard to differentiate between a coach and a rehearsal pianist, and often the two overlap. A coach must be a watchdog in matters of intonation. Ideally, a coach should work with singers on matters of interpretation. I remember with pain the earlier days of my career when I would often pound out notes of a song or an aria for a singer who had a fine voice and not much else.

"When I arrived at the piano I discovered that Rostropovich had pasted a Playboy centerfold across the first two pages of the music!"

Accompanying is a field that can act as a springboard to other music-making activities. For example, a number of conductors such as Julius Rudel, Judith Somogi, and Richard Woitach labored as rehearsal pianists in opera companies before the baton replaced the piano as their means of musical expression. Charles Wadsworth has been for a number of years the artistic administrator of one of the most important chamber music societies in the world, The Chamber Society of Lincoln Center; at one time, he was one of the most active recital accompanists. My own teacher, Sergius Kagen, was renowned as a vocal coach, accompanist, and voice teacher, but he was becoming increasingly involved with composing at the time of his death.

If a person chooses accompanying as a livelihood, he should truly enjoy making music with others as a steady diet. The accompanist must be flexible in dealing with many schools of thought on how a piece should be interpreted. This flexibility will be strengthened by the accompanist's own knowledge and conviction of the music at hand. More and more, today's musician is one who not only can play his instrument or sing well, but is also stylistically and musicologically informed.

Fortunately, a great deal has happened in the accompanying field in the past twenty years, and the accompanist is no longer the black sheep in the musical community. A number of universities have degree programs, both graduate and undergraduate, in the field of accompanying and/or chamber music (in my own estimation, accompanying is chamber music). This trend seems to be growing. I always feel that the pianist who wishes to become a professional accompanist should understand certain basic facts: the repertoire is vast; certain skills such as transposition, ornamentation, and sight reading can be acquired (these are skills which improve simply by doing them frequently); and the love of music rather than the love of the limelight is needed to sustain an extremely difficult life with a financial reward that is hardly concomitant with the amount of labor and effort invested.

I would like to quote my dear English colleague Graham Johnson about our field. He says, "There is a double-edged sword between certain soloists and accompanists which requires total dedication, even intimacy in a musical context, which would seem to suggest equality and close friendship. But the confusing and saddening thing for many accompanists is that when the going is tough (over schedules, publicity credits, fees), the relationship evaporates to that of lordly employer and hired hand. The greatest pity is that trust and friendship are built into the character of chamber music, and it becomes increasingly difficult for an accompanist to function openheartedly when he or she has been too often disillusioned by disloyalty and lack of trust." When would-be accompanists understand these very real facts of life, they have already become professionals. **SS**

How To Tape Yourself Seriously

"Through this way of working we can develop an attitude which often prevents mistakes from happening."

BY FREDERICK MOYER

The tape recorder has been an invaluable aid in my piano practice for almost as long as I have been playing the piano. It has provided me with the opportunity to compare what my playing really sounds like with what I think it sounds like while I'm coping with all those involved physical motions. This article describes the variable ways a tape recorder has aided my practice time. Other people have, undoubtedly, found many more applications; I would be interested to hear what they are.

**Performing For
A Tape Recorder**

One of the best ways to use a tape recorder is to play a complete piece for it, and then listen back. This has given me great insights — both technical and interpretive. Playing for a tape recorder provides a performing opportunity, a time to practice being on the "hot seat." This is an excellent way to test memory under pressure.

Normally, as I listen back to what I have just played, I follow along with the score. This enables me to refresh my memory on some of the subtler details of a piece. Thus, a tape recorder provides a format through which one can get into the habit of playing from memory (under pressure), while maintaining constant contact with the score.

Have you ever tried to make an audition tape? It is tremendously educational. If you don't have any taped auditions coming up, try to make a tape that you can proudly send to your friends. Or, with a specific piece or group of pieces, try to make a tape every day that is better than the tape you made yesterday. Although this is easier said than done, such a project is destined to get results!

With a tape recorder, you can become your own teacher. If you feel the need to develop your own style of playing — your own interpretations and aesthetic values, the tape recorder will provide you with an avenue of critical evaluation.

Using A Tape Recorder To Find Technical Problems

What I have found most intriguing about the tape recorder is its ability to dissect technical problems. Instead of concluding that some section just isn't right, with the help of a tape recorder, one can trace exactly what happened all the way down to what part of what key, what part of what 16th note, or which side of which finger is causing the problem. This clarity of analysis often suggests the most effective approach to a solution.

When playing back fast music, the use of the ½ speed (and ¼ speed) button is invaluable. Here are some examples of what ½ speed playback has brought to light about my playing:

In a difficult jump between two notes, I often play either or both of these notes too soon (e.g.), thus making the jump even more difficult.

During a 2-3 or 2-4 right hand trill my thumb tends to develop a tension which causes its arrival to be late ( ).

In fast 16th-note runs ( ), I often play the 2nd and sometimes the 4th notes early (like this: or).

During fast octaves, my 2nd, 3rd and 4th fingers sometimes inadvertently hit black keys. With ½ speed, I can find out exactly which fingers are hitting which keys and why.

A tape recorder at ¼ speed can point out which notes in a single-strike chord are coming in too soon or too late.

Even a tape recorder with one speed can enlighten technical problems. For example, I have noticed through work with a one-speed recorder that, within a group of notes, I tend to shorten the long ones. I have also noticed a ripple effect; if my concentration is somehow distracted in one section, often, half a minute down the road, I will bungle some other place. The original distraction can take many forms: a mistake, a feeling that I don't know what to do musically with a certain section, a worry that I may forget, the sudden realization that I am daydreaming, or even the self-conscious elation that I have just played some spot particularly well(!).

Through analytic work, we can not only fix the specific technical problem at hand, but also develop an attitude toward mistakes which often prevents future mistakes from happening. As all of us know, the fear of making mistakes causes a large percentage of them. (It also causes inhibited playing.) Instead of mistakes being psychologically categorized into some chaotic realm where there are no rules and where we have no control over events which cannot be understood — or into some indescribable void somewhat analogous to death — they now can be seen as they really are: complete, logical, understandable systems of cause and effect, whose study offers tremendous educational benefits, as well as the potential for their modification. The word "mistake," with its emphasis on the negativism of the occurrence, omits the description of the perfection and neutrality of that occurrence. To me, a more constructive and realistic way to describe a "mistake" is: "Something interesting happened . . . let's check it out . . ." Not only is this approach a lot of fun, but one's playing will improve 100 percent as a result.

Getting Rhythm

A tape recorder can be used to help you feel and play difficult rhythms. It becomes a metronome of sorts, except that the "ticks" are not necessarily even; they change with the music. I make rhythm tapes all the time with modern music, and to clarify trills and embellishments in classical music. With a little ingenuity, all sorts of rhythms can be taped; it helps to have a tape recorder with ½ and ¼ speed for fast music, a metronome whose speed can be changed while it is ticking (for accelerations, ritards, etc.), and a second tape recorder for dubbing in one rhythm over another (polyrhythms). I use a rhythm tape in two ways:

I listen to it over and over in order to "feel" the rhythm, and I try to play along with it. For playing along with tapes in fast music, it helps to have a tape recorder with a gradual variable speed control knob for building up your tempo.

Ensemble Playing

If I am working on an ensemble piece, I often play along with commercial recordings of the work. This teaches me the practical aspects of how to fit my part in with the whole, and points up details of the ensemble that I may have missed. It also forces me to be flexible. I find playing along with records gives me an idea of what that instrumentation is capable of in terms of timing and volume. This is particularly important in concerti; with the practical consideration of limited rehearsal time, it is good to present an interpretation that an orchestra can follow with reasonable ease. (However, regarding concerti, I have noticed that if I do too much playing along with records, my own playing becomes reactive, rather than commanding. Although there is a vast difference between a second piano and a real orchestra, practicing with a warm body who accompanies YOU is still an extremely valuable step in preparing for a concerto appearance.

General Concepts

One of the more offbeat uses I have made of tape recorders stems from the difficulty I have had incorporating certain general concepts into my playing. When I really put a great effort into being vigilant about these concepts, I cannot concentrate on the music. So I have actually made tapes that talk to me. A tape will consist of a concept of a few words, . . . silence, . . . then another concept, . . . more silence, . . . another concept, etc. I then play this tape while I practice. It allows me to keep a check on those basic points without losing musical concentration. The results of this have been terrific. While the subject matter on my tapes is, perhaps, of the up-in-the-clouds variety, I can see this technique working for those with more nuts and bolts concerns, like relaxing the shoulders, or keeping the fingers curved.

The use of a tape recorder in these ways can contribute to clarity of mind by developing focus, relaxation, confidence, and fewer technical problems, leading to better over-all playing and a positive attitude. These qualities will allow you to save time on technical work — time that you are now free to spend on more artistic matters.

*B*orn in 1957, Frederick Moyer of Wayland, Massachusetts, began piano studies with his mother at the age of seven. He attended the Curtis Institute and Indiana University and studied with Theodore Lettvin, Eleanor Sokoloff, and Manahem Pressler. At Tanglewood he participated in master classes taught by Andre Watts and during the summer of 1977 studied with Leon Fleisher.

Mr. Moyer's extensive and varied concert experience includes appearances with the Philadelphia and Minnesota Orchestras, the Buffalo Philharmonic, the Opera Orchestra of Genoa, and the Boston Pops Orchestra. In 1978 he toured Japan as soloist with the Japan Philharmonic and Sapporo Symphony Orchestras. His 1983 world tour took him across the United States to Hong Kong, India, Greece, and Japan, where he once again toured with the Japan Philharmonic. His two-week tour of India was sponsored by the Arts America program of the USIA.

Getting Your Music
Published
A Game Plan For Today

You say you're a brilliant young composer struggling with your latest opus in a small shack in the Florida marshlands, or in a garret (do they still have garrets?) on Manhattan's Upper West Side. You have glorious visions of your work being published and distributed internationally to orchestras and individual musicians who immediately sing its praises in performances throughout the world?

Well, get ready for the sharp slap across the face. As the golden mists clear, we're back to reality. Music publishers, composers, and professional organizations all agree that publishing is not only secondary to a composing career, but that it is practically impossible for an unknown to achieve print without an established history of performance.

There have been many changes in the music publishing industry over the past twenty or thirty years, and the emphasis on performance is understandable. A publishing house can no longer merely print and distribute sheet music. According to established composers Ned Rorem and Eric Salzman, a good publisher must also act as a composer's agent, helping actively to promote his or her works. "Today," Salzman says, "it would be sheer vanity to pay fifty percent of your earnings to a publishing house for the prestige of having them make copies of your score."

Rorem feels music publishing as we've known it might not exist in another fifteen years or so. "Soon it will all be

> *"The real publishing of music today is recording. You've got to get your notes down on disc."*
> Eric Salzman

computerized. There'll be no pretty covers, no binding. You'll just punch up the score you want and out it will come."

Publishing, though, has not yet become an obsolete enterprise. "Semiobsolete" Salzman calls it. "The real publishing of music today is recording. Once, publishing was the only available means of distribution; everyone read music and everyone had a piano in their living room. Today you've got to get your notes down on disc instead of on paper."

ASCAP, the American Society of Composers, Authors and Publishers, which represents over 6,000 music

publishers, collects and disburses royalty payments for performances. Surprisingly, the society offers little information on classical publishing, although it provides an extensive booklet of hints for the pop music sector. Margaret Jory, Director of the Symphonic and Concert Department of ASCAP, was firm in agreeing that performance should be a young composer's first priority. "Publishing is not the be-all and end-all of composing; performance is. You shouldn't begin to approach a publisher until you have established a performance career. Those days when a young composer, music manuscript under his arm, could

> *"If you want to get your music published write specifically to a publisher's needs."*
>
> Ned Rorem

approach a publisher and gain acceptance are gone—if they ever existed at all. Even with established composers, it's impossible to get more than one piece at a time handled by a publisher."

She does suggest a course of action, however. "Keep performing, or having your music performed. Save all your clips. Above all, keep people interested in your work; build up a good mailing list. From this, amass a substantial portfolio. Then do some research. Check out publishers catalogs and see what kind of material they seem to want. Your best bet is a small press with special interests. If you find a house that specializes in flute or marimba music, say, and you can write that, your odds of success are increased."

Appealing to a specialized market within a larger publishing house's province will also increase your odds. Composer Rorem suggests you "write very specifically to a publisher's needs. Generally, they accept easy choral pieces with one, two, three or four parts, with or without piano accompaniment. They'll also look at band music (for educational facilities like high schools and colleges) and easy piano pieces (also in the educational sector)."

A spokesman for the National Music Publishers Association, an organization devoted to copyright protection of its membership, suggests arming yourself with knowledge about a publishing company's specific needs "Shawnee Press, for instance, favors choral works. In general, choral and piano music are the most in demand. Often, a special interest house will look to expand its catalog, or will need something on a specific level of performance difficulty. Dramatic music for performance—whether it be opera, ballet, or concert—is an extremely limited market in the U.S. A young composer in these areas might consider approaching a foreign publisher through a representative here, or might even go directly to Europe."

Now that you've been properly warned, you may still wonder what the chances are for getting into print. Bruce MacCombie, Vice-President and Director of Publications of G. Schirmer, offers some dismaying statistics. "Schirmer publishes in three main areas: the professional market, the educational market, and the amateur market. We get many works submitted to us, some 2,000 annually. We publish about 150 pieces each year. Most works we actually publish are solicited by us. Thirty percent of our output is serious music for professional performance. This is produced solely by the fifteen or twenty composers under contract to us—Gian Carlo Menotti, Gunther Schuller, Lenny Bernstein and John Corigliano among them. Sixty-five percent of Schirmer's published work is educational material for college conservatories: choral pieces, piano methods, or literature for teaching. Most of this comes from established composers whom we use regularly but who are not contracted to us. The last five percent is the amateur and leisure market.

"We do look at everything that comes in to us, but we prefer to have some indication of a new composer's performance or recording credits instead of simply receiving a manuscript cold. Our policy is to examine all submissions and judge them by a number of factors: instrumentation, length of piece, difficulty level, production costs, and our catalog needs at the time. It's not always an aesthetic judgment. We accept or reject pieces without explanation; otherwise we'd be spending enormous amounts of time on explanatory letters."

"Out of 2,000 works submitted annually we accept about 150. It's not always an aesthetic judgment."
Bruce MacCombie

Stewart Pope, Chairman of Boosey & Hawkes, Inc., was a bit less liberal in the area of unsolicited manuscripts. "Do *not* send your music; we will send it straight back, unexamined. There have been incidents in which publishing houses have become involved in plagiarism suits. It's best to write a letter first, describing your music and style. We'd like to know whether you're re-writing Chopin or Henry Cowell," he jests. "Send us a résumé, tell us what you have had performed or recorded. Then wait for a response; any good publisher always responds."

Boosey & Hawkes' statistics are even more depressing than Schirmer's. The firm prints about 200 pieces a year; this covers *both* the United States and Europe. B&H prefers to handle all the music of a handful of composers instead of the odds and ends of a great many. There are a mere twelve composers on retainer with the house. "We choose to help establish the careers of a very few composers. We are a serious music house. We do have a series

of band music publications, but for that we solicit only composers we know."

Ned Rorem feels lucky to be one of Boosey & Hawkes' blessed dozen. He has had an exclusive contract with B&H for twenty years, and has had hundreds of his works published. "If I wrote something for seven bass flutes and

"Do not send your music. Write a letter first. We'd like to know whether you're re-writing Chopin or Henry Cowell."
Stewart Pope

twenty harpsichords, they'd publish it. They feel even my unsaleable works may have some future value. I was lucky. I didn't paper my room with rejection slips when I started. I had my first work, three songs on a religious text, published in 1945 when I was twenty-one. David Diamond gave them to Associated Music Publishers and they were published immediately on his recommendation." Stewart Pope and Bruce MacCombie both agree that an established composer's recommendation will strongly influence their decision.

One last route out of the Florida swamps and into publication is competition. The NMPA spokesman suggests you get your works involved in competitions like those sponsored by ASCAP and BMI. Seek out other organizations responsible for competitions. He claims publishers will look more closely at award-winning works. Then, besides submitting awards, recording, and performance information along with a manuscript, include a tape as well. "Most publishers want both," he states.

Even if you follow all these astute suggestions, you may not turn up an instant winner in the publishing game, it will almost certainly take time. Eric Salzman's *Civilization and Its Discontents*, which he describes as a "music-theater comedy," was first performed in 1977, and was recorded about two years later by National Public Radio and then by Nonesuch. The work won the Prixe Italia, and has been broadcast to a large portion of the English-speaking world, achieving much critical acclaim. Salzman signed a publishing contract for the work in 1979 or 1980, and despite all the accolades, the piece is first scheduled to be published as a piano and vocal score this year. Salzman also claims to have had difficulties earlier in his career; some years back, another firm reneged on publishing his works in spite of an exclusive contract to do so.

A young composer can avoid these headaches and heartaches by exploring alternate sources of distribution, or by starting his or her own publishing company. Rorem points to three successful composers—Harry Partch, Donald Martino, and Alan Hovhaness—who did so out of sheer desperation. Salzman joins Rorem in touting self-publication, adding that "modern print reproduction methods like the Xerox machine make it easy and cheap for a composer to copy and distribute his own scores." The two composers independently praise the American Composers Alliance, an organization that makes unpublished music available to performers.

So, all you composers up there in those dusty garrets or marshy shacks—maintain your glorious vision: just change the emphasis. You still have a chance. ∎

PW

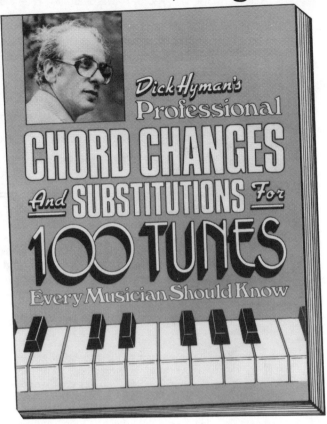

The Shortcut To Great Keyboard Technique!

For Adults & Kids Who Hate To Practice!

- **The Amazing 20 Minute, 20 Week Program!**
- **See and Hear Super Results In One Week!**
- **For All Keyboard Players!**

Here's the *easy* way to a solid keyboard technique. No scales . . . no finger breaking, mind-boggling studies . . . no repetitive arpeggios until you're blue in the face. Just great, common sense mini-exercises and pieces which are easy enough to play at sight for practically everyone. And you play them *at your own pace.*

A NEW YOU AT THE KEYBOARD

Internationally renowned concert pianist Douglas Riva has created this 20-week program with the early and intermediate grades in mind. It's easy to read, fun to play, and super effective in its results. You won't believe it's you when you. begin to play the kinds of things you could never play before. You will be amazed at your control, at the evenness of tone, at the speed at which your fingers suddenly move.

WHEN EVERY MINUTE COUNTS

"The 20 Minute Workout" proves that you *don't* have to practice hours a day to gain a respectable keyboard technique. On the very first day, you will see that Mr. Riva asks you to play four different pieces, spending only a few minutes on each. The program always keeps you moving, keeps you interested, demonstrating new finger and hand applications all the while.

WEEKLY CHARTS FOR DAILY ROUTINES

Before you begin each new week, you will review the chart for the entire week's activities. Each mini-exercise and piece has simple-to-follow instructions which put more variations and interest into each section. Not only will "The 20 Minute Workout" give you much greater technical ability, but you'll find yourself a better sight-reader too. You'll even get an introduction to the concept of transposition — though it's presented so smoothly and casually that you'll hardly realize it!

MONEY BACK GUARANTEE

Whether you *hate* to practice or whether you simply just don't have the time, "The 20 Minute Workout" is guaranteed to be big on results and big on enjoyment. If you don't agree that it is both of these things, if you are not fully satisfied in every way, simply return it to us for a complete refund. *No questions asked.*

We are confident, however, that this will be one book you will *not* put down until you're finished. And when you are, you will have achieved a foundation in keyboard technical mastery that you never realized you could have.